The Literature of Education
A Critical Bibliography
1945–1970

The Literature of Education
A Critical Bibliography 1945-1970

W. KENNETH RICHMOND

METHUEN & CO LTD
11 New Fetter Lane London EC4

First published 1972 by Methuen & Co Ltd
11 New Fetter Lane, London EC4
© 1972 W. Kenneth Richmond
Printed in Great Britain by
Butler & Tanner Ltd
Frome and London

SBN hardbound 416 60190 1
SBN paperback 416 60200 2

Distributed in the U.S.A.
by Barnes & Noble Inc.

Contents

Abbreviations

C	Cambridge
CSE	Certificate of Secondary Education
DAVI	Department of Audio-Visual Instruction
HMSO	Her Majesty's Stationery Office
L	London
NCET	National Council for Education Technology
NFER	National Foundation for Educational Research
NY	New York
O	Oxford
OECD	Organization for Economic Cooperation and Development
SCMP	Student Christian Movement Press
SCRE	Scottish Council for Research in Education
SPCK	Society for the Promotion of Christian Knowledge
UP	University Press

Introduction

Bookmen who set themselves impossible tasks have only themselves to blame if they fail disastrously. Both as a guide and as a critique, *The Literature of Education 1945–1970* is almost certain to be found deficient in many respects. With fresh publications coming thick and fast all the time the chances are that, as a guide, it will be well on the way to being obsolete by the time it sees print. As a critique, the commentaries in each of the various sections will be thought to be distorted by personal bias or, worse, by sheer ignorance, at any rate by specialists in the fields concerned.

The near certainty of failure, nevertheless, is no deterrent seeing that the task itself seems so essentially worthwhile, not to say urgent. Without resorting to special pleading, then, the reason for daring to make the attempt should be made plain at the outset.

A great deal is known about maze-learning in rats, precious little about the problems encountered by students (lecturers, too, for that matter) in finding their way through the labyrinths of prescribed and non-prescribed reading in their courses of study. Since 1945 the volume of writing on educational topics has increased so prodigiously as to be quite unmanageable by any individual. This survey, accordingly, is confined to a selection of some of the more notable books and major official reports which have appeared in the English language (some of them in translation) during the last twenty-five years, with only an occasional reference to outstanding research papers. It is true that most of the important research findings are reported in the learned journals, that many of the livelier contributions are made in the professional quarterlies and weeklies, and that some of the most highly talented and perceptive authors do not answer to the description of educationists. To scan all this scattered literature clearly *is* out of the question.

Even with these limited terms of reference it would require a team of educational librarians and the services of a large computer to do the job properly; and given these, it seems unlikely that the outcome would be very helpful for the average student. To obtain the synoptic view that is needed calls for more than omniscience: it calls for a miracle of compression and a lucidity of exposition which can hardly be accomplished in a single volume.

Why invite disaster and derision, then, it may be asked? After all, it is arguable that any intelligent person can safely be left to find his way around unaided. For the advanced research student this may well be the case: for him, there is no lack of guidance and advice when it comes to looking up the relevant sources in his chosen area of inquiry. For the rank and file, however, and for those who want to survey the field of educational studies as a whole, the chances of becoming utterly lost and overwhelmed are very real. Faced with a bewildering range of offerings, and with no means of deciding what is good, bad or indifferent, they frequently opt for the first book which happens to present itself, or they waste time in riffling through half a dozen when a thorough grasp of one key text is all that is needed. For them, a *mappa mundi* may have its uses. Without one, route-finding is a matter of trial and error, full of wrong turns and blind alleys.

But why 1945 to 1970? As to that, the answer must be obvious enough. So far as education is concerned, the past quarter of a century has been a period of unprecedented growth and expansion. This was the period when, after a longish standstill, the number of British universities doubled within a decade; when the old two-year training establishments multiplied and took on a new lease of life as colleges of education, launching their own B.Ed. degrees; when the size of sixth forms assumed greater proportions than ever before; when the educational services at all levels were subjected to the stresses and strains imposed upon them by remorseless pressures of demand. With the numbers of school leavers proceeding to some form of higher education steadily mounting, the catchment from non-graduate and graduate courses of teacher training has provided a more substantial infrastructure for educational studies at the B.Ed., Diploma, M.Ed. and advanced degree levels. It has also provided the economic base for a flourishing trade in educational books of all kinds, the take-off point for which may be said to date from the early 1960s.

In the process, the scope of educational studies has widened very considerably. In 1945, to take only one obvious example, programmed learning was unheard of and the concept of educational technology, if it could be said to exist at all, amounted to nothing more than a vague conglomeration of audiovisual aids. Network analysis, systems theory and the rest had yet to gain a hearing. As late as 1955 the sociology of education had still to find an assured place in most courses devoted to the training of teachers. As for the economic aspects, hindsight suggests that considerations of cost-effectiveness never entered the minds of the majority of academic educationists until quite recently. Similarly, in the teaching of educational administration there has been a significant move towards a more dynamic approach which has been strongly influenced by theories and techniques derived from organizational and management studies. Some of the airy-fairiness of educational theory, too, has been dissipated in the practical business of curriculum renewal.

Even in psychology, once the undisputed queen of the social sciences in education, drastic changes have occurred. Before 1950 any suggestions that intelligence might in larger or smaller measure be regarded as an acquired characteristic were roundly poohpoohed and those who were rash enough to voice them were given short shrift. The consensus of informed opinion still clung to the myth of the Limited Pool of Ability until the *Robbins Report* (1963) finally discredited it, though the after effects of the earlier *Norwood Report* (1943) – one of the biggest confidence tricks ever perpetrated – still linger on and show themselves in the stubborn belief that children can and need to be classified as first, second and third class citizens at a relatively early age. The lessons to be learned from developmental and social psychology, from the latest findings on creativity, in group dynamics, role theory, organization theory and interpersonal behaviour have yet to be assimilated.

The 'education explosion' is not merely a bravado term. It has produced its own fall-out. By the year 2000 it is estimated that the U.S. Library of Congress catalogue will list 100 million volumes, enough to fill a bookshelf as wide as the equator. It seems that the time is approaching when, for storage reasons alone, the microbook will replace the paperback just as the latter has already to some extent ousted the bulkier hardback editions. With miniaturization it is now possible to reproduce a 1000-page tome, illustrations, statistical tables, index and all, on a plastic fiche no bigger than a visiting card. Accommodating 20,000 works on a coffee table is no longer an insuperable problem apparently: digesting the contents of them all certainly *is*!

Granted, the proliferation of educational books is no more remarkable than it is in other branches of human knowledge. Some ten years ago it used to be said that it would take two and a half professors, working full time and on a seven-day-week basis, to read through all the research journals in chemistry alone. Bearing in mind the exponential growth of such publications, the probability is that at least twice as many would be required to cope with this fiendish assignment today.

It is no use saying that the days of the polymath are over anyway or that the problem will be alleviated once on-line facilities for data banking and data processing become widely and easily available. As things are, the inescapable fact is that each of us has to act as his own computer and carry vastly greater loads of information in his head than scholars have needed to do in the past.

No doubt this heavy burden explains why 1945–70 was an age of big ideas and little men. In Britain, certainly, it produced no educational thinker of the calibre of A. N. Whitehead or John Dewey, no figure commanding international status and stature. In philosophy and the humanities generally these were the lean years when the recovery from the post-war *crise de conscience* was beset with all manner of doubts and misgivings. In sociology, Karl Mannheim, if not the last of the giants, was the last of the pioneers to display any direct interest in educational problems. Only in psychology, where from start to finish the influence of Jean Piaget has dwarfed all others, can it be said that a survivor from the era of the Great Educators is still to be found.

The period divides into two roughly equal and dissimilar halves – the Drift and the Trend. To those of us who worked our passage through it, the first half now seems strangely remote, a little unreal. Just how remote and how unreal may be gauged by the fact that for practical purposes little or nothing can be salvaged from the wreckage of the 1945–55 literature, reflecting as it does an ethos and intellectual climate of opinion very different from that of today. Looking back, nothing is more instructive or more chastening than to observe how the same authors who were singing one tune in the 1940s and 1950s had either fallen silent or were singing quite another tune after 1960 (what tune will they be singing ten years hence, one wonders?). The watershed – turning-point, rather – may be dated from the White Paper on *Technical Education* (1956) or, more accurately perhaps, from the *Crowther Report* (1959). Thereafter, undoubtedly, the mood changed and the freshening winds of change began to blow in new directions.

The Years of Drift (1945–1960)

Seeing that so much was accomplished, and in the face of so many difficulties, why call it drift? The immediate post-war years were flushed with hope, resolve and enthusiasm. Reconstruction and development plans were bold, none bolder than the 1944 Education Act itself. Sired during the darkest days of the Blitz, this, it was generally agreed, was what England had long been waiting for, the grand design that would help to bring order out of the mess and muddle of a century and more of *laissez-faire*. With a Minister at the head of affairs, charged with the duty of promoting and directing national policy, it was believed that the time was ripe for all-round, coordinated advances. While allowing that the progress stemming from this monumental piece of legislation has been very considerable, both in the short run and the long run, the high hopes entertained in 1944 gradually gave way to a sense of disenchantment verging on apathy. First, the clauses relating to the establishment of county colleges were quietly pigeonholed, then left as dead-lettered in the Statute Book. One by one, the carefully prepared development plans of the local education authorities were approved and it became clear that the crazy-paving pattern of English secondary education, long rationalized as 'diversity', was there to stay. The promise of 'parity of esteem', dangled in front of the secondary modern schools ever since the pre-1939 Hadow reorganization, was seen to be illusory. There was growing public dissatisfaction with selection procedures for admission to grammar schools – of all social injustices the 11-plus examination was the one that rankled most – and growing disquiet in the minds of educational psychologists and others who were 'in the know'. The Act had nothing to say about types of school or types of pupil, only a vague reference to 'age, ability and aptitude', which was capable of widely different interpretations.

In all this, 'the note of authority at the centre', which W. O. Lester Smith saw as the key to the situation, was missing; for if stop-go-stop was the rule in the economic policy of the governments of the day educational policy turned out to be no less vacillating under a succession of Tweedledum and Tweedledee ministers. It was not simply that ambitious plans were foiled by shortage of cash, shortage of materials, shortage of teachers and shortage of clear goals. In the absence of a positive lead, it was as though a war-weary society lacked both the means and the will to implement an Act which remains to this day the next-best-thing to a national education plan.

In passing, and by way of extenuation, it may be observed that American education, too, was in the doldrums until the mid-1950s and that the same shilly-shallying was experienced in France over the controversial Langevin Plan (1946) during the topsyturvy political conditions which prevailed until de Gaulle came to power. Caught between conflicting cross currents, the western world was uneasily becalmed.

The first educational books to be published in Britain after the

Second World War scarcely reflected this troubled background. To begin with, they amounted to no more than a trickle, for, with paper and print in short supply, government publications, Command Papers, directories, yearbooks, etc., were given first priority. Still, 1945 got off to a good start with several writers of distinction airing their views. There was Bruce Truscot, that damned elusive Pimpernel of the academic world, with his *Redbrick in These Vital Days*, Rex Warner waxing eloquent on *The English Public School*, Wilson Knight on *The Dynasty of Stowe* and the indefatigable C. E. M. ('It all depends on') Joad's *About Education* – not forgetting J. A. Lauwerys's thoughts on *The Content of Education* (price 4*d*, believe it or not).

As a first offering, the 1945 output did not add up to much. Vital days, possibly, but the vital issues were left untouched. Compared with the Harvard Committee's report, *General Education in a Free Society*, published in the same year, the British contribution must be reckoned lightweight and vapid.

In 1946 the professional educationists weighed in, M. L. Jacks with *Total Education: A Plea for Synthesis*, an impassioned appeal for an all-out concerted drive on the lines of the national war effort which sounded more rhetorical than convincing even at the time. Bruce Truscot was having his final fling in *First Year at the University*, but his pen, too, had lost its earlier bite. The reissue of Nunn's popular minor classic, *Education: its Data and First Principles*, was symptomatic of the general willingness to carry on from where things had left off abruptly in September 1939. And (since it is only fair to write one's own obituary) W. K. Richmond's *Education in England*, a hotchpotch of garbled history and reformist zeal, was a naive effort to popularize the great expectations of a New Order that seemed nearer then than it does today. One title alone, Marjorie Reeves's *Growing up in a Modern Society*, pointed the way ahead to the systematic sociological analysis which was needed to put an end to complacent thinking.

Some idea of the slow build-up in the market for educational books can be gained from the number of notices appearing in *British Book News*: 22 in 1945, down to 16 in 1946, up to 39 in 1947, 43 in 1948, 47 in 1949, 50 in 1950.

In 1947 the country was settling down to normal peacetime conditions. After the austerity of rationing, coupons and utility goods, J. W. Adamson's *The Illiterate Anglo-Saxon*, a slim collection of consummate essays on medieval educators, seemed the height of luxury. Educational studies were back to normal with C. M. Fleming's *Research and the Basic Curriculum,* R. A. C. Oliver's *Research in Education,* M. V. Daniel's *Activity in the Primary School* and J. J. B. Dempster's *Education in the Secondary Modern School.* Out of the common run was M. V. C. Jeffreys's *Glaucon.* It is conceivable, if unlikely, that posterity will single out this as one of the truly great texts of the period. A Christian existentialist's reflections on the ultimate purposes of education, which it sees as nothing less than providing the learner with a faith to live by, this unusual book has suffered the not unusual fate of falling on stony ground, lost among the tares of a rampant secular humanism. It is none the worse for being temporarily out of fashion.

Apart from Sir Richard Livingstone, urbane as always in drawing attention to *Some Tasks for Education,* the writers of 1947 avoided the larger issues (other than the religious one, that is). Once again, discussions about the place of liberal studies in general education had to be prompted from abroad, this time by Ortega y Gasset's radical and visionary *Mission of the University.*

1948 brought another varied crop, first and foremost Sir Fred Clarke's *Freedom in the Educative Society.* Had he lived, this master teacher's blend of international experience, cultural wisdom and religious conviction might well have resolved the false antitheses – between freedom and authority, individual and the collective, work and leisure, liberal studies and technical training – which continued to plague educational theory and policy-making alike after his death. Not being blinkered by insular-mindedness, he saw, as others did not, that education, as distinct from schooling, was to be conceived as a function of the social life as a whole. As he said, 'Great simple ideas – like the Golden Rule – are notoriously difficult to translate into practice. So it is with democracy. The heart of the idea, I take it, is Equality, the *Recognition of Man.* Equality is an ideal we understand with our hearts rather than with our heads. It is not "one plus one plus one". . . . The real problem of Equality is to interpret the idea in terms of an *organic society.*'

Not so unassuming but no less a sage, that spokesman for the Classics Sir Richard Livingstone returned to the fray once more with *Some Thoughts on University Education.* D. A. Winstanley's *Later Victorian Cambridge* came as a welcome reminder of the palmier days of historical scholarship. James Hemming spoke up vehemently for the progressives in *Teach Them to Live,* John Newsom put in a good word for *The Education of Girls* (not before time, either), and Randolph Laban gave a novel twist to teaching of eurhythmics in *Modern Educational Dance*. Meantime, across the Atlantic, a portent no bigger than a man's hand appeared in the shape of Norbert Wiener's *Cybernetics*.

In 1949 H. C. Dent took the slogan of the day for his title, *Secondary Education for All*, and, like everyone else, found no way of lifting it out of the tripartite rut in which it was lodged. Mary Atkinson's *Junior Community* was a more than usually enlightened portrayal of 'activity and experience' methods with young children. Eric (now Lord) James proffered *An Essay on the Content of Education* in Platonic vein, confessing that no adequate curriculum for the mass of non-academic pupils had yet been discovered. Anti-egalitarian, sceptical of the viability or the desirability of the new comprehensive schools, he concluded that any attempt to devise a common course must be ruled out once and for all. 'The problem of devising a general education that shall satisfy the need which Milton felt of combining academic, scientific and moral elements is still before us.' It still is. J. F. Wolfenden's *The Public Schools Today* was not in the least perturbed. The Book of the Year, Sir Walter Moberly's *Crisis in the University* sounded perturbed: the trouble was that no one could bring themselves to believe that there *was* a crisis. Sir Walter spoke gravely of the neglect of 'the issues that are momentous': sad to say, the issues he had in mind were religious and philosophical, not the ones to interest most academics, administrators or students.

By way of a *bonne bouche*, the 1949 offerings included a gem of a pamphlet issued by the Ministry of Education and simply called *The Story of a School*. It told how a junior school in one of the seedier slums of Birmingham transformed itself from a Fagin's den into a veritable Aladdin's cave, a Palace of Many Delights. As an antidote to the commonly held view that 'progressive' methods are impracticable under normal classroom conditions in the state-maintained system it remains as good as any.

So we arrive at mid-century. 1950 was a somewhat drab year, memorable mainly for two titles which marked the parting of the ways. One was Vicars Bell's aptly named book *The Dodo*, the nostalgic *apologia pro vita sua* of a rural school headmaster who saw that he and his world were coming to the end of the line. The other was a little-known work by C. S. Segal, *Backward Children in the Making*, a study of the depressive effects of the bricks and mortar life situation in North Kensington. In its small way it anticipated a whole series of investigations into the influences of social class, family background and neighbourhood on the measured intelligence and achievement of school children. For the next ten years research workers sought to unravel the snarled-up web of inequalities in the education system, to throw light on the formation of subcultures and the causes of alienation in urban industrial society. The full impact of this cumulative evidence was not felt until 1957 when Jean Floud, A. H. Halsey and F. M. Martin reported their findings in Middlesbrough and south-west Hertfordshire in *Social Class and Educational Opportunity*, which seemed at the time (and still does) an unanswerable case for abolishing the *status quo*, at least as regards the 11-plus and all that.

Not that the sociologists were the only ones who were on the move. Innovation was in the air. Robin Pedley's *Comprehensive Education: A New Approach* (1956) was a manifesto for reform which was suitably contentious. B. F. Skinner's 1954 essay on 'The science of learning and the art of teaching' in the *Harvard Educational Review* was a manifesto of a different kind which was soon to have worldwide repercussions in educational technology:

> A country which annually produces millions of refrigerators, dishwashers, automatic washing machines, automatic clothes driers and automatic garbage disposers can certainly afford the equipment necessary to educate its citizens to high standards of competence in the most effective way.
>
> There is a simple job to be done. The task can be stated in concrete terms. The necessary techniques are known. The equipment can easily be provided. Nothing stands in the way but cultural inertia. . . . We are on the threshold of an exciting and revolutionary period, in which the scientific study of man will be put to work in man's best interests.

Arresting words. The fact that they were largely untrue – that the job to be done was very far from simple, that the necessary techniques were *not* known, and that educational problems were not akin to those of garbage disposal – did not prevent their being infectious.

In the event, cultural inertia in the U.S.A. was soon to receive its biggest jolt when Sputnik I went into orbit in 1957. For instant reform in education there is nothing to equal a sudden threat to national security. Within months the veiled and unveiled criticisms which had centred on the American high schools since 1945 came to a head and found their expression on the grand get-together of the Woods Hole Conference, as well as in a flurry of massive curriculum projects.

Distilled from this public debate, J. S. Bruner's *The Process of Education* (1960) ushered in a new era.

True to form in missing the point, England at the time was enjoying its own storm in a teacup, stirred up by C. P. Snow's Rede Lecture, *The Two Cultures and the Scientific Revolution* (1959). For all that, the end of the years of drift was now in sight.

The Trend (1960–1970)

An educational Rip van Winkle who fell asleep in 1960 and awakened ten years later could hardly fail to be puzzled by the subtle changes in vocabulary which have occurred. 'Models', 'modules', 'media', 'systems', 'strategies', 'feedback', 'subculture', 'reinforcement', 'interface', 'behavioural objectives', 'simulation and gaming', 'input-output analysis', 'research and development' – these are only a few of the trendy terms he might be hard put to understand.

How to explain what has happened? That the twenty-five years can be characterized as a period of social-cultural flux is fairly evident, as is the fact that the process of change has been speeding up and gathering momentum. So long as the tide of events or the 'stream of consciousness' is so slow as to be barely perceptible a man may allow himself to be carried along willynilly because it never occurs to him that he needs to do anything else. For him, as for his forefathers, 'The old order changeth, yielding place to new', with the same inevitability that night follows day or summer wanes into autumn. It is only when the tempo of innovation accelerates that he realizes that it is up to him to regulate its flow and chart his course. That, or something like it, is the difference between the drifter and the trendsetter. For the latter, prediction and control are of the essence whether he calls himself a cyberneticist, a sociologist, a behavioural psychologist, a programmer, an economist or a curriculum theorist.

The loosening of the log-jam in British educational thought, which began with the *Crowther Report* in 1959, was completed in 1963 by the *Robbins Report (Higher Education)* and the *Newsom Report (Half Our Future)*. All three were strongly influenced by the evidence regarding the effects of social class and the disclosure of serious wastage in the nation's potential manpower and brainpower. Between them they spelled out a message which had been carefully suppressed ever since Robert Owen first gave it utterance in *A New View of Society* as long ago as 1813. Robbins summed it up in a sentence: 'If there is to be talk of a pool of ability, it must be of a pool which surpasses the widow's cruse in the Old Testament, in that when more is taken for higher education in one generation more will tend to be available in the next.' The same note of confident optimism was being sounded simultaneously, though with less reason, by the *enfants terribles* of programmed learning and teaching machines, some of whom were brash enough to claim '95 per cent success with 95 per cent of the population' for their wares. And if these claims turned out to be premature, if not absolutely false, at least the experience gained in clarifying learning objectives and assessing their achievement lent colour to the belief that the mass of ordinary children were capable of feats of learning which previously had been judged to be too difficult for them.

Again, one of the main conclusions drawn from the spate of experimental curriculum projects has been that the capacities and capabilities of the average and below-average pupil – the 'Newsom children', as they have come to be called – have been seriously underestimated in the past. Curriculum study and educational technology, indeed, are rapidly converging in the same direction. Both emphasize the need for clearly stated objectives, for careful analysis of the structure and sequence of the learning process, and for regular feedback of 'knowledge of results' to pupil and instructor alike. In a word, more *can* mean better if only the problems of facilitating learning are tackled with ingenuity and an open mind. Any lack of ability is not to be laid solely at the door of the learner, rather on the *conditions* to which he is subjected. To that extent, the philosophy of the Trend is unashamedly environmentalist. It is convinced that human resources can be managed, that it is not good enough to leave developments to take their own haphazard course. Latterly, this same conviction has led economists to take a greater interest in the cost-effectiveness of the educational services.

As a result of all this, the educational book trade has ceased to be a cottage industry. Since 1960 it has enjoyed phenomenal rates of growth, with the number of new publications plotted on a steeply rising curve. There are indications that this curve may level off after 1970, but there is clearly no possibility of repeating the kind of résumé for the years 1945–50 attempted in the first half of this introduction. In any case, the place for such attempts is in the commentaries which preface the various sections of *The Literature of Education*. All that remains to be done here is to draw attention to some of the less praiseworthy features of the current Trend.

In the first place, as the range of educational studies has widened so has the scope of each of them narrowed. Whatever the subject, the treatment now tends to be more specialized, more technical – and more ephemeral. At the beginning of the period a professor of education was expected to be catholic in his interests and versatile in accomplishments, if not exactly a jack-of-all-trades: today, if he has any thought for his reputation he is much more likely to concentrate on one aspect and make his name as an educational psychologist, an educational sociologist, an authority on educational technology or management and administration. With the social sciences in the ascendant, it seems that the days of the all-purpose professor are numbered.

Seeing that the times favour the expert in this or that rather than the all-rounder (never a star player at the best of times) it may seem to be wildly unrealistic to expect anyone to be *au fait* with all ten sectors of the field of educational studies represented in this survey:

> Philosophy of Education
> Educational Theory
> Curriculum Study
> Educational Psychology
> History of Education
> Sociology of Education
> Educational Administration
> Comparative Education, Education in Developing Countries
>   and Educational Planning
> Economics of Education
> Educational Technology

A tall order and no mistake. It is fair to say that nowhere is there a diploma or degree course so broad-based or so demanding as to require a high level of proficiency in all of these; and if there were, only *l'uomo universale* could be expected to take it in his stride.

Paradoxically, on the other hand, a contextual approach to educational problems is now seen to be essential. Whether we call it 'systems thinking' or 'interdisciplinary study' is really immaterial. The chief impediment to the writing of great poetry, said Keats, was the fact that the poet did not know enough. It is an impediment which is only now beginning to be overcome in many-sided educational thought and decision-making.

The list should not be regarded as closed. Other desiderata are certain to be added sooner or later. It will be noted that cultural anthropology and politics, two essential studies for seeing all the others in perspective, have not been included. This is because both must be ranked as virtual non-starters for the great majority of British students. How much longer their arrival on the scene will be delayed can only be conjectured.

The fall-out from the education explosion is apt to throw more dust in his eyes than the innocent reader imagines. On the face of things, each and all of these reading lists looks impressive, not to say daunting. In fact, the multifarious titles conceal an enormous amount of duplication, a repetitious raking over of other people's research findings, other people's ideas. Marshall McLuhan confides that when the manuscript of *Understanding Media* was submitted for their consideration the publishers protested that it was unsuitable because 75 per cent of the material was entirely new. By contrast, it is a safe bet that less than 5 per cent of the contents of any new book on education will be in any way original.

This would not matter so much if lack of originality were offset by grace and felicity of style. As the literature proliferates, unfortunately, the trend is towards a flat uniformity. Admittedly, it is unusual to come across a really trashy or incompetent book about education nowadays. But the *magnum opus* looks like becoming a thing of the past and even minor classics seem to be becoming fewer and fewer. The style is no longer the man.

One way of sensing the change that has taken place is to sample the writings of the Victorians. Thomas Arnold, for example, never altered a word from the moment he laid pen to paper to the moment he finished what he had in mind, yet every sentence he wrote bears the unmistakable stamp of the man's character. Since books about education became the province of technical experts, the 'Nelson touch' has gradually disappeared. It is as though there is no longer any place for human warmth, only for clinical concepts, desiccated statistics and aseptic analysis. For flair, invention, verve and ready wit the Americans are, on the whole, better than the British, though it goes against the grain to admit it. Quite apart from their professional qualifications, authors like Norbert Wiener and J. S. Bruner are essayists of some distinction.

Trendy-minded students should bear in mind that most educational books have a pitifully short half-life. To be acclaimed today and forgotten tomorrow is the fate of nine out of ten. Suffering from built-in obsolescence as they do, it is necessary to ask just why the latest publications should be considered more acceptable or more reliable than those they are supposed to supersede. Could it be that what we have to do with in this welter of information-peddling is a form of cultural pollution? How, in Thomas Jefferson's phrase, to 'sort the genius from the rubbish'?

In retrospect, the verdict must be that the literature *is* mostly 'rubbish' – at least in the sense that yesterday's ice cream carton or last year's cast-off clothing is said to be rubbish – and that works of genius are depressingly rare. Of the thousands of titles scanned there are, at most, a dozen that this reviewer would gladly read again and again. There are, to be sure, plenty of studies which earn a cliché mention as 'notable' 'important' or 'standard work'.

One of the reasons for this pervasive drabness is that educational writers, particularly those who like to think of themselves as social scientists, rarely indulge in the luxury of writing in the First Person Singular. The conventions of their profession prevent it. Yet if old-timers' books like *The Dodo* remain fragrant in the memory, and if Kurt Hahn's or A. S. Neill's personality has left its mark, it is because these were the odd men out who were never afraid to speak their minds. The rest, the clever convergers, took refuge in the dead-pan jargon of educationese.

If educational writers have a common fault it is that of taking themselves and their subject too seriously. As a result, they are so obsessed with abstract expertise that what they write about bears little or no resemblance to concrete, grim and gay realities of life as it is lived in the average classroom. A film like *Kes* or a television documentary or play like *Roll on Four o'Clock* may contain moments of truth for the viewer which are too often denied him as a reader. Unless, that is, he goes right outside the field of conventional educational reportage and tries an author who can actually *write*. Cassandra, for instance, in *John Bull's Schooldays* (1961): 'The main thing that I learnt at the Secondary School, apart from Doppler's Principle, Playfair's axiom, and the specific gravity of mercury (thirteen point something or other), was how to acquire an Acute Sense of Failure. I still possess it.'

So, it may be thought, does Britain.

But why end on a sour note? In the contemporary flux it may appear to be a case of everything by fits and nothing long, but the very fact that so many developments are taking place and in such different directions means that the mood is invigorating. With so much going on around him it may be difficult, if not impossible, for the student of education to keep track of all these developments or to see their implications. Since he cannot excel in every corner of the field simultaneously, he is probably well advised to concentrate his interests and energies in one or two sectors. Come to think of it, the complexities arising from the division of labour in a technological society are no more intractable than those that are triumphantly resolved in the performance of any symphony orchestra. In one sense, the various instrumentalists are all musicians, bound by a common set of rules which keeps them in harmony: in another, they are all specialists. For strings, brass, wood-wind and percussion read historian, psychologist, technologist and economist (not necessarily in that order!) and the analogy is obvious enough. Or would be if only we could find a philosopher-king to serve as our conductor – and a few great composers. True or false, the orchestral analogy at least holds good in so far as it underlines the need for specialists to work and play together, to understand what they and their colleagues are doing, when and where to make their appropriate entries. Educationists, like musicians, must know the score.

1 *Philosophy of Education*

'The question of the relation of subject matter and method is fundamentally the same question that appears in philosophy as the problem of the relation of the subject and object, or of the relation of intelligence, mind, to the world.'

The words are John Dewey's, transcribed by one of his students at a lecture given on 1 February 1899 (Archambault, 1965). Much the same relationship exists between philosophy of education and educational theory, which interact at all points. If there is no saying just where or how the one merges into the other the reason is that philosophy and education alike refuse to be pinned down by nice definitions. Was Rousseau a philosopher? World opinion continues to think so despite sneering references to him as a militant lowbrow by thinkers who cannot stomach what he had to say. Socrates' stature as a philosopher, certainly, is in no way diminished simply because Bertrand Russell happened to have a low opinion of him. Was Karl Mannheim, usually ranked among the sociologists, a philosopher? Is Marshall McLuhan (scarcely the kind of thinker who can be said to excel in the realm of 'clear and distinct ideas')?

These questions are pertinent in view of recent trends, which foster the opinion that the right to pronounce on fundamental educational issues properly belongs only to those who have received their training in the formal schools of philosophy. There is a certain arrogance in this academic notion, which needs to be dispelled at the outset. It has been said with justice that a philosopher is not a special kind of man, rather that every man is a special kind of philosopher.

True, from Plato to Whitehead, most of the great educators were philosophers by profession. Until 1960 or thereabouts, then, students training to become teachers were expected to imbibe such philosophy as was thought necessary for them either from courses labelled 'Principles and Theory' or 'History of Education'. For the former the prescribed reading was as often as not a textbook such as Nunn's *Education: Its Data and First Principles* (3rd ed. 1945: cited under Educational Theory, p. 54) or J. S. Ross's *Groundwork of Educational Theory* (1942: cited under Educational Theory, p. 55); for the other, perhaps,

W. Boyd's *History of Western Education* (9th ed. 1969: cited under History of Education, p. 104) or R. R. Rusk's *Doctrines of the Great Educators* (4th ed. 1969: cited under History of Education, p. 106), standard works that have withstood the passage of time remarkably well. Alternatively, the course might take the form of a review of the main schools of philosophical thought – Idealism, Realism, Pragmatism and the rest (in the U.S.A. the list of Isms tended to be well nigh endless) – with some attempt being made to point out the implications of each for educational theory and practice. Here again, the course leaned heavily on some such textbook as J. S. Brubacher's *Modern Philosophies of Education* (4th ed. 1969) or T. Brameld's *Philosophies of Education in Cultural Perspective* (1955), with a rather more readable symposium like A. V. Judges's *Education and the Philosophic Mind* (1957) thrown in by way of light relief.

In the event, none of these approaches proved to be very satisfactory. In the U.S.A., as in Britain, a common verdict has been that 'All courses called "Philosophy of Education" operate under a cloud of academic suspicion' (Broudy *et al.*, 1967). Both in university departments of education and in the colleges of education, courses of the 'Principles and Theory' type were frequently criticized, sometimes rightly, as being a mishmash of half-baked chat; those on the 'History of Education' as being largely irrelevant to the on-the-job situation (always uppermost in the students' minds); those on 'Philosophy of Education' as being no better than a travesty, crammed with inert ideas, besides being taught in a fashion which could only be described as amateurish.

In the meantime British philosophy had been undergoing a radical sea-change. As if suddenly apprised of, and appalled by, the inherent pitfalls in language usage, professional philosophers decided that the age-old questions which they had previously posed – questions concerning the nature of man and his destiny – were improper because unanswerable. Between them, such thinkers as Ludwig Wittgenstein, A. J. Ayer and Gilbert Ryle helped to forge the techniques of logical empiricism and linguistic analysis and set the styles of inquiry which were soon to find favour in the attack on educational problems. Following on from the work of Rudolf Carnap, similar moves were being made simultaneously in the U.S.A., where Israel Scheffler's *The Language of Education* (1962) and P. H. Phenix's *Realms of Meaning* (1964) were very much in line with the drive towards a strictly discipline-centred approach to curriculum reform.

The new style was coolly rational, spectatorial rather than committed, clinical rather than constructive, above all analytical. Disavowing doctrines, it offered criticisms instead. Possibly its clearest formulation is to be found in Ayer's *Language, Truth and Logic* (2nd ed. 1946). According to this, sentences were to be regarded as meaningful only in so far as they were statements of verifiable fact: metaphysical considerations were ruled out as being literally nonsense. If philosophy was going to 'make sense' it must cut its losses or, as Langford (1968) puts it, 'only by devouring its capital of past error'.

This stoic determination on the part of the analysts and the logical empiricists has left them so far out on a limb that the wonder is that they have been as influential as they have in the field of educational studies. Could it be that the 'error' was theirs, not their predecessors'? After all, an obsessive distrust of language is by no means peculiar to philosophers in the twentieth century: from E. E. Cummings and T. S. Eliot ('shabby equipment always deteriorating') to James Joyce and Samuel Beckett it has been a constant source of dissatisfaction among poets, novelists and dramatists, yet this has not prevented them from finding new modes of expression through the medium of the written and spoken word. Unlike the linguistic analysts, they have not been driven to the extremity of severing all connections with the past or of excluding from their terms of reference religious, moral and political commitments which 'make sense' to the ordinary man.

As to that, of course, the logical retort will be that philosophy is not literature. But it is this very insistence on logical explanations which provides a second reason for seeing the cult of analysis as a *trahison des clercs*. If the simple logic derived from grammar and common sense is incapable of coping with the complexities of quantum theory, say, what reliance can be placed on its axioms in the conduct of human affairs? Traditionally, the philosopher has been cast in the role of the wise man, a lover of truth. In recent years it has been left to personalist and existentialist thinkers to assume such a role which is now abjured by the logic-and-language fraternity. In education, as in everything else, it has become fashionable to disparage any forms of thought which look even faintly transcendental; and the result, in Britain at least, is that the more deeply pondered works of men of genius – Buber, Jaspers, Teilhard de Chardin – have been quietly cold-shouldered. The prevailing impression has been that linguistic analysis and logical empiricism between them constitute *the* philosophy. What makes it all the odder, as Northrop Frye says, is that 'We do not now think of the wise man's mind as a dictatorship of reason. We think, rather, in Freudian terms, of a mind in which a principle of normality and balance is fighting for its life against a thundering herd of chaotic impulses.' ('The university and personal life', in W. R. Niblett (ed.), *Higher Education: Demand and Response*, 1969: cited under Educational Administration, p. 158.)

In his *Philosophy and Education* (1962) Louis Arnaud Reid foresaw that the analysts' preoccupation with language and logic might well lead to a New Scholasticism as sterile as its medieval counterpart – what A. N. Whitehead in an earlier generation had castigated as a 'celibacy of the intellect which is divorced from the concrete contemplation of complete facts'. In Reid's memorable phrase, 'it is important for the student of education not to let himself be inhibited by arbitrary notices "No Road" posted across ancient rights of way'. In view of what has happened in the interim it is a warning that needs to be borne in mind today.

The declared intention of the analytical school was to serve as a corrective, to strip away the woolliness of unexamined assumptions, to give greater precision to concepts and terms which had become fuzzy through being popularized as slogans – 'activity and experience', 'child-centredness', 'equality of opportunity', etc., etc. To begin with, its pundits enjoyed fair sport, finding plenty of sitting targets for criticism in the literature; and they lost no time in picking holes in the writings of authors like Susan Isaacs (see Archambault, 1965, for some typical examples). Their rigorous scrutiny was a good deal slower in turning its attention to some of the major issues which had exercised the minds of educationists ever since 1945.

Of these, the most vexing centred around the apparently conflicting claims of general and special education. This problem may as well be aired here in the first instance, though it will be necessary to discuss it again in the section on educational theory (pp. 46–8). It was stated fairly and squarely in the Harvard Committee's report, *General Education in a Free Society* (1945: cited under Educational Theory, p. 51): 'How can general education be so adapted to different ages and, above all, to different abilities and interests, that it can appeal deeply to each, yet remain in goal and essential teaching the same for all?'

As the Harvard Committee said, it was (and remains) the question of the age. It was emphatically *not* the kind of question which appealed to analytical philosophers, most of whom studiously avoided it. Although the solution proposed in *General Education in a Free Society* represented at best an uneasy compromise (i.e. in seeing social studies as a

link between science and the humanities), the Harvard Committee
report must be reckoned one of the key documents of the period. In
Britain, where early specialization in the sixth form had long been
causing concern, Sir Eric Ashby propounded an alternative solution,
summed up in his assertion that the way to culture in the modern world
is through a man's specialism, not by by-passing it (*Technology and the
Academics*, 1958: cited under Educational Theory, p. 49). This en-
visaging of technology as the core of a new humanism marked a
significant departure in the philosophy of education. Earlier thinkers,
notably A. N. Whitehead, had urged the falsity of any antithesis
between liberal-general and technical-special aims or between science
and the humanities. In Sir Fred Clarke's estimate (1948), so far as
Britain was concerned, any controversy merely arose from the septic
debris of past social history. This did not prevent the controversy
flaring up anew after C. P. Snow's Rede Lecture *The Two Cultures and
the Scientific Revolution* (1959). In retrospect, the Snow-Leavis confrontation, unlike the one between Matthew Arnold and Thomas
Huxley a century earlier, seems a rather unseemly episode, lacking in
subtlety and dignity alike, and engendering more heat than light. This is
not to say that it was a case of much ado about nothing: on the contrary,
it was sparked off by a growing awareness of the predicaments created
by the exponential growth and fissiparous tendencies in modern
knowledge (no longer a seamless web) and the realization of the sheer
impossibility of learning something about everything. The division of
labour in advanced industrial societies being so complex, the demand
everywhere is for highly specialized qualifications. Increasingly, therefore, the problem as stated in 1945 has come to seem an insoluble
riddle. The plea for a synthesis, so frequently and plaintively voiced in
the 1940s, remains unanswered: the search for a common core curriculum which will 'appeal deeply to each' continues. The arts *v.* science
debate has more or less petered out, mainly because the participants
have found nothing significant or useful to add to what has been said
over and over again. Amid the hullabaloo over the Two Cultures,
Michael Polanyi's *Personal Knowledge* (2nd ed. 1962), which effected a
brilliant reconciliation between objective-scientific ways and knowing
and subjective-humane value judging, went for the most part unnoticed.

In some respects, the difficulty of finding a common core is greater in
an élitist system of education than it is in one organized on egalitarian
lines. In this connection, the role of the secondary school is everywhere
seen to be crucial. In the U.S.A., where the high school has been

nonselective since 1890, recent curriculum projects have attempted to raise overall academic standards and requirements. In Britain, wedded in 1944 to a tripartite organization, 'secondary education for all' has gradually and uncertainly moved towards the adoption of the comprehensive principle. This movement derives its support partly from economic arguments – Britain's poor record in the international growth league, it is alleged, stems from the persistent failure to exploit the reserves of human capital in the mass of children who are excluded from a full-length secondary course. Beginning with Crowther (1959: cited under Educational Theory, p. 50), the point has been driven home in a series of official reports which have exposed the inadequacy of the weak definition of equality of opportunity and the futility of *laissez-faire* concepts of 'parity of esteem'. If the cause of social justice has taken a new turn since the mid-1950s, however, it is not because politicians, still less philosophers, have rallied to it, but because public opinion has felt the groundswell of discontent with selection procedures for grammar school and university places – 11-plus, 18-plus and all that. In the main, the evidence that has effectively changed policy-making has come from the sociologists.

A shift of emphasis from the individual and his 'needs' to the community and its 'claims' is one of the most obvious changes which have taken place in educational thought during the last quarter of a century. Whereas Nunn took his stand on the belief that no good enters this world except through the endeavours of individual human beings, Sir Fred Clarke's vision of an educative society (1948), like Mannheim's, insisted that education, as distinct from schooling, was a function of the social life as a whole. Subsequent developments in the social sciences have strengthened the latter view. Though the relationship between individual and society, like those between arts and science, liberal and technical education, etc., can easily degenerate into a false dualism there is no denying that the centre of gravity has been moved and that the focus of interest today tends to be placed more and more on demographic trends, on organizations and on interpersonal relationships.

No less obvious has been the steady drift away from religious interpretations of life and the ascendancy of secular humanism. Just as the 1944 Education Act took it for granted that the Christian ethic provided the orthodoxy and terms of reference for national policy-making, so most of the post-war educational writers, Clarke included, were men with sincere religious convictions. M. V. C. Jeffreys (1950, 1955) typifies this vein of high seriousness, strongly influenced as it was by existential philosophy and Protestant theology. For him, the purpose of education was nothing less than providing the learner with a faith to live by, and the key word was 'commitment'. W. R. Niblett (1954) maintained a similar if less openly evangelical position. Both stressed the sacramental and spiritual nature of the educational process and the importance of treating the learner at all stages and at all times as a person.

After the mid-1950s, however, this meditational style cut precious little ice – too numinous, too holy-joey for a reading public which was more inclined to put its trust in empirical research findings and utilizable techniques. Looking back, books like Jeffreys's *Glaucon* (1950) and Blamires's *Repair the Ruins* (1950) seem to belong to an entirely different era, an age of lost causes. The genres which have taken over from them have no use for Angst. Philosophically speaking, Skinner's behaviourism was a non-starter, yet his 1954 essay in the *Harvard Educational Review* (vol. 24, No. 2), 'The science of learning and the art of teaching', soon triggered off a chain reaction in the form of worldwide developments in the field of programmed learning and teaching machines. By contrast, the ideas of Norbert Wiener (1951) were at once more sophisticated and advanced, foreshadowing the emergence of technology as *the* humane discipline of the future. Unlike Skinner, Wiener underlined the dangers arising from an uncritical acceptance of the gospel of social engineering – dangers which provided the main theme for Jacques Ellul's tract for the times, *The Technological Society* (1965).

As a philosophy of education, idealism never really recovered from Popper's hatchet job in *The Open Society and Its Enemies* (1945), which sought to debunk Plato and derided Hegel as the prince of windbags. Later still, D. J. O'Connor's *An Introduction to the Philosophy of Education* (1957) fairly put the cat among the pigeons of educational theory. His round assertion that the conventional wisdom of the Great Educators was not to be trusted and that the term 'educational theory' was normally bestowable only as a courtesy title caused a good deal of consternation, not to say offence, in academic circles. Briefly stated, his case was that any theory worth the name should satisfy three requirements: (1) prescribe a course of action, (2) predict the outcome and (3) explain that outcome.

In passing, it may be observed that this is what most educational theories signally fail to do. Indeed, the popularity of techniques like programmed learning is attributable to the fact that they are the exceptions which prove the rule. O'Connor's thesis has been rebutted, not very convincingly, by Hirst (in J. W. Tibble (ed.), *The Study of Education*, 1966) on the grounds that he has taken as his paradigm the kind of theory used in the natural sciences. The ensuing debate about what constitutes an educational theory has not yet cleared the air of conceptual confusions and like the earlier one over the Two Cultures may be thought to have been less than helpful.

'Bacon once said that the discourse of philosophers is like the stars: it sheds little light because it is so high. But when it is brought nearer the earth . . . it can still only shed light on where empirical research needs to be done and where practical judgements have to be made,' says R. S. Peters (in W. R. Niblett (ed.) *Moral Education in a Changing Society*, 1963: cited under Educational Theory, p. 57). More than any other's, his name is associated with the vogue of logical empiricism in British education. If that philosophy has had little to say concerning the issues which men like Jeffreys, Niblett and Sir Walter Moberly held to be momentous, there is a fourth issue on which the critical-analytic approach has endeavoured to shed some light. This is the search for a new basis for morality in an age in which existing codes of conduct are being called in question and age-old faiths quietly eroded. In some respects Peters is representative of the English tradition of shrewd common sense exemplified by Hobbes, Locke and Burke, all of whom he quotes with approval. That tradition has always been averse to radical proposals: it is solidly behind the 'Establishment', sceptical or contemptuous of forms of thought which appear to be in any way emotionally charged. Peters is masterly at serving up a tightly marshalled argument which leaves no logical stone unturned in arriving at its conclusion. His most substantial book to date is *Ethics and Education* (1966), which his many devotees place on a par with Dewey's *Democracy and Education* (1916: cited under Educational Theory, p. 51) as one of the most outstanding contributions to the philosophy of education in the twentieth century. Unlike Dewey, however, Peters offers no explicit programme for educational theory and practice unless it be that of persuading teachers to think hard and carefully about what they are doing. Not *what* to think but *how* to think: that is the question. His overriding concern is to find rational justifications for fundamental concepts in educational theory like 'knowledge', 'interest', 'freedom', 'authority', 'discipline', 'worthwhileness', 'respect for persons', etc. As a philosopher, his declared intention is to find and follow reasons and to disregard any considerations which are logically irrelevant. R. F. Dearden (1969) has followed these same procedures to good effect in analysing the slipshod terminology and loose talk which have gained something like common currency in primary schools ever since the 1931 report of the Consultative Committee of the Board of Education (Chairman W. H. Hadow) first encouraged the adoption of a curriculum in terms of 'activity and experience'.

But if the criticisms are trenchant and if the arguments adduced are difficult to fault, the conclusions themselves are often disappointing and occasionally banal. Throughout, there is an ill-disguised hostility to egalitarian principles, to 'progressive' practice, indeed to any innovation which looks like threatening the *status quo*. There is also, despite self-conscious disclaimers to the contrary, the tacit assumption that education is first, last and all the time an intellectual process. This belief that learning and teaching are pre-eminently cognitive is shared by members of the discipline-centred axis in contemporary American educational thought, Marc Belth for example (1965). It seems out of keeping with the native English tradition which has always held fast to the Wykehamist motto, 'Manners makyth man'.

The flaw in the analytical philosopher's make-up is that he can never bring himself to agree that the only rational course is to recognize the existence of non-rational elements and forces in human experience: in sticking close to logical arguments he misses the mystery and the magic which for others are the heart of the matter. It remains to be seen, therefore, whether the pride of place awarded by the analytical school of thought to conceptual problem-solving will carry the day or whether it will be modified by the developmental approach recommended by the psychologists.

The indications are that a reconciliation between discipline-centred and child-centred frames of reference, long overdue, may be near. In *The Logic of Education* (1970), Hirst and Peters write: 'When . . . we stress the importance of the development of knowledge and under-standing as being central to education, we are acutely aware that the cognitive and affective aspects of such development are intimately connected. Our sympathies are with the progressives in their emphasis on the motivational factors in education, to which they draw attention with their talk about the needs and interests of children. But our con-viction is that this kind of motivation, which is crucial in education, is unintelligible without careful attention to its cognitive core.' That they are acutely aware of the advisability of protesting that their hearts are in the right places is at least reassuring: too often the analytical philoso-pher's obsession with the 'forms of knowledge', as he is pleased to call them, leaves the impression that he is a bloodless rationalist. As John Wilson observes (1968), 'Rationality in morals involves more than attention to logic, language and the overt facts. It involves attention to one's feelings and *controlled* use of imagination.'

And if the pretensions of analytical philosophy to be regarded as *the* philosophy for the second half of the twentieth century now begin to look somewhat exaggerated, there is another school of thought – the literary intellectuals – which seems well on the way to becoming *passé*. W. Walsh (1959) earns an honourable mention in this connection, if only for upholding the place of sensibility in an examination-ridden system which leaves the affective side of learning to look after itself. The most consistent and redoubtable exponent of the Eng. Lit. viewpoint, however, has been G. H. Bantock (1952, 1963, 1965, 1967). A Leavisite and a disciple of T. S. Eliot, Bantock is a traditionalist who plays the part of Nestor, one who is appalled by the low level of the quality of life in modern society, pessimistic about the potentialities of the mass of school children and scornful of the superficiality of the general run of educational discourse. For him Rousseau and Dewey are the arch-enemies. Here, too, it may be thought that there is certain unconscious arrogance in the insistence that literary intellectualism is the supreme arbiter in the realm of value judging.

A not unfair verdict might be that analytical philosophy has, on the whole, performed a useful service by applying a cold douche to sentimental and muddled thinking; that literary intellectualism has played its part, necessarily a defensive one, in opposing the dehumanizing effects of mass education and scientism. Both lay themselves open to the charge of being in some respects reactionary; and it seems probable that both have had their day. Neither of them is in sympathy with the moods and aspirations of large sections of modern youth, or sufficiently well acquainted with the wide range of knowledge and techniques drawn from psychology, sociology, cultural anthropology, theology, ethology, economics, policial science and other fields which together will provide the constituents for a genuinely overarching theory of education. The one-dimensional approach, whether it be linguistic, logical or literary is clearly inadequate. It results only in that kind of restrictive humanism which T. S. Eliot had in mind when he said that 'No humanist *qua* humanist ever had anything to offer the mob'.

Curiously enough, there is one offshoot from literary intellectualism which may well be a pointer to the future. 'Our need today is culturally the same as the scientist's who seeks to become aware of the bias of his instruments'. Thus McLuhan (1962). Not only must education come to terms with the mob; it must also come to terms with the 'logic' and 'language' of the new non-verbal media of communication which have transformed the learning situation. The symbolic forms which crave to be understood go far beyond those of literacy. In short, the plea for a modern synthesis, so prematurely urged in the post-war years, has become more urgent.

From now on, would-be philosophers in the field of education will need to know vastly more than they did in the past. Significantly, the latest attempts to devise a coherent theory and practice – for example, R. A. Hodgkin (1970) – are fused from a richly varied background knowledge. Hodgkin's *Reconnaissance on an Educational Frontier* may not be to everyone's taste with its blend of psychoanalysis, communication theory, mountaineering adventure, logical indeterminacy and Christian existentialism, but at least it marks a return to the kind of philosophy which is not afraid to ask and answer questions about the nature of man and his destiny.

If interaction is the clue to such problems as the relation between Nature and Nurture, general and special education, arts and science, individual and society and so *ad nauseam*, the inference must be that only an all-embracing philosophy arising from the interaction of many minds and many disciplines will suffice. To call it a 'systems approach', i.e. the viewing of a problem in a contextual frame of reference with all its interior connections and all its exterior ramifications, is, of course, to invite immediate derision. The place for general systems theory, it may be thought, is in the sociology of education (see pp. 121–8) or in educational technology (see pp. 194–7), not here; and in any case it is too inchoate to place much reliance on its applications at present. Possibly so: but if a philosophy of education is to succeed in its attempt to see life whole, as a many-splendoured thing, it might do worse than to cultivate the habit of systems thinking.

Bibliography

For advanced students two guides to the literature on philosophy of education are available:

POWELL, J. P. (ed.) *Philosophy of Education: A Select Bibliography.* 2nd ed. Manchester UP, 1970. pp. 51. Items numbered but not annotated. Author index. Topics classified ranging from 'General

Works on Philosophy', 'Nature of Philosophy of Education', etc., to 'Indoctrination', 'Equality', 'Punishment' and 'Educational Theories'. Most of the entries refer to articles from the relevant learned journals in the English-speaking world. Only twenty-nine book titles are listed.

BROUDY, H. S., PARSONS, M. J., SNORK, I. A. and SZOKE, R. D. *Philosophy of Education: An Organization of Topics and Selected Sources.* Urbana, U of Illinois P, 1967. pp. 287. This is based on a major curriculum project on the teaching of philosophy of education in colleges and universities in the U.S.A. The project had two objectives: (1) to identify, (2) to classify the topics and the literature. All sources published in the English language were scanned. After classification, each of the various items was allocated to a cell in a grid system in order to facilitate quick reference.

Not being intended for the research scholar, the compilation presented here does not pretend to be either systematic or exhaustive. It adopts a dual classification: 1 Formal Studies, 2 Informal Studies.

Category 1 refers to books by professional philosophers and includes a number of important works on general philosophy (asterisked), which have a direct or indirect bearing on educational issues. Category 2 refers to books by authors who would not necessarily describe themselves as philosophers. Inevitably, these straddle the borderline between Philosophy of Education and Educational Theory (see pp. 37–48).

For the doctrines of the Great Educators, see the section on History of Education (pp. 106–10).

1 Formal Studies

ARCHAMBAULT, R. D. (ed.) *Philosophical Analysis and Education.* L, Routledge, 1965. pp. 222. Although L. A. Reid utters a caveat against going overboard on analysis in the Introduction, the other contributors ignore it. Chop-logic of the New Scholasticism, mostly.

—— (ed. with Introduction) *Lectures in the Philosophy of Education 1899 by John Dewey.* NY, Random House, 1966. pp. 366. Transcripts from one of his student's shorthand notes; for progressives the next best thing to a recording of His Master's Voice.

ARNSTINE, D. *Philosophy of Education: Learning and Schooling.* NY, Harper & Row, 1967. pp. 588.

*AYER, A. J. *Language, Truth and Logic.* 2nd ed. L, Gollancz, 1946. pp. 160. A key text.

* AYER, A. J. *The Concept of a Person and Other Essays.* L, Macmillan, 1963. pp. 272.

——— Man as a Subject for Science. L, Athlone P, 1964. pp. 26.

BEREDAY, G. Z. F. and LAUWERYS, J. A. (eds.) *The Year Book of Education 1957: Education and Philosophy.* L, Evans, 1957. pp. 578. Mishmash of comparative religion and other odds and ends; the sort of thing that the analytical school has rightly reacted against.

BELTH, M. *Education as a Discipline.* Boston, Mass., Allyn & Bacon, 1965. pp. 317. Argues that the school is a school is a school, i.e. that the process of education is strictly intellectual.

BLAU, J. L. *Men and Movements in American Philosophy.* Englewood Cliffs, Prentice-Hall, 1952. pp. 403. From the colonial period to Dewey.

BRACKENBURY, R. L. *Getting Down to Cases.* NY, Putnam, 1959. pp. 222. A problems approach to educational philosophizing.

BRAMELD, T. *Philosophies of Education in Cultural Perspective.* NY, Holt, Rinehart & Winston, 1955. pp. 446. Standard American textbook prior to 1960.

——— Cultural Foundations of Education. NY, Harper & Row, 1957. pp. 330.

——— Toward a Reconstructed Philosophy of Education. 2nd ed. NY, Holt, Rinehart & Winston, 1962 (first pub. 1956). pp. 417. Combines Perennialism, Essentialism and Progressivism in a philosophy dedicated to a worldwide democratic New Order.

——— Education as Power. NY, Holt, Rinehart & Winston, 1965. pp. 146. 'Reconstructionism' as social action and reform.

BRAUNER, C. and BURNS, H. W. *Problems in Education and Philosophy.* Englewood Cliffs, Prentice-Hall, 1965. pp. 165.

BROUDY, H. S. *Building a Philosophy of Education.* 2nd ed. Englewood Cliffs, Prentice-Hall, 1961 (first pub. 1954). pp. 480. Uses Aristotelian straw to make its bricks.

BRUBACHER, J. S. *Modern Philosophies of Education.* 4th ed. NY, McGraw-Hill, 1969 (first pub. 1939). pp. 393.

——— A History of the Problems of Education. 2nd ed. NY, McGraw-Hill, 1966 (first pub. 1947). pp. 659.

*BUBER, M. *I and Thou.* 2nd ed. NY, Scribner, 1958. pp. 137.

——— Between Man and Man. L, Fontana, 1961. pp. 256. Personalism tends to have a quasi-mystical ring, carries the reader into deep waters.

BURNS, H. W. and BRAUNER, C. J. (eds.) *Philosophy of Education: Essays and Commentaries.* NY, Ronald P, 1962. pp. 442.

30 *Philosophy of Education*

CAHN, S. M. *The Philosophical Foundation of Education.* NY, Harper & Row, 1969. pp. 433. Textbook-cum-anthology of classical, modern and contemporary analytical schools of thought.

CURTIS, S. J. *An Introduction to the Philosophy of Education.* L, U Tutorial P, 1958. pp. 258. Solid, reliable, unexciting.

DEARDEN, R. F. *The Philosophy of Primary Education.* L, Routledge, 1969. pp. 196. Neat sniping, often on target, directed mainly against 'activity and experience', etc.

*DE CHARDIN, T. *The Phenomenon of Man.* L, Collins, 1959. pp. 320. Lofty thinking on Christian science.

ELAM, S. (ed.) *Education and the Structure of Knowledge.* Chicago, Rand McNally, 1964. pp. 277. Interdisciplinary discussions about the place of arts, science and social studies in general education.

*FLEW, A. G. N. (ed.) *Logic and Language.* O, Blackwell, 1953. pp. 242.

FRANKENA, W. K. *Three Historical Philosophies of Education.* Glenview, Ill., Scott Foresman, 1965. pp. 216. Idealism (Kant), Realism (Aristotle) and Pragmatism (Dewey).

GRIBBLE, J. *Introduction to the Philosophy of Education.* Boston, Mass., Allyn & Bacon, 1969. pp. 198. A good textbook. Section 2 (Training, Instruction, Conditioning, Indoctrination) is particularly useful.

HIRST, P. and PETERS, R. S. *The Logic of Education.* L, Routledge, 1970. pp. 147. Extends an olive branch to progressives and developmental psychologists but insists that attention to the cognitive core of learning is the first priority.

HOLLINS, T. H. B. (ed.) *Aims in Education: The Philosophic Approach.* Manchester UP, 1964. pp. 154. Symposium; interesting critique of the concept of mental health by R. S. Peters.

*HOSPERS, J. *An Introduction to Philosophical Analysis.* L, Routledge, 1967. pp. 629. Definitive work.

JOHNSTON, H. *A Philosophy of Education.* NY, McGraw-Hill, 1963. pp. 362. Neo-Thomism.

JUDGES, A. V. (ed.) *Education and the Philosophic Mind.* L, Harrap, 1957. pp. 208. Lectures on the various Isms; eminently readable.

KILPATRICK, W. H. *Philosophy of Education.* NY and L, Macmillan, 1951. pp. 465. Swansong of the progressive movement.

KNELLER, G. F. *Existentialism and Education.* NY, Wiley, 1964. pp. 173. Sees the individual, not the group, as the authentic unit in education.

—— *An Introduction to the Philosophy of Education.* NY, Wiley, 1964. pp 139.

KNELLER, G. F. *Logic and the Language of Education*. NY, Wiley, 1966. pp. 252. All three above titles are good examples of lucid exposition.

LANGFORD, G. *Philosophy and Education: An Introduction*. L, Macmillan, 1968. pp. 160. As good a textbook for British students as any.

LUCAS, C. J. *What is Philosophy of Education?* L, Collier-Macmillan, 1969. pp. 352. It's a good question; ably answered, too.

MORRIS, V. C. *Existentialism in Education*. NY, Harper & Row, 1966. pp. 163. Brings some elusive issues into focus.

MORRISH, I. *Disciplines of Education*. L, Allen & Unwin, 1967. pp. 336. Good chapters on Plato, Rousseau and Dewey.

NASH, P. *et al. Authority and Freedom in Education*. NY, Wiley, 1966. pp. 342. Analytical-dialectical examination of controversial themes.

NATIONAL SOCIETY FOR THE STUDY OF EDUCATION. *Fifty-Fourth Year Book: Modern Philosophies and Education*. U of Chicago P, 1955. pp. 374. Covers the gamut of Isms.

NEFF, F. C. *Philosophy and American Education*. New York, Center for Applied Research in Education, 1966. pp. 116.

O'CONNOR, D. J. *An Introduction to the Philosophy of Education*. L, Routledge, 1957. pp. 156. Bombshell or damp squib? Title is something of a misnomer, more an exposition of logical empiricism; for all that, stimulating and challenging.

PAI, Y. and MYERS, J. T. (eds.) *Philosophic Problems and Education*. Philadelphia, Lippincott, 1967, and L, Pitman, 1968. pp. 467.

PARK, J. (ed.) *Selected Readings in the Philosophy of Education*. 3rd ed. NY, Macmillan, 1968. pp. 433.

—— *Bertrand Russell on Education*. L, Allen & Unwin, 1965. pp. 147.

PETERS, R. S. *Authority, Responsibility and Education*. 2nd ed. L, Allen & Unwin, 1963. pp. 137.

—— *Ethics and Education*. L, Allen & Unwin, 1966. pp. 319.

—— (ed.) *The Concept of Education*. L, Routledge, 1967. pp. 223.

—— (ed.) *Perspectives on Plowden*. L, Routledge, 1969. pp. 116. See also HIRST, P. and PETERS, R. S. (above).

PHENIX, P. H. *Philosophy of Education*. NY, Holt, Rinehart & Winston, 1958. pp. 623.

—— *Realms of Meaning: A Philosophy of the Curriculum for General Education*. NY, McGraw-Hill, 1964. pp. 391. Sees human learning in six categories: Symbolics, Empirics, Aesthetics, Synnoetics, Ethics and Synoptics.

*POLANYI, M. *Personal Knowledge: Towards a Post-critical Philosophy.* 2nd ed. L, Routledge, 1962 (first pub. 1958). pp. 442. Stresses the essentially subjective nature of 'objective', scientific knowledge.

PRICE, K. *Education and Philosophical Thought.* Boston, Mass., Allyn & Bacon, 1962. pp. 511. Doctrines of the Great Educators as seen from an analytical viewpoint.

REID, L. A. *Philosophy and Education.* L, Heinemann Educ., 1962. pp. 224. Unlucky in its timing, this mature work has been somewhat overshadowed by the *succès fou* of the analytic junta. Retains a personalist flavour now out of fashion.

RUSSELL, B. *Education and the Social Order.* L, Allen & Unwin, 1956. pp. 254.

—— *On Education, Especially in Early Childhood.* L, Allen & Unwin, 1960 (first pub. 1926). pp. 171.

*—— *History of Western Philosophy.* 2nd ed. L, Allen & Unwin, 1961 (first pub. 1946). pp. 916. Monumental, entertaining, quixotic.

—— *Education of Character.* NY, Philosophical Library, 1961. pp. 160. No modern philosopher of comparable stature has been so strangely neglected in the field of educational studies – at any rate in Britain. Too progressive, no doubt!

*RYLE, G. (ed.) *The Revolution in Philosophy.* L, Macmillan, 1947. pp. 126.

*—— *The Concept of Mind.* L, Hutchinson, 1949, reprinted 1967. pp. 336. Demolishes the Cartesian myth of the 'ghost in the machine'.

*SARTRE, J.-P. *Existentialism and Humanism.* L, Methuen, 1948. pp. 70.

SCHEFFLER, I. *The Language of Education.* Springfield, Ill., Thomas, 1962. pp. 113. Influential in the U.S.A. and Britain; astringent criticism of terms which tend to be blurred in common usage.

—— *Conditions of Knowledge.* Glenview, Ill., Scott Foresman, 1965. pp. 117. An introduction to epistemology and education.

—— (ed.) *Philosophy and Education.* Boston, Mass., Allyn & Bacon, 1966. pp. 387. Modern readings.

SMITH, B. O. and ENNIS, R. H. (eds.) *Language and Concepts in Education.* Chicago, Rand McNally, 1961. pp. 221.

SOLTIS, J. F. *An Introduction to the Analysis of Educational Concepts.* Reading, Mass., Addison-Wesley, 1968. pp. 100.

*STRAWSON, P. F. *Individuals.* L, Methuen, 1959. pp. 255. Essay in descriptive metaphysics by a philosophers' philosopher.

ULICH, R. R. *Philosophy of Education.* NY, Van Nostrand Reinhold, 1961. pp. 286. A cosmic view.

—— (ed.) *Three Thousand Years of Educational Wisdom.* 2nd ed. Cambridge, Mass., Harvard UP, 1954 (first pub. 1947). pp. 668. Source book anthology.

*WARNOCK, G. J. *English Philosophy Since 1900.* 2nd ed. L, OUP, 1969. pp. 200.

*WARNOCK, M. *Ethics since 1900.* 2nd ed. L, OUP, 1966. pp. 220.

WEBER, C. O. *Basic Philosophies of Education.* NY, Holt, Rinehart & Winston, 1960. pp. 333.

*WILSON, J. *Philosophy.* L, Heinemann Educ., 1968. pp. 124.

WILSON, J., WILLIAMS, N. and SUGERMAN, B. *An Introduction to Moral Education.* Harmondsworth, Penguin Books, 1968. pp. 480. Progress report on team research involving a philosopher, a psychologist and a sociologist.

*WITTGENSTEIN, L. *Philosophical Investigations.* O, Blackwell, 1953, pp. 232. *Locus classicus* for linguistic analysis.

WYNNE, J. P. *Philosophies of Education.* NY, Prentice-Hall, 1947. pp. 427. From the standpoint of the philosophy of experimentalism. Authoritarianism, *laissez-faire* and experimentalism. Dated.

2 Informal Studies

BANTOCK, G. H. *Freedom and Authority in Education.* L, Faber, 1952. pp. 212.

—— *Education in an Industrial Society.* L, Faber, 1963. pp. 238.

—— *Education and Values: Essays in the Theory of Education.* L, Faber, 1965. pp. 182.

—— *Education, Culture and the Emotions.* L, Faber, 1967. pp. 202.

BARNES, K. C. *The Involved Man: Action and Reflection in the Life of a Teacher.* L, Allen & Unwin, 1969. pp. 246.

BARZUN, J. *The House of Intellect.* L, Secker & Warburg, 1959. pp. 288.

BLAMIRES, H. *Repair the Ruins.* L, Bles, 1950. pp. 192. Reflections on education from a Christian point of view.

CHOMSKY, N. *Language and Mind.* NY, Harcourt, Brace & World, 1968. pp. 88. Hypothesis is that language learning is only possible because humans have an inborn 'code' for generative grammar. Seminal study of profound significance for educationists.

CLARKE, SIR F. *Freedom in the Educative Society.* U of LP, 1948, reprinted 1966. pp. 104.

CONSULTATIVE COMMITTEE OF THE BOARD OF EDUCATION (Chairman W. H. Hadow). *The Primary School.* L, HMSO, 1931. pp. 290.

ELIOT, T. S. *Notes Towards the Definition of Culture.* L, Faber, 1948, 1967. pp. 124. Argues that societies cannot cohere without a class structure; derides some popular assumptions, e.g. that education makes people happier, that education is something everyone wants, that education should be organized so as to give equality of opportunity, etc.

ELLUL, J. *The Technological Society.* L, Cape, 1965. pp. 496. Gloomy appraisal of world situation in which 'things are in the saddle and ride men'.

FROMM, E. *The Sane Society.* L, Routledge, 1956. pp. 402.

—— *The Art of Loving.* L, Allen & Unwin, 1957. pp. 143. By the author of *The Fear of Freedom.*

HODGKIN, R. A. *Reconnaissance on an Educational Frontier.* L, OUP, 1970. pp. 108. Essay of rare distinction by headmaster-mountaineer in search of the numinous.

JACKS, L. P. *The Education of the Whole Man.* U of LP, 1931, 1966. pp. 155. A plea for a new spirit in education. But the Age of Analysis can only ask what is meant by the concept of the 'whole man'.

JASPERS, K. *The Idea of the University.* L, Peter Owen, 1965. pp. 176. A little masterpiece. Part I on the nature of science and scholarship is in a class of its own.

JEFFREYS, M. V. C. *Glaucon.* L, Pitman, 1950. pp. 173.

—— *Beyond Neutrality.* L, Pitman, 1955. pp. 60.

—— *Mystery of Man.* L, Pitman, 1957. pp. 111.

—— *Personal Values in the Modern World.* Harmondsworth, Penguin Books, 1962. pp. 174.

LAUWERYS, J. A. (ed.) *Ideals and Ideologies.* L, Evans, 1969. pp. 127. Essays on philosophy, morals and education from recent issues of the *Year Book of Education.*

LEWIS, C. S. *That Hideous Strength.* L, John Lane, 1945. L, Pan Books, 1968. pp. 256.

—— *The Abolition of Man.* L, Bles, 1946. pp. 64.

MCLUHAN, M. *The Gutenberg Galaxy.* L, Routledge, 1962. pp. 300. Diagnosis of print-dominated modes of thought.

—— *Understanding Media.* L, Routledge, 1964. pp. 384. Seer or charlatan? Probably the most talked-of book in a decade. Readers must sift the stuff from the nonsense themselves.

MAKARENKO, A. S. *The Road to Life*. Moscow, Foreign Languages Publishing House, 1955. 3 vols. pp. 444, 342 and 428. The great Soviet educator's account of an experiment in the rehabilitation of delinquents. Reads like a Dostoevsky novel.

NEILL, A. S. *Summerhill*. Harmondsworth, Penguin Books, 1962, reprinted 1970. pp. 336.

—— *Talking of Summerhill*. L, Gollancz, 1967. pp. 144. G.O.M. of progressive education, incorrigible, provocative.

NIBLETT, W. R. *Education and the Modern Mind*. L, Faber, 1967 (first pub. 1954). pp. 160. A plea for education in *depth*.

ORWELL, G. *Nineteen Eighty-Four*. Harmondsworth, Penguin Books, 1970 (orig. pub. 1949). pp. 256. Prophetic allegory, tract for the times.

*POPPER, K. R. *The Poverty of Historicism*. 2nd ed. L, Routledge, 1960. pp. 184.

*—— *The Open Society and Its Enemies*. 4th ed. L, Routledge, 1962 (first pub. 1945). Vol. 1 *The Spell of Plato*, pp. 364. Vol. 2 *The High Tide of Prophecy*, pp. 428. Hegel, Marx and the aftermath. Devastating attack on historicism. 'History has no meaning'. Idealism as the breeding ground for dictatorship.

*—— *Conjectures and Refutations*. L, Routledge, 1963. pp. 426.

*RAMSEY, I. T. (ed.) *Christian Ethics and Contemporary Philosophy*. L, Student Christian Movement P, 1966. pp. 400.

—— *Religious Language*. NY, Collier-Macmillan, 1965. pp. 192.

*SKINNER, B. F. *Science and Human Behaviour*. NY, Macmillan, 1953. pp. 461. The case for social engineering.

—— *Walden Two*. NY, Macmillan, 1969. pp. 266. Utopia in a technological society; 1984 through rose-coloured spectacles.

SNOW, C. P. *The Two Cultures and the Scientific Revolution*. Rede Lectures. CUP, 1959. pp. 58.

TIBBLE, J. W. (ed.) *The Study of Education*. L, Routledge, 1966. pp. 240.

*TOULMIN, S. *An Examination of the Place of Reason in Ethics*. CUP, 1960. pp. 228.

*TOULMIN, S. and GOODFIELD, J. *The Discovery of Time*. L, Hutchinson, 1965. pp. 288. Third of a four-volume *magnum opus* on 'The Ancestry of Science'. How human life acquired a history and a genealogy.

WALSH, W. *The Use of Imagination*. L, Chatto & Windus, 1959. pp. 252.

*WHITEHEAD, A. N. *Science and the Modern World*. CUP, 1936, and various eds. pp. 266.

*WHITEHEAD, A. N. *Adventures of Ideas*. CUP, 1933, and various eds. pp. 302.

—— *The Aims of Education*. L, Benn, 1932, and various eds. pp. 256. Three classic texts from the pre-1945 period, unequalled since.

*WIENER, N. *Cybernetics*. 2nd ed. NY, Wiley, 1961 (first pub. 1948). pp. 212.

—— *The Human Use of Human Beings*. L, Eyre & Spottiswoode, 1951. New ed. Sphere, 1969. pp. 192. Cybernetics in the service of men?

*YOUNG, B. Z. *Doubt and Certainty in Science*. L, BBC, 1950. The Reith Lectures 1950.

2 *Educational Theory*

Universities endow chairs for it, colleges prescribe courses for it, students answer questions about it, so why baulk at calling it the *Theory of Education*? One good reason for doing so is the difficulty of deciding just what 'it' is. What to include and what to omit in this haziest of all corners in the field of educational studies? Is it even a corner? Rather a limbo, many of its critics would say – a ragbag for whatever is left over after the politicians, the philosophers, the psychologists, the sociologists, the historians and the rest have had their say. The contrary view, which maintains that educational theory draws its raw materials from these varied sources, might be more convincing if it succeeded in making something distinctive out of them.

'Far from being an autonomous discipline, educational theory would seem to be rather as complex as any field of knowledge can be, and different from those fields not because some unique form of understanding is involved but because the elements are used in the making of practical principles', writes Paul Hirst (in J. W. Tibble (ed.), *The Study of Education*, 1966).

As to that, the obvious rejoinder must be that it is precisely the failure to adduce practical principles that has helped to bring educational theory into disrepute. More often than not the impression created has been that there *is* no demonstrable end product, nothing solid to bite on, no take-home pay for the intellectual efforts expended in chasing this nebulous will-o'-the-wisp. Students are left in no doubt that theories *about* education abound, and that each and all of them are riddled with question marks. To speak of a theory of education, therefore, let alone *the* theory of education, sounds to most of them suspiciously like a misnomer. Claptrap, they call it.

Understandably, then, many authors nowadays are careful to avoid any mention of the word in choosing their book titles. Techniques, yes; models, yes; theory, no. Classroom interaction analysis, microteaching, simulation and gaming, group dynamics, organization theory, systems theory and the rest – students nowadays can get their teeth into these, it seems, but when it comes to 'theory of education' many of them draw a blank. It is not simply that the credibility gap between theory and

37

practice is too great for them to surmount: more serious is the feeling that what passes for theory is so generalized as to be utterly amorphous. At one extreme, the issues discussed are indistinguishable from those raised in the philosophy of education; at the other, they tend to interpret themselves at the humdrum level of tips for teachers – principles of classroom management. What lies between is not so much a bridge as a no-man's-land.

All the same, this dislike of the sloppy usage of the term 'theory', like the analytical philosophy that first prompted it, is no more than a passing phase. We need reminding that in the language of everyday discourse the word is legitimately applied in a wide range of contexts. To look for a common core of meaning is as idle as to insist on a single, strict definition since the most that can be said is that there is a recognizable family resemblance in these different usages.

In *The Concept of Mind* (1949: cited under Philosophy of Education, p. 32), Gilbert Ryle rightly differentiated between *having* a theory, *using* a theory and *finding* a theory. The latter he likened to the task of making paths where none as yet exist. In this sense, any book that is concerned to explore any unresolved problem in education may be classified under the heading of 'theory'. The extent to which that exploration is guided by rational hypothesis, personal belief, emotive thinking, blind hunch or even black prejudice represents a difference of degree rather than of kind.

It is often said that the trouble with education is that it is an activity in which everyone feels entitled to express his own opinion. It may well be the case that much of what passes for 'theory of education' consists of nothing more reliable than expressions of individual points of view. But even if theory were to be thus demoted to the status of opinion, no one doubts that some opinions are more worthy of consideration than others. They have survival value because they are seen to embody a measure of truth, or at least wisdom – and wisdom is not necessarily demeaned by describing it as conventional.

In a relativistic age absolute theories, like absolute truths, are no more to be expected or desired than are final solutions. Uncertainty is a *sine qua non* in any human enterprise. Learning to live with the knowledge that a fully prescriptive theory of education is an impossibility may be hard, but there is no escaping it. To be told that there is nothing for it but to find one's own way through the bewildering thicket of theories (shades of opinion) which surrounds us left, right and centre may be cold comfort, but in so far as we are all in the same predicament there is no alternative to the exercise of the right and duty of private judgement. The more widely informed that judgement is, however, the more hopeful will become the task of creating paths where none as yet exist, if only because it is sustained by the knowledge that others have been this way before, that the ground leading to the way ahead has been partly cleared, that we are never entirely alone. This, presumably, is what Hirst and Peters have in mind when they refer (in *The Logic of Education*, 1970) to 'the intellectual challenge involved in trying to make up one's mind about complex questions to which there are not as yet, and perhaps never can be, definite answers'.

Educational theory has long been bedevilled by false dualisms – Nature versus Nurture, liberal studies versus technical training, discipline-centred versus child-centred approaches to teaching, élitist versus egalitarian policies, etc., etc. Occasionally, as in the Snow – Leavis fracas over the Two Cultures, these give rise to lively controversy, but in general they have a way of leading only to conclusions in which little or nothing is concluded. Once the shouting has died down the impression left behind is that agreement to differ is the most that can be bargained for. 'A plague o' both your houses!' say the bystanders.

This is a pity, for the last twenty-five years have seen educational theory converging in a number of broad directions. It is true that these have been power-steered by developments in psychology, sociology, technology and other fields, and that it is too early to claim that they point to anything like a consensus, still less to a set of rules which teachers can follow in the classroom. Even so, there are signs that educational theory *is* capable of making something distinctive out of the raw materials it uses, and that it can offer end products that are not entirely nebulous. How long it will be before educational theory once again commands the authority that formerly enabled it to lay down explicit basic principles with complete assurance remains to be seen. In the meantime it is worth noting some of the points that now meet with wide assent among educationists:

(1) 'Intellectual talent is not a fixed quantity with which we have to work but a variable that can be modified by social policy and educational approaches . . . the kind of intelligence which is measured by the tests so far applied is largely an acquired characteristic. This is not to deny the existence of a basic genetic endowment; but whereas that endowment, so far, has proved impossible to isolate, other factors can be identified.'

This key passage from the *Newsom Report* (*Half Our Future*, 1963) sets the tone and summarizes the arguments for the contemporary rev-olution in educational theory. Revolution because it marks a breakaway from negative, fatalistic concepts of educability, which it seeks to replace with positive, optimistic concepts. Environmental influences are now seen to be of crucial importance in deciding the learner's school performance. The ways in which factors other than the genetic one (social class, family background, language, neighbourhood, the organiza-tion of schools, etc.) interact and combine to produce an interlocking network of inequalities in the education system are now tolerably well known. Whether or not the practical implications are well enough realized is another matter. British culture being what it is, the probability is that a sneaking love of inequality will persist, regardless of the evidence. So much the worse for Britain if it does. At any rate, there is no longer any excuse for resurrecting the 'Limited Pool of Ability' myth, nor any resisting the conclusion that policy-making hitherto has woefully underestimated the potential capabilities of the mass of children.

(2) 'We begin with the hypothesis that any subject can be taught effectively in some intellectually honest form to any child at any stage of development.' This sentence from J. S. Bruner's book *The Process of Education* (1960) is as hackneyed as any in the literature, and deservedly. Reminiscent of Makarenko's dictum, 'If the pupil fails to learn the fault is in the teaching', it typifies the spirit of the new pedagogy. Here again, to British ways of thinking such a declaration of faith is apt to seem widely unrealistic, a piece of nonsense on a par with Helvetius's 'L'éducation peut tout' or James Mill's 'Any man may learn any thing, one person as well as another'. Bruner's hypothesis and his advocacy of a spiral curri-culum with its progressive stages of enactive, iconic and symbolic levels of understanding have been criticized as being no better than a revamp of Whitehead's well-known 'Rhythm of Education'; and the objection is often made that his adumbration of a prescriptive theory of instruc-tion in *Toward a Theory of Instruction* (1966) is not really very helpful to the practising teacher. Nevertheless, it is to Bruner more than to any other individual that we owe the initial impetus which has led to the growing interest in curriculum reform. The 'new' mathematics, Nuffield Science and humanities projects, French in the primary school – these and a host of fresh departures are backed by the same underlying conviction that all-round standards of attainment can be raised if only a concerted effort is made to enhance styles of presentation. Just as the modern concept of educability implies that the average child is capable

of better things, so the new pedagogy rises to the challenge of heightened competence and professionalism on the part of teachers. To this end it may be necessary in some cases to provide teachers with high quality, field-tested learning materials, in others to assist them in exploiting the opportunities afforded by modern technologies of communication; in short, to smooth the changeover from their role as *instructors* to that of *managers* in a school which is slowly but surely being transformed into a resources for learning centre. And if this sounds unnecessarily futuristic, at least it can be said that experimental work in the fields of curriculum development and educational technology has underlined once and for all a number of fundamental principles which hold good for any methodology of teaching.

(3) One of these is the prior need for a clear statement of objectives. As if taking their cue from the linguistic analysts, educationists have become increasingly dissatisfied with so-called ultimate aims, which seem at best to amount to nothing more than the expression of pious hopes. Instead, they prefer to concentrate on learning tasks which allow of visible, tangible achievements. Hence the cult of stating objectives in behavioural terms.

Unlike an 'aim', an objective leaves neither the teacher nor the pupil in any doubt about what has to be done or what the outcome is to be: moreover, it ensures that both can assess the progress they are making.

This is not to say that educational theory has excluded any possibility of having a final goal, simply that, in the first instance, it recommends the pursuit of immediate, short-term ones. Obviously, stating objectives in behavioural terms, i.e. saying precisely what the learner will be capable of doing as a result of the instruction he has received, is a good deal easier for a lesson lasting forty-five minutes than it is, say, for the year's work as a whole. Higher-order objectives are now conceived hierarchically on the lines set out in B. S. Bloom's *Taxonomy of Educational Objectives, Handbook 1: The Cognitive Domain* (1956) in which they are arranged in six classes in ascending order:

1.00 Knowledge
2.00 Comprehension
3.00 Application
4.00 Analysis
5.00 Synthesis
6.00 Evaluation

While the present vogue in favour of behavioural objectives has much to commend it, however, certain reservations need to be made. The first arises from the fact that the popularity of the 'taxonomy' has centred more or less exclusively on *Handbook 1*. *Handbook 2: The Affective Domain* (Krathwohl *et al.*, 1964) has proved to be decidedly less successful and is arguably misconceived. As a consequence, the trend of educational thought in recent years – a trend encouraged by B. F. Skinner's work in programmed learning and by R. W. Tyler's in assessment – might well be characterized as Neo-Herbartian. A second reservation concerns the vital distinction which has to be drawn between higher-order objectives which admit of little or no dubiety in their outcome and those which must, in the nature of things, be permanently hedged about with uncertainty. The longer the time span, the greater the tendency for new-style objectives to merge into old-fashioned aims!

The decision to settle for tangible objectives and for identifiable long-term goals is, no doubt, understandable. This liking for 'knowledge of results' is praiseworthy in so far as it permits teacher and pupils alike to see where they are going and how they are faring. A good deal of the disenchantment with the profession of theoretical aims springs from the flagrant discrepancies between such a profession and its actual outcome in practice. The current disillusion over the effects of compulsory religious instruction in English schools is only one illustration of this. If the rationalists had their way, presumably, religion would forthwith cease to be the final court of appeal in education, in which case some alternative ideology would have to be found to replace it. To be sure, this is not a problem that educational theorists can be expected to solve on their own: it raises fundamental issues in the national life which are unlikely to be resolved until some agreement has been reached about 'that for the sake of which everything else is done'. As things are, no such agreement is in sight. Ultimate goals are seemingly no more part of the educationist's business than the eternal verities are of the analytical philosopher's. If so, there is more than a rough grain of truth in the notion that Britain has lost an empire and has yet to find a role in the modern world.

(4) As a corollary of the preoccupation with objectives, there is now a much stronger insistence on the need for systematic *assessment*. The traditional end-of-course examination still has its place (and a mighty big one) but it is no substitute for a policy of continuous testing-as-you-go. Only by building assessment into the learning and teaching process can the pursuit of objectives be regulated and the dangers of off-course drift avoided.

(5) Yet another principle stresses the need for careful analysis of the

structure of the course of study, area of knowledge, skill or whatever it is that pupils are expected to learn. 'Grasping the structure of a subject is understanding in a way that permits many other things to be related to it meaningfully. To learn structure, in short, is to learn how things are related', says Bruner in *The Process of Education*; and again, 'The curriculum of a subject should be determined by the most fundamental understanding that can be achieved of the underlying principles that give structure to that subject. Teaching specific topics or skills without making clear their context in the broader fundamental structure of a field of knowledge is uneconomical in several deep senses.' In the first place, such teaching makes it difficult for the pupils to see the relevance and significance of what they are learning; in the second, it is likely to be dull: in the third, it will tend to be easily forgettable. 'Organizing facts in terms of principles and ideas from which they can be inferred is the only known way of reducing the quick loss of human memory.' Only connect . . .

(6) 'Nature observes a suitable time', as Comenius noted three and a half centuries ago. If the emphasis on the importance of *structure* has boosted the claims of discipline-centred curriculum theory, the need for equally careful analysis of the *sequence* that the learning process must follow if it is to be effective is also realized. This sequence is necessarily psychological rather than logical, i.e. it must be in keeping with the stage of mental development through which the learner is passing. Today, the essential rightness of a developmental approach to learning and teaching is generally accepted in primary schools if nowhere else. Despite its detractors, child-centred education has shown that the soundness of any theory and practice is ratified by psychological justifications, not solely by adhering to logical proofs. There is indeed a kind of poetic justice in the historical process by which the ideas of romantic dreamers like Rousseau and Froebel have been vindicated by modern empirical psychologists, among whom Piaget is beyond question the most influential.

The developmental approach has made relatively little headway in the grammar schools, where it is blocked by external examination requirements, but it has been responsible for a measure of emancipation in the work of many secondary modern schools. Although the quarrel between 'progressive' and 'traditional' theory and practice has yet to be composed, it is becoming easier to see that the extremists on both sides – A. S. Neill and R. F. Mackenzie on the one, the Black pamphleteers on the other – represent two polarities which between them define a single process. Each has its suitable time and its proper place. On the whole, child-centred approaches seem to be more at home during the pre-school and primary stages, discipline-centred study in the upper reaches of the academic secondary school. The error lies in advancing all-out claims on behalf of one or the other. *Pace* theorists like Belth (1965), no useful purpose is served by pretending to treat education as if it were exclusively intellectual. If it has done nothing more, child-centred theory has at least underlined the importance of the affective aspects of learning. The fact that 'progressive' schools have so far failed to flourish in the state system tells us something about the conditions prevailing inside that system: it is not to be taken as an aspersion on the theory underlying their practice. Never let it be forgotten that the antithesis of 'progressive' is not 'traditional', as the die-hards fondly suppose, but quite simply 'unprogressive'.

In the U.S.A. the 'return to learning', as it has been called, was a necessary corrective in view of the low levels of scholastic attainment during the slap-happy era of Life Adjustment courses and the twilight of the 'progressive' movement. In the general disarray of American high schools between 1945 and 1955 a discipline-centred approach proved to be as timely as it was salutory. Since these conditions have never been typical of the British situation, however, there is no excuse for aping the American example in this respect. On the contrary, it is to the developmental approach as a humane and civilizing influence that we must look if we are ever to rid ourselves of the divisive after effects of a Two Nations mentality.

(7) Hitherto the content of education has been thought of primarily in terms of existing subject matter. In the case of liberal studies it has been customary to justify the selection of the content of courses on the grounds that they possessed intrinsic worth, exemplifying 'the best that has been thought and said in the world'. Against this, contemporary curriculum theory insists that 'Content is important only in so far as it helps to bring about intended outcomes. . . . Content has no intrinsic worth, indeed no place, until man does something with it as a result of experience in which behaviour is learned.' So D. K. Wheeler in *Curriculum Process* (1967: cited under Curriculum Study, p. 71).

At first sight this is a hard saying, flying in the face of accepted practice as it does. But although the rank and file of teachers would probably say that their main job is to teach 'subjects' there is, nevertheless, a perceptible and growing tendency to view the curriculum in a contextual frame of reference. Gone, or going fast, is the mindless habit of teaching a 'subject' for no better reason than 'because it's there'. Amid all the loose talk about 'the learning situation', 'conditions of learning' and 'the learning environment', there is the dawning recognition that the secret of success or failure in the pupil's school performance resides not so much in the difficulty of a 'subject', its inherent worth or even the method of teaching it as in the social setting in which the learning process takes place.

In the same way, and for the same reason, that theology has been to some extent demythologized (Religion without God) and morality has parted company with the established codes of yesteryear, so educational theory is less and less disposed to worship some of its sacred cows. This is not to say that 'the best that has been thought and said in the world' has been discredited, only that it is no longer held to be an adequate rationale for deciding what is and what is not to be taught.

This emphasis on the contextual aspects of learning is part and parcel of a wider social movement which David Riesman characterizes as the transfer from an inner-directed to an other-directed way of life (*The Lonely Crowd*, 1964: cited under Sociology of Education, p. 137). The danger is, of course, that it may leave us with a concept of education which is virtually contentless. Conceivably, this, or something like it, has already happened in philosophy, in ethics and in religion.

(8) 'Most learning occurs outside the classroom.' Of all McLuhan's *obiter dicta* this is the one that should occasion the least surprise seeing that it has always been the case that the school has been only one agency for the transmission of culture. With the advent of new technologies of communication (which should not be equated with the mass media) the contrast between formal, school-bound learning and the informal learning which finds its expression in the television lounge, the discotheque and elsewhere has been accentuated. For many children the *vade mecum* is no longer the book but the transistor radio. It is true that research findings on the effects of media exposure tend to be inconclusive and that many investigators have reported no significant differences, but it seems likely that this is because the tests employed so far have been designed to measure cognitive learning and little else. Just as a standardized intelligence test tells us nothing about an individual's creative potential, so a literate-minded test tells us nothing about the psychic effects of watching television, say. What is being called in question here is the adequacy of existing concepts of learning, in particular the assumption that learning is closely identified with verbal reasoning. Cognitive learning has always been the chief stock in trade

of the schools, but it is now recognized that even cognitive learning assumes a variety of forms, each of which calls for special treatment. By comparison, affective and attitudinal learning has been played down, not being so amenable to examination.

Throughout the nineteenth century *literacy* was the first priority in the education of the masses. In the twentieth this heavy premium placed on reading and writing has been offset by the growing demand for *numeracy*. Latterly, a third desideratum, which, for want of a better, goes by the name of *oracy*, has been brought to the notice of teachers. It seems possible that a fourth – *picturacy*, i.e. the ability to 'make sense' of kaleidoscopic visual configurations – will be added in the not-so-distant future. In any case, radical rethinking about the so-called basic skills will become necessary sooner or later.

All of which may seem to pose questions that are far too open-ended for the average student and practitioner, constrained as they are by forces inside and outside the education system which combine to make 'business as usual' the rule. Even so, it is difficult to envisage the school carrying on with its well-worn routines in a world which will have at its disposal a vaster array of learning experiences at the touch of a switch than ever before. As it is, the formal learning it dispenses is restrictive, being tied to mental disciplines based almost entirely on the manipulation of verbal and mathematical symbols, which leads to a situation in which too many competitors are left chasing too few rewards. The divorce of school from life, so often bemoaned by educationists in the past, remains as pronounced as ever; and the drop-out phenomenon is a symptom of the profound sense of alienation felt by many teenagers. From now on, no question about it, understanding media must be the first commandment for any viable educational theory.

Name-dropping is a contemptible habit. Still, it can hardly have escaped notice that not one of those mentioned in this cursory review – Bruner, Bloom, Makarenko, Piaget, Tyler, McLuhan – is British; or that none of them answers to the usual description of an educationist. As A. V. Judges noted in *The Function of Teaching* (1959), 'the vital impulses now sustaining discussions about the role of education spring up in places quite remote from the usual debating grounds of the professional educators'. It is no accident that most of the significant departures during the past quarter of a century, notably those in curriculum study and educational technology, have originated abroad.

There remains the knottiest of all problems in educational theory, the relationship between general and special education, previously touched on in the section on philosophy of education. To conclude, as was done there, that it is an insoluble riddle is not necessarily defeatist, merely another reminder of the uncertainty which the quest for a wholly satisfying theory of education invariably entails. A gloomier view might be that we are all in the same boat as Sir Richard Livingstone was when he wrote *Education for a World Adrift* (1943).

Which is it to be: breadth of studies on the lines recommended in the Harvard Committee's report (1945) or specialization in depth as the *Crowther Report* (1959) and Sir Eric Ashby (*Technology and the Academics*, 1958) were inclined to think? Or is this just another pseudo-problem arising from yet another false dualism? Clearly, no solution is going to be possible so long as intellectual prowess is taken to be the acid test of human worth. The dilemma of educationists is the dilemma in which all rational humanists now find themselves. Language is the tool of their trade: they are nothing if not experts in the written word. The question is whether this expertise is the only one that is required. As Ernest Gellner says in *Crisis in the Humanities* (edited by J. H. Plumb, 1964): 'When the age of chivalry was over, Don Quixote was a joke. The military equipment of a knight could no longer be taken seriously. The question now is: how seriously does one now take the *cognitive* equipment of the *clerk*? The answer is, alas, not very much.'

At the risk of being accused of anti-intellectualism, therefore, the one hope of finding some principle of unity-in-diversity is to be found in the markedly egalitarian trend in contemporary educational thought. Certainly, this trend is vigorously contested by the forces of élitism for whom the shibboleth and rallying cry is 'Excellence' (usually evaluated in terms of A-levels and Open Scholarship awards). Britain, as we have seen, cherishes its time-honoured inequalities with the same affection it reserves for its stately homes. In America, where the tension between Jeffersonian and Jacksonian democracy has seen the latter gain the upper hand for long periods, the education system has developed more on by-the-people-for-the-people lines than it has anywhere in Europe. Of the three political ideals which the Founding Fathers borrowed from the French *philosophes* – liberty, equality and fraternity – the first has been universally conceded. The idea-ideal of equality, on the other hand, is openly questioned and frequently derided as nonsensical. As for fraternity, it stands little chance of winning more than lip-service in a competitive, acquisitive society. No matter: some ideas, as White-head saw, are so seminal that they carry within themselves the prophecy of their eventual fulfilment. Liberty, equality and fraternity are to the secular humanism of the modern world what the supernatural virtues of faith, hope and charity were to medieval Christendom. Just as in Wilberforce's day many educated people found it easy to query the necessity of freedom as human right, so today many seek to rationalize their prejudice against the idea of equality. That is at once the mark of their immaturity and an indication of the arrested development that has yet to be overcome in the life of certain ideas.

It should be a chastening thought that there have been few even moderately good books about education and only one great one – and it took the greatest philosopher of all time to write that one, as Sir Eric (now Lord) James remarked in *An Essay on the Content of Education* (1949: cited under Curriculum Study, p. 68). By rights, 'the best that has been thought and said' in the field of education studies should be located here. The sorry truth is that there is precious little that is worth preserving and a great deal that deserves no better than to be categorized as mush. In the U.S.A. publishers still advertise textbooks on the 'Foundations of Education'. Not in Britain. Most of the steam which formerly energized educational theory is now being transferred to curriculum study (see pp. 60–71) and educational technology (see pp. 190–206), two fields in which contemporary model-building finds happier hunting grounds than it does in the realm of philosophy. The fact remains that in the last analysis the heart of the matter must always be philosophical in nature.

Bibliography

Not surprisingly, no systematic bibliography of educational theory is available. The list that follows has been loosely grouped under the broad headings of:

1 General works
2 Religious education
3 Moral education
4 Aesthetic education
   4.1 Art
   4.2 Creative writing

1 General Works

ARCHAMBAULT, R. D. (ed. and Introduction) *Tolstoy on Education*. Tr. L, Wienet. U of Chicago P, 1967. pp. 360. Reflections on the progressive school run by the greatest Russian novelist; general message-permissiveness.

ASHBY, SIR E. *Technology and the Academics.* L, Macmillan, 1958. pp. 118. Specialism as the key to culture in the modern world.

BANDER, P. (ed.) *Looking Forward to the Seventies: A Blueprint for Education in the Next Decade.* Gerrards Cross, Colin Smythe, 1968. pp. 336. Fudged; contributions from most of the big names in British education, none of them very adventurous.

BANTOCK, G. H. *Freedom and Authority in Education.* L, Faber, 1952. pp. 212. Sets the tone for the rest of this writer's *œuvre* – antiprogressive, anti-egalitarian, yet commanding attention by its high seriousness.

—— *Education in an Industrial Society.* L, Faber, 1963. pp. 238. Ah-the-past ruminations.

—— *Education and Values: Essays in the Theory of Education.* L, Faber, 1965. pp. 182. Educational problems not reducible to technological solutions.

—— *Education, Culture and the Emotions.* L, Faber, 1967. pp. 202.

BELTH, M. *Education as a Discipline.* Boston, Mass., Allyn & Bacon, 1965. pp. 317. Sees educational theory as the study of verifiable hypotheses, models for the construction of knowledge.

BEREDAY, G. Z. F. and LAUWERYS, J. A. (eds.) *The World Year Book of Education 1965: The Education Explosion.* L, Evans, 1965. pp. 498. Mine of information on the problems of meeting the world-wide demands for expansion.

BESTOR. A. E. *Educational Wastelands.* Urbana, U of Illinois P, 1953. pp. 226. Scathing indictment of the retreat from learning in American schools at the time; one of several angry books (see also entries for LYND and NEATBY in this section), which has left its mark.

BLACKIE, J. *Good enough for the Children?* L, Faber, 1963. pp. 160. Chief Inspector's thoughts on the lack of quality in primary education; a minor classic.

BLAMIRES, H. *Repair the Ruins.* L, Bles, 1950. pp. 192. Reflections on education from the Christian point of view; makes nostalgic reading twenty years on when all sense of sacredness seems to have evaporated into thin air.

BLOOM, B. S. *et al. Taxonomy of Educational Objectives. Handbook 1: The Cognitive Domain.* NY, Longmans, 1956. pp. 207. Hierarchy of the intellect; trend-setter for recent educational thought.

BROWN, B. B. *The Experimental Mind in Education.* NY, Harper & Row, 1968. pp. 301.

BRUNER, J.S. *The Process of Education.* C, Mass., Harvard UP, 1960. pp. 97. Required reading, a study of rare distinction. Chapters 2 to 4 give the kernel.

—— *OnKnowing: Essays for the Left Hand.* C, Mass., Harvard UP, 1962. Underlines the need for intuitive, heuristic problem-solving as distinct from deductive and algorithmic thinking.

—— *Toward a Theory of Instruction.* C, Mass., Belknap P, 1966. pp. 176. Predispositions, structure, sequence, reinforcement.

CENTRAL ADVISORY COUNCIL FOR EDUCATION (ENGLAND). *15 to 18 (The Crowther Report).* L, HMSO, 1959. pp. 520. Draws attention to the low level of general education of the majority of school-leavers; sees no alternative to specialization in sixth-form studies, but recommends the use of 'minority time' to correct undue imbalance.

—— *Half Our Future (The Newsom Report).* L, HMSO, 1963. pp. 299. Advocates a new deal for children of average and below-average ability.

—— *Children and Their Primary Schools (The Plowden Report).* Vol. 1. L, HMSO, 1967. pp. 555. Chapters 15 to 22 are the most relevant; difficult to see the wood for the trees elsewhere.

CENTRAL OFFICE OF INFORMATION/MINISTRY OF EDUCATION. *Story of a School.* L, HMSO, 1949. pp. 36. A gem from the slums of Birmingham.

CLARKE, SIR F. *Freedom in the Educative Society.* U of LP, reprinted 1966. pp. 104. Minor classic from the World War II years.

CONANT, J. B. *On Understanding Science.* NY, New American Library, 1951. pp. 144. Differentiates between the public consensus among scientists and its lack in the humanities where 'to stick to ascertainable facts is to limit the discourse to the banal'. One of the many important books by this distinguished American educationist.

—— *Education and Liberty.* C, Mass, Harvard UP, 1953. pp. 168. Role of the schools in three modern democracies: U.K., Australia and U.S.A.

CONNEL, W. F., DEBUS, R. L. and NIBLETT, W. R. (eds.) *Readings in the Foundations of Education.* L, Routledge, 1967. pp. 398. Comprehensive anthology drawn from essays ancient and modern; a good source book.

COX, C. B. and DYSON, A. E. (eds.) *The Crisis in Education: Black Paper Two.* L, Critical Quarterly Society, 1969. pp. 160. Right-wing fulminations.

Crowther Report – see CENTRAL ADVISORY COUNCIL FOR EDUCA-
TION.

DEWEY, J. *Democracy and Education.* NY, Macmillan, 1916 and various
eds. pp. 378. Magnum opus unequalled in the twentieth century.
—— *Experience and Education.* NY, Collier–Macmillan, 1938, 1963.
pp. 91. The most concise, readable statement of Dewey's position,
written in the light of criticisms of progressive theory and practice.
—— *Selected Educational Writings.* L, Heinemann, 1966. pp. 334.
Introduction and commentary by F. W. Garforth.

ELVIN, H. L. *Education and Contemporary Society.* L, Watts, 1965.
pp. 220. An exemplary study, broad-based, shrewd. Part 1 reviews the
state of the art in sociology, psychology, philosophy and comparative
education. Part 2 relates this varied background knowledge to
practical issues, e.g. democratization, élites, intellectual, moral and
social values. Highly recommended.

ENTWISTLE, H. *Child-Centred Education.* L, Methuen, 1970. pp. 222.
Sober weighing of the pros and cons.

FLANDERS, N. A. *Analyzing Teacher Behavior.* Reading, Mass.,
Addison-Wesley, 1970. pp. 448. Outlines techniques of classroom
interaction-analysis, microteaching, etc.

FLETCHER, B. A. *A Philosophy for the Teacher.* L, OUP, 1961. pp. 154.
A study of the child and human knowledge.

FOSS, B. M. *Education as Art, Science and Technology.* L, Harrap, 1967.
pp. 28. A psychologist's view.

FRASER, W. R. *Residential Education.* O, Pergamon P, 1968. pp. 320. A
little-known book of some quality.

HARVARD COMMITTEE. *General Education in a Free Society.* C, Mass.,
Harvard UP, 1945. pp. 298. One of the great documents of the period.
Social studies as the link between science and the humanities.
Chapter 2, 'Theory of General Education', remains essential reading.

HIGGINSON, J. H. *Changing Thought in Primary and Secondary
Education.* L, Macmillan, 1969. pp. 148.

HIGHET, G. *The Art of Teaching.* L, Methuen, 1951. pp. 182. Classical
scholar's apologia for great teachers from Socrates and Jesus to the
present day.

HIRST, P. H. and PETERS, R. S. *The Logic of Education.* L, Routledge,
1970. pp. 147.

HUDSON, L. *Contrary Imaginations.* L, Methuen, 1966. pp. 181.
Harmondsworth, Penguin Books, 1967, pp. 205. Convergent and
divergent frames of mind.

HUTCHINS, R. M. *The Learning Society.* Harmondsworth, Penguin Books, 1970. pp. 142.

HUTCHINSON, M. and YOUNG, C. *Educating the Intelligent.* Harmondsworth, Penguin Books, 1962. pp. 240. Proposals for reforming the secondary schools.

JACKS, M. L. *Total Education: A Plea for Synthesis* L, Kegan Paul, 1946. pp. 160. But the Age of Analysis has passed it by.

—— *The Education of Good Men.* L, Gollancz, 1955. pp. 192.

JACKSON, B. *Streaming: An Education System in Miniature.* L, Institute of Community Studies/Routledge, 1964. pp. 176. Hard-hitting attack on the vices of ability-grouping in English primary schools.

JEFFREYS, M. V. C. *Glaucon.* L, Pitman, 1950. pp. 173. Christian existentialist's inquiry into the purposes of education; a notable work of the kind not much favoured at the moment, but due for a come-back.

—— *Beyond Neutrality.* L, Pitman, 1955. pp. 60. Essays on the need for responsible choice in an age in which 'our ethical foundations are crumbling, our religious beliefs are evaporating'.

—— *The Unity of Education.* O, Religious Education P, 1966. pp. 128.

JENKINS, D. *The Educated Society.* L, Faber, 1966. pp. 258. Examination of the wider social implications of educational expansion.

JUDGES, A. V. (ed.) *The Function of Teaching.* L, Faber, 1959. pp. 172. Lectures on T. S. Eliot, Mannheim, Maritain, Buber, Freud, William James and Archbishop William Temple.

KING, E. J. *The Education of Teachers.* NY, Holt, Rinehart & Winson, 1970. pp. 153.

—— (ed.) *The Teacher and the Needs of Society in Evolution.* O,Pergamon P, 1970. pp. 319. Symposium on the changing role and status of teachers.

KNELLER, G. F. *Educational Anthropology: An Introduction.* NY, Wiley, 1965, pp. 171. American textbook for which there is no adequate British equivalent.

—— (ed.) *Foundations of Education.* 2nd. ed. NY, Wiley, 1967. pp. 678.

KOERNER, J. D. *Reform in Education.* L, Weidenfeld & Nicolson, 1968. pp. 332. American observer's perceptive criticisms of British education.

KRATHWOHL, D. R., BLOOM, B. S. and MASIA, B. B. *Taxonomy of Educational Objectives. Handbook 2: The Affective Domain.* NY, David McKay, 1964. pp. 196.

LAUWERYS, J. A. (ed.) *Teachers and Teaching.* L, Evans, 1969. pp. 147. Essays on curriculum, training and social position of teachers from recent *Year Book of Education* issues.

LIVINGSTONE, R. W. *Education for a World Adrift.* CUP, 1943. pp. 158.

—— *Some Tasks for Education.* L, OUP, 1946. pp. 106. Eloquent defence of 'Greats', swansong of the Classics.

—— *Education and the Spirit of the Age.* L, OUP, 1952. pp. 124.

LYND, A. *Quackery in the Public Schools.* Boston, Mass., Little Brown, 1953. pp. 282. *Saeva indignatio* against progressive education; a best-seller in its day.

MACKENZIE, R. F. *A Question of Living.* L, Collins, 1963. pp. 160. Biting attack on the Establishment by a Scots headmaster with fire in his belly.

MCLUHAN, M. *The Gutenberg Galaxy.* L, Routledge, 1962. pp. 300. Diagnosis of print-dominated modes of thought; baffling book by a master of discontinuous prose, but an important one.

—— *Understanding Media.* L, Routledge, 1964, and various eds. pp. 384. Essential reading despite its obscurantism and eccentricities of style.

MARITAIN, J. *Education at the Crossroads.* New Haven, Conn., Yale UP. 1943, 1955. pp. 120. Notable contribution by eminent Catholic thinker; castigates as misconceptions a disregard of ends, false ideas concerning the End, pragmatism, intellectualism, voluntarism and the notion that everything can be learned.

MOBERLY, SIR W. *The Crisis in the University.* L, Student Christian Movement P, 1949. pp. 316. Pietist plea for more attention to 'the issues that are momentous' in higher education.

MORRISH. I. *Disciplines of Education.* L, Allen & Unwin, 1967. pp. 336. Useful textbook.

NEATBY, H. M. *So Little for the Mind.* Toronto, Clarke Irwin, 1953. pp. 384. Canadian onslaught on progressive education; on a par with BESTOR and LYND (see above).

NEILL, A. S. *The Free Child.* L, Jenkins, 1953, pp. 180.

—— *Summerhill.* Harmondsworth, Penguin Books, 1962. Reprinted 1970. pp. 336.

—— *Talking of Summerhill.* L, Gollancz, 1967. pp. 144. Sums up a lifetime's experience of this bonny fighter in the cause of freedom as self-regulation.

NEWSOM, J. H. *Education for Girls.* L, Faber, 1948. pp. 160.

Newsom Report – see CENTRAL ADVISORY COUNCIL FOR EDUCATION.

NIBLETT, W. R. *Education and the Modern Mind.* L, Faber, 1967 (first pub. 1954). pp. 160.

NUNN, SIR T. P. *Education: Its Data and First Principles.* 3rd ed. L, Arnold, 1945. pp. 283. Textbook widely used in the pre-war period; classic exposition of the case for individualism.

OESER, O. A. *Teacher, Pupil and Task.* L, Tavistock, 1966. pp. 210.

OLLERENSHAW, K. *Education for Girls.* L, Faber, 1961. pp. 196.

ORTEGA Y GASSET, J. *Mission of the University.* L, Routledge, 1946. pp. 81. Updating the concept of liberal education by the author of *The Revolt of the Masses.*

PETERS, R. S. (ed.) *The Concept of Education.* L, Routledge, 1967. pp. 223.

—— *Perspectives on Plowden.* L, Routledge, 1969. pp. 116.

PETERSON, A. D. C. *Educating Our Rulers.* L, Duckworth, 1957. pp. 93.

—— *The Future of Education.* L, Cresset P, 1968. pp. 256. Sane assessment of the prospects.

PICKERING, G. *The Challenge to Education.* L, Watts, 1967. pp. 167. Argues that the British system was designed to meet nineteenth-century conditions and is ill suited to face up to the challenge of the times.

Plowden Report – see CENTRAL ADVISORY COUNCIL FOR EDUCATION.

PLUMB, J. H. (ed.) *Crisis in the Humanities.* Harmondsworth, Penguin Books, 1964. pp. 176. Scholarly essays on the dilemma of intellectual humanism in the classics, history, philosophy, divinity, literature. etc.

RAMANATHAN, G. *The Quest for General Education.* India and L, Asia Publishing House, 1969. pp. 237. Indian follow-up on the Harvard Committee report.

RICHARDSON, E. *The Environment of Learning.* L, Nelson, 1967. pp. 247. Conflict and understanding in the secondary school.

RICHMOND, W. K. *An Apology for Education.* L, Redman, 1952. pp. 247.

—— *Culture and General Education.* L, Methuen, 1963. pp. 184. Two Cultures hypothesis using makeshift culture tests.

—— *Readings in Education.* L, Methuen, 1968. pp. 246. Programmed extracts dealing with main topics arising in educational theory.

ROSS, J. S. *Groundwork of Educational Theory*. L, Harrap, 1942, 1952. pp. 264. Quasi-philosophical textbook, dated but durable.

ROSS, S. C. *Arts v. Science*. L, Methuen, 1967. pp. 158. Symposium on the Snow line.

SCHAEFER, R. J. *The School as a Centre of Inquiry*. NY, Harper & Row, 1967. pp. 77.

SCOTTISH EDUCATION DEPARTMENT. *Primary Education in Scotland*. Edinburgh, HMSO, 1965. pp. 230. Official blessing for 'activity and experience'.

SKINNER, B. F. *Science and Human Behaviour*. NY, Macmillan, 1953. pp. 461.

SMITH, L. M. and GEOFFREY, W. *The Complexities of an Urban Classroom*. NY, Holt, Rinehart & Winston, 1968. pp. 277. Towards a general theory of teaching; micro-ethnographic analysis of conditions in a slum classroom in Washington, D.C.

SNOW, C. P. *The Two Cultures and the Scientific Revolution*. CUP, 1959. pp. 52. Sees modern knowledge as divided into two self-contained hemispheres with communication between them increasingly difficult and near-impossible 'at the top of the Establishment'.

—— *The Two Cultures* and *Second Look*. CUP, 1964. pp. 108.

STENHOUSE, L. *Culture and Education*. L, Nelson, 1967. pp. 156. A sociological interpretation; sees culture as the medium in which formal education exists.

TAYLOR, W. *Society and the Education of Teachers*. L, Faber, 1969. pp. 304.

—— (ed.) *Towards a Policy for the Education of Teachers*. L, Butterworth, 1969. pp. 262. Many-sided interdisciplinary symposium.

TIBBLE, J. W. (ed.) *The Study of Education*. L, Routledge, 1966. pp. 240. Many-sided approach to problems in educational theory; standard work.

VAIZEY, J. *Education in the Modern World*. L, Weidenfeld & Nicolson, 1967. pp. 256. A good factual survey; useful background reading.

WALSH, W. *The Use of Imagination*. L, Chatto & Windus, 1956. pp. 256. Seeks insight into child development and the growth of sensibility in poetry (especially the Romantics) and the novel (D. H. Lawrence).

WHITEHEAD, A. N. *Science and the Modern World*. CUP, 1936, and various eds. pp. 266.

—— *The Aims of Education*. L, Benn, 1932, and various eds. pp. 256. Included here mainly because there has been nothing to touch them since 1945.

WYNNE, J. P. *Theories of Education*. NY, Harper & Row, 1963. pp. 521. An introduction to the foundations of education.

YATES, A. (ed.) *Grouping in Education*. NY, Wiley, 1966. pp. 314. International research studies on the effects of ability-grouping in schools.

YOUNG, M. *The Rise of the Meritocracy*. L, Thames & Hudson, 1958, and various eds. One of the liveliest books in the literature; two-edged satire on life in a competitive society obsessed with the need for economic growth.

2 Religious Education

One of the most striking developments in educational theory since 1945 has seen religious issues receding more and more into the background. During the same period Protestant theologians like Niebuhr, Tillich, Bultmann and Bonhoeffer have sought new interpretations of Christian doctrine. Significantly, however, the lofty vein of writers like M. V. C. Jeffreys and W. R. Niblett tends to get short shrift nowadays.

ARGYLE, M. *Religious Behaviour*. L, Routledge, 1958. pp. 224. Title speaks for itself.

BULTMANN, R. *Jesus Christ and Mythology*. L, Student Christian Movement P, 1960. pp. 96. Essential reading for the serious-minded.

COX, E. *Changing Aims in Religious Education*. L, Routledge, 1966. pp. 128.

—— *Sixth Form Religion*. L, SCMP, 1967. pp. 188.

GOLDMAN, R. *Religious Thinking from Childhood to Adolescence* L, Routledge, 1964. pp. 276.

—— *Readiness for Religion*. L, Routledge, 1965. pp. 238. A Piagetian approach; a highly influential study.

LOUKES, H. *Teenage Religion*. L, SCMP, 1961. pp. 160.

—— *New Ground in Christian Education*. L, SCMP, 1965. pp. 200.

MADGE, V. *Children in Search of Meaning*. L, SCMP, 1965. pp. 142.

MAY, P. R. and JOHNSTONE, D. R. *Religion in Our Schools*. L, Hodder & Stoughton, 1968. pp. 125.

MURRAY, A. V. *Education into Religion*. Welwyn, Nisbet, 1953. pp. 230.

RAMSEY, I. T. (ed.) *Christian Ethics and Contemporary Philosophy*. L, SCMP, 1966. pp. 400.

SMITH, J. W. D. *Religious Education in a Secular Setting*. L, SCMP, 1969. pp. 128. A down-to-earth textbook.

UNIVERSITY OF SHEFFIELD INSTITUTE OF EDUCATION. *Religious Education in Secondary Schools.* L, Nelson, 1961. pp. 96.
World Year Book of Education: Church and State in Education. L, Evans, 1966. pp. 386. Source book.

3 Moral Education

Morals without religion become increasingly problematical in a permissive society. There is no easy way out by saying that *how* we teach is more important than *what* we teach. 'Moral education is a name for nothing clear', we are informed.

ACLAND, SIR R. *We Teach Them Wrong.* L, Gollancz, 1963. pp. 192.

BIBBY, C. (ed.) *Aspects of Education: Morality and Education.* U of Hull Institute of Education, 1964. pp. 96.

BOWLBY, J. and FRY, M. *Child Care and the Growth of Love.* Harmondsworth, Penguin Books, 1965. pp. 254.

BULL, N. J. *Moral Education.* L, Routledge, 1969. pp. 192.

EPPEL, E. M. and EPPEL, M. *Adolescents and Morality.* L, Routledge, 1966. pp. 254.

ERIKSON, E. H. *Childhood and Society.* Harmondsworth, Penguin Books, 1965. pp. 430. Neo-Freudian approach; a major work.

FLUGEL, J. C. *Man, Morals and Society.* Harmondsworth, Penguin Books, 1955. pp. 415.

GRAINGER, A. J. *The Bullring: A Classroom Experiment in Moral Education.* O, Pergamon P, 1970. pp. 158.

HOLLINS, T. H. B. (ed.) *Aims in Education: The Philosophic Approach.* Manchester UP, 1964. pp. 154. See the papers on 'Education and Indoctrination' by J. Wilson and on 'Adolescents into Adults' by R. M. Hare.

MACY, C. *Let's Teach Them Right.* L, Pemberton, 1969. pp. 214. But can virtue be taught?

NIBLETT, W. R. (ed.) *Moral Education in a Changing Society.* L, Faber, 1963. pp. 172. Symposium.

PHENIX, P. H. *Education and the Common Good.* NY, Harper & Row, 1961. pp. 271. Search for values based on objective worth.

WARD, L. O. *Teaching Moral Values.* O, Religious Education P, 1969. pp. 72. Concise review of problems, research trends and the role of the teacher.

WILSON, J. *Moral Thinking.* L, Heinemann Educ., 1970. pp. 88.

WILSON, J., WILLIAMS, N. and SUGERMAN, B. *An Introduction to*

Moral Education. Harmondsworth, Penguin Books, 1968. pp. 480.
Philosopher, psychologist and sociologist combine in search for
rational criteria which should recommend themselves to anyone who
takes the trouble to think about the matter intelligently. A notable
contribution, strongly recommended. But the Socratic question
remains: *Can* virtue be taught?

4 Aesthetic Education

Some voices crying in the wilderness here. Among the learning objectives prescribed by the vast majority of schools aesthetic ones tend to
get low priority, despite constant assertions of their importance. The
usual excuse given is that aesthetic activities are not readily examinable.
A more honest explanation might be that the education system is
essentially philistine.

4.1 ART

BHATIA, H. R. *Craft in Education.* 2nd ed. India and L, Asia Publishing House,1962. pp. 196. Gandhi-inspired philosophy and psychology
of Craft in Basic Education.

BRITTON, J. (ed.) *The Arts and Current Tendencies in Education.*
U of L Institute of Education/Evans, 1963. pp. 153.

CARLINE, R. *Draw They Must.* L, Arnold, 1968. pp. 325. Strictly a
history, but contains excellent chapters on child art and primitive
art, imaginative composition, art appreciation and methods of
teaching.

MUNRO, T. *Art Education: Its Philosophy and Psychology.* Indianapolis,
Bobbs-Merrill, 1956. pp. 387.

READ, H. *Education Through Art.* 3rd ed. L, Faber, 1958 (first pub.
1943). pp. 328. Apologia for art as *the* basis for all education; a major
work, somewhat marred by high-flown, doubtful psychological
interpretations.

—— *The Redemption of the Robot: My Encounter with Education Through
Art.* L, Faber, 1970. pp. 271.

RICHARDSON, M. *Art and the Child.* U of LP, 1964. pp. 134. Sympathetic study by a well-known and well-loved exponent of 'free-
enterprise' methods.

STEVENI, M. *Art and Education.* L, Batsford, 1968. pp. 40. Good
introduction to the theory and practice of creative work in the
classroom.

VIOLA, W. *Child Art.* 2nd ed. U of LP, 1944. pp. 206.

4.2 CREATIVE WRITING

The constraints on self-expression through the written word are not so easily thrown off as they are in child art. If it is agreed that the latter speaks for itself, the reason is that adult appraisals of what is good, bad or indifferent in the visual arts are less arbitrary than they used to be. Can evaluation of children's poetry and prose be similarly open-ended ? Too often, it may be thought, the champions of creative writing spoil their case by resorting to highfalutin' theory or, worse, sentimental gush.

ABBS, P. *English for Diversity*. L, Heinemann Educ., 1969. pp. 148. Acidulous diatribe.

BRIDGES, S. A. *Gifted Children and the Brentwood Experiment*. L, Pitman, 1969. pp. 160.

CLEGG, A. B. (ed.) *The Excitement of Writing*. L, Chatto & Windus, 1964. pp. 160. West Riding anthology.

DRUCE, R. *The Eye of Innocence: Poems*. Leicester, Brockhampton P, 1965. pp. 128. Children and their poetry.

HOLBROCK, D. *English for the Rejected*. CUP, 1964. pp. 292. Thesis is that non-academic, below-average ability pupils are capable of self-expression through the written word; arguably the most convincing of several books on the subject by this author.

HOURD, M. L. *The Education of the Poetic Spirit*. L, Heinemann Educ., 1949. pp. 192. Bears re-reading, better than most of its successors in the same Wordsworthian vein.

MACKINLAY, E. *The Shared Experience*. L, Methuen Educ., 1970. pp. 144. Sensitive study of creative writing in schools and colleges of education.

3 Curriculum Study

'Curriculum' is a slippery word. Broadly defined, it means nothing less than the educative process as a whole. Narrowly defined, as it usually is, the term is regarded as being more or less synonymous with 'the syllabus', 'a scheme of work' or simply 'subjects'. According to the one, no sharp distinction can be drawn between curricular, cocurricular and extracurricular activities, all of which are held to play their part in the pupils' total experience; according to the latter, the line between formal instruction and informal learning needs to be drawn much more firmly. The difference between the two positions corresponds to the difference between child-centred and discipline-centred theories discussed in the previous section. It can be caricatured not altogether unfairly as the difference between a philosophy that insists that learning is all one with living and one that is content to identify learning with schooling.

Curriculum study is concerned with the analysis and elucidation of the complex factors – historical, cultural, political, economic, technological, etc. – which determine what is taught and learned in the process of education. In the U.S.A. it is commonly referred to as *curriculum theory*, a designation that is apt to seem slightly pretentious to British ways of thinking.

Curriculum development, a vastly more ambitious undertaking, represents a deliberate attempt to manage innovations in the schools, which would otherwise be left to chance. Its proponents argue that in view of the exponential growth of all forms of modern knowledge and the ever-accelerating tempo of social change we are faced with an unprecedented situation and can no longer afford to sit back and let events take their own course. In the past, curriculum revision was a gradual process involving no more than piecemeal modifications in the content of courses. Today, nothing less than a policy of continuous adaptation to change – and the machinery to implement it – will meet the needs of the times.

In so far as this spells the end of *laissez-faire* theory and practice it seems certain that the curriculum development movement will join forces with educational technology (see pp. 190–206) and the managerial

60

revolution now taking place in educational administration (see pp. 144–162), with both of which it has obvious affinities. Clearly, if it is to be successful, any attempt to coordinate, let alone control, innovation must be undertaken on the basis of a massive combined operation. Airy talk of 'systems approaches' should deceive nobody. W. G. Bennis, K. P. Benne and R. Chin, authors of *The Planning of Change* (1961), see planning as 'the application of systematic and appropriate knowledge in human affairs for the purpose of creating intelligent action and change', which sounds fine, but so long as there is no agreement about what constitutes appropriate knowledge and no certainty about its applications if and when agreement is reached such formulations are bound to be Utopian. Model-building in curriculum theory is fast becoming a fine art but remains for the most part an academic exercise. True, the impressive assembly of theories and techniques now available in educational administration has been put to good use in places and promises well for the future. Being new and intellectually exciting, these theories and techniques encourage the belief that social engineering may at last be feasible.

As regards the host of experimental curriculum projects which have been carried out so far, however, the verdict must be that they are the merest skin grafts, some of which have not 'taken', not organic transplants. A state of mild euphoria has been brought about by the reported success of alphabet-soup curriculum making in the U.S.A. since 1957 and latterly of similar ventures in the United Kingdom. A decade hence the tone of self-congratulation to be found, for example, in R. W. Heath's *New Curricula* (1964) and W. Wooton's *SMSG: The Making of a Curriculum* (1965) will almost certainly appear naive. A fact that should never be forgotten is that the forces of innovation are easily exaggerated and that in any case they are not within the control of educationists. Even if they were, the inertia of tradition – 'dynamic conservatism' as it has been called – is not to be underestimated. A. G. Oettinger's *Run, Computer, Run* (1969) comes as a welcome antidote to the current wave of optimism in the fields of curriculum development and educational technology alike. No Luddite – Oettinger is in fact one of the leading authorities on computer-assisted instruction – he points out that: 'In Boston, which has enough trial programs and experiments to fill a book, the life of the average child in the average classroom is virtually unaffected. The teachers, the curriculum, the school committee are the same. The books are the same. The attitudes are the same.'

Evidently the impossible takes decidedly longer than the enthusiasts like to suppose. While it would be wrong to infer that the billions of dollars poured into curriculum projects in the U.S.A. – in mathematics, physics, chemistry, biology, etc. – have made little or no difference to scholastic standards in the high schools, it is now recognized that a strategy which involves moving one piece on the board at a time is fated to fail. Redesigning the curriculum as a whole cannot be accomplished by a feat of technological giganticism. With the possible exception of Sweden, no national planning board has yet shown that a systems approach to the problem may be viable.

Possibly because there is so much double talk about the need for curriculum renewal, there are as yet very few British books on the subject. The relevant literature is dispersed in the numerous bulletins and working papers issued by the Schools Council, the Nuffield Foundation, the Consultative Committee on the Curriculum (Scottish Education Department) and various regional bodies. For beginners, the best source is the *Journal of Curriculum Studies*. The pre-1969 literature is sparse and largely outmoded. Apart from one or two ineffectual reports from the immediate post-war years, Eric (now Lord) James's *An Essay on the Content of Education* (1949) and S. Nisbet's *Purpose in the Curriculum* (1957) are the only titles worthy of mention. Significantly, both take the existing subject matter as given, 'because it's there'. The new order ushered in by Bruner's *The Process of Education* (1960) and Bloom's *Taxonomy of Educational Objectives* (1956), two works whose importance as trend-setters has been stressed in the previous section, preferred to take a different starting point. In fairness, however, it should be pointed out that most of the spadework in curriculum study – in particular the insistence on the prior need for behavioural objectives and the need for improved assessment techniques – had been done by American educationists like R. W. Tyler (1950), H. Taba (1949), V. E. Herrick (1950) and W. O. Stanley (1957) long before the Sputnik scare lent them publicity value. D. K. Wheeler's *Curriculum Process* (1967) is typical of this highly doctrinaire genre: unfortunately, it is couched in so abstract a style as to be almost unreadable. Slighter but more appealing is J. F. Kerr's *Changing the Curriculum* (1968), an interdisciplinary symposium. Standing apart from the general run of books advertising themselves as innovation-minded, there are also one or two outstanding studies that have a direct bearing on the updating of methods of teaching, e.g. M. A. K. Halliday's *The Linguistic Sciences and Language Teaching* (1964), Z. P. Dienes's *An Experimental Study of Mathematics-Learning* (1964) and F. R. Jevons's *The Teaching of Science*

(1968). R. Goldman's *Readiness for Religion* (1965: cited under Educational Theory, p. 56) is another influential work.

All of which may encourage the belief that serious curriculum study in Britain is making up for lost time. The fact remains that it is still in its infancy. As for *curriculum development*, the less said about it the better until the prodigious snags that stand in its way have been reconnoitred and ways and means of outmanoeuvring them have been discovered; otherwise, it may turn out that the would-be planners of change have bitten off more than they can chew. Prestigious as they are, policies for the conservation of the natural environment all too easily reduce themselves to a topic for polite conversation and the same is likely to be true of some of the efforts now being made to rearrange the learning environment. As things are, and quite apart from the lack of adequate financial resources for research and development, educationists simply do not know enough to warrant the belief that they are capable of tackling the job.

The strategies for innovation adopted in different national systems provide an interesting comparative study. Why is it, for example, that Sweden is leading the field with a flow chart of across-the-board reforms, whereas its next-door neighbour, Denmark, is content to remain relatively conservative? Why must England have a Schools Council if Scotland can do without one? Why is it that in France legislation and ministerial decree between them have done more to transform the ethos of *culture générale* in the schools than all the expensive curriculum projects put together have succeeded in doing in the U.S.A.? Each strategy, it seems, is *sui generis*.

On the whole, nations with long histories tend to reverence the continuity of tradition, which is not the same as saying that they cling to the past. From John Locke and Dr Johnson to Winston Churchill and T. S. Eliot (English by adoption), great Englishmen have expressed their contempt for *avant garde* thinkers who urge the need for wholesale, radical reforms. The paradox is that these are the very men who have been mostly committed to the cause of time-honoured tradition and the ones who have helped to give it new directions and new leases of life. A policy of hastening slowly comes more naturally to the British way of life and may prove to be more effective than one which openly proclaims itself 'agin the system'. Like other myths, the English teacher's right to teach how he pleases is largely fictitious, but, as the early experience of the Schools Council suggests, the myth is real enough to arouse active opposition to any move that looks like foisting a packaged deal on the schools. The tactics employed in the U.S.A., where academics and specialist subject teachers put their heads together to produce new textbooks, are unlikely to meet with success here; and those that have found favour in Sweden, where a central planning board is responsible for a prearranged production schedule leading to the general adoption of mass produced learning materials, are virtually unthinkable in a British climate of opinion.

Inevitably, this sounds defeatist. Maybe it *is* defeatist. Certainly, the advocates of a systems approach have a point when they stress the dangers of go-slow in the schools at a time when the outside world is in a state of flux. Certainly, the credibility gap between 'learning' and 'living' is growing all the time and needs to be reduced. Even so, it is necessary to sound a cautionary note until the necessary strategies have been worked out. To this end, the advances now being made in educational technology and in management and organization studies will undoubtedly enhance the prospects for genuine curriculum development. Nevertheless, the discrepancy between the all-out claims of the model-builder and the practical problems which have to be faced is the discrepancy between what-might-be and what-can-be done to re-orientate the process of education. The larger the system, the greater the difficulty of controlling it. Organizing the staff and timetable of a school is one thing; administering the affairs of a local authority is another; implementing a national policy yet another. Managing a *culture* (the system of all the systems) is too tall an order in the present state of human knowledge and may, for all we know, be permanently out of the question. Which explains why this section prefers to call itself 'Curriculum Study'.

For an account of the North West Regional Curriculum Development Project, see the article on 'Curriculum model building' in *Educational Research in Britain 2*, edited by H. J. Butcher and H. Pont (1970: cited under Educational Psychology, p. 94). Launched in 1967, this project involves a consortium of fifteen local development centres, maintained by thirteen local education authorities and coordinated by the University of Manchester School of Education. In its early stages, the project was mainly occupied with organizational problems and is still undergoing its field trials. Even so, its emergent pattern, with its emphasis on the preliminary setting up of objectives, followed by the preparation of new courses which are continuously evaluated and modified in the light of feedback from teachers and pupils, foreshadows the shape of things to come.

For obvious reasons, curriculum development tends to be a good deal more viable in developing countries than it is in firmly established education systems (see section on comparative education). Despite the rough-handling of it in this review, the principles embodied in the concept of curriculum development – and the techniques of prediction and control – are the same as those to be found in the 'systems approach' now favoured in educational administration (see pp. 146–50) and educational technology (see pp. 194–7). A rationale for them is ably expounded by C. E. Beeby, J. F. Kerr and others in *Developing a New Curriculum*, edited by A. G. Howson (1970).

Bibliography

Curriculum study does not gain by being narrowly circumscribed. Team teaching and organizational changes in the schools are as much a part of it as are accounts of experimental projects, designs for new courses and new techniques of assessment. No excuse is offered, therefore, for listing works which feature in the bibliographies of other sections of *The Literature of Education* – in particular those dealing with Educational Theory, Educational Technology, Educational Administration (Politics, Management and Organization) and Comparative Education (Planning). Where necessary, cross references to annotations in these are indicated.

BAIR, M. and WOODWARD, R. G. *Team Teaching in Action.* Boston, Mass., Houghton Mifflin, 1964. pp. 229.

BEAUCHAMP, G. A. *Curriculum Theory.* 2nd ed. Wilmette, Ill., Kagg P, 1968. pp. 186. Highly abstract.

BENNIS, W. G., BENNE, K. P. and CHIN, R. *The Planning of Change.* NY, Holt, Rinehart & Winston, 1961. pp. 781.

BEREDAY, G. Z. F. and LAUWERYS, J. A. *The Year Book of Education 1958: The Secondary School Curriculum.* L, Evans, 1958. pp. 559. Still a useful source book, to some extent superseded by events.

BIDDLE, J. B. and ELLENA, W. J. (eds.) *Contemporary Research on Teacher Effectiveness.* NY, Holt, Rinehart & Winston, 1964. pp. 352.

BLOOM, B. S. *et al. Taxonomy of Educational Objectives. Handbook 1: The Cognitive Domain.* NY, Longmans, 1956. pp. 207. See under Educational Theory.

BRISTOL UNIVERSITY INSTITUTE OF EDUCATION. *The Curriculum of Secondary Schools Offering Advanced Studies.* Bristol U Inst. of Educ. Publications, 1962. pp. 67. Survey of sixth-form work.

BRITISH COUNCIL. *New Approaches to Teaching Mathematics.* L, British Council, 1970. pp. 16. A book list.

BRUNER, J. S. *The Process of Education.* C, Mass , Harvard UP, 1960. pp. 97. See under Educational Theory.

CENTRE FOR CURRICULUM RENEWAL AND EDUCATIONAL DEVELOPMENT OVERSEAS. *Modern Curriculum Developments in Britain.* L, CEDO, 1968. pp. 36.

CENTRAL ADVISORY COUNCIL FOR EDUCATION (ENGLAND). *Enquiry into the Flow of Candidates in Science and Technology into Higher Education (The Dainton Report).* L, HMSO, 1968. pp. 180. Examines bottlenecks to numeracy in schools and recommends their removal in order to increase the supply of scientific manpower.

CLARK, L. H. (ed.) *Strategies and Tactics in Secondary School Teaching.* NY, Macmillan, 1968. pp. 453. American anthology of (mostly) discipline-centred essays.

CONSULTATIVE COMMITTEE ON THE CURRICULUM. *Science for General Education: Curriculum Paper No. 7.* Edinburgh, HMSO, 1967. pp. 111. Sets out objectives in behavioural terms and outlines a course which cuts across the subject divisions of physics, chemistry and biology; now widely adopted in Scottish secondary schools.

COUNCIL FOR CURRICULUM REFORM. *The Content of Education.* U of LP, 1945. pp. 198. An early, wistful, wishful look at the problems.

DIENES, Z. P. *An Experimental Study of Mathematics-Learning.* L, Hutchinson, 1964. pp. 207. Penetrating research-based study of a Brunerian approach to mathematics in the primary school involving the use of structural apparatus.

EGGLESTON, J. F. and KERR, J. F. *Studies in Assessment.* L, English Universities P, 1969. pp. 256. Case studies of new-style curriculum evaluation, fixing objectives, moderating teachers' estimates, etc.

ELAM, S. (ed.) *Education and the Structure of Knowledge.* Chicago, Rand McNally, 1964. pp. 277.

FLEMING, C. M. *Research and the Basic Curriculum.* U of LP, 1947. pp. 120. Early guide to research findings on the relevance of school subjects from spelling and handwriting to history and geography and new methods of teaching.

FORD, G. W. and PUGNO, L. (eds.) *The Structure of Knowledge and the Curriculum.* Chicago, Rand McNally, 1964. pp. 105. A discipline-centred approach to curriculum planning.

FREEMAN, J. *Team Teaching in Britain.* L, Ward Lock Educ., 1969. pp. 424.

GOODLAD, J. I. *School, Curriculum and the Individual.* Waltham, Mass., Blaisdell, 1966. pp. 259.

GROBMAN, H. *Evaluation Activities of Curriculum Projects: A Starting Point.* American Educational Research Monograph Series on Curriculum Evaluation No. 2. Chicago, Rand McNally, 1969. pp. 136.

HALLIDAY, M. A. K., MCINTOSH, A. and STEVENS, P. *The Linguistic Sciences and Language Teaching.* L, Longmans, 1964. pp. 322. Highly influential study of the applications of modern linguistics.

HAPPOLD, F. C. *The English Subjects Synthesis.* L, Christophers, 1951. pp. 126. Suggests bringing history, geography, etc., under the same roof as English studies.

HARDING, D. H. *The New Pattern of Language Teaching.* L, Longmans, 1967. pp. 212.

HEATH, R. W. (ed.) *New Curricula.* NY, Harper & Row, 1964. pp. 292. Progress reports on all the major U.S. curriculum projects in physics, mathematics, biology, chemistry, English, etc., with some valuable second thoughts arising from them.

HERRICK, V. E. and TYLER, R. W. *Toward Improved Curriculum Theory.* U of Chicago P, 1950. pp. 124. Early, near-classic text by two doyens of curriculum reform; stress placed on systematic assessment.

HOWSON, A. G. (ed.) *Developing a New Curriculum.* L, Heinemann, 1970. pp. 149. CEDO (Centre for Educational Development Overseas) symposium, mainly devoted to problems of planning in developing countries; chapters 1–3 give a useful outline of general principles.

HOWSON, A. G. and ERAULT, M. R. *Continuing Mathematics: A proposal for a systems approach to the mathematical education of sixth-formers specializing in the arts and in social or life sciences.* L, Councils & Education P/NCET, 1969. pp. 30.

JACKSON, B. (ed.) *Verdict on the Facts: The Case for Educational Change.* C, Advisory Centre for Education, 1969. pp. 60. Urges the need for radical overhaul.

JAMES, E. *An Essay on the Content of Education.* L, Harrap, 1949. pp. 125. Elegant argument takes its stand on the intrinsic worth of study in depth, ends before means and the virtues of intellectual prowess; belongs to an earlier era.

JEVONS, F. R. *The Teaching of Science.* U of LP, 1968. pp. 208. Thoughtful, perceptive vindication of science as an integral part of general education.

KAZAMIAS, A. M. and MASSIALAS, B. G. *Tradition and Change in Education.* Englewood Cliffs, Prentice-Hall, 1965. pp. 182.

KERR, J. F. (ed.) *Changing the Curriculum.* U of LP, 1968. pp. 112. A British symposium which brings together the views of an educationist, a psychologist, a philosopher, a sociologist and a historian. Notable paper on 'The Problems of Curriculum Reform' by J. F. Kerr.

KRATHWOHL, D. R., BLOOM, B. S. and MASIA, B. B. *Taxonomy of Educational Objectives. Handbook II: The Affective Domain.* NY, David McKay, 1964. pp. 196.

LAUWERYS, J. A. and HANS, N. (eds.) *The Year Book of Education 1952.* L, Evans, 1952. Post-war reforms.

LOVELL, K. *Team Teaching.* U of Leeds Institute of Education, 1967. pp. 52. Brief, lucid progress report from the U.S.A.

MACCIA, E. S. (ed.) *Methodological Considerations in Curriculum Theory Building.* ASCD Commission in Curriculum Theory, 1965. Strictly for model builders.

MACLURE, S. (for the Schools Council) *Curriculum Innovation in Practice.* L, HMSO, 1968. pp. 100. Entertaining report of the proceedings of an Anglo-American-Canadian conference, reflecting different national viewpoints.

MARTIN, W. T. and PINCK, D. C. (eds.) *Curriculum Improvement and Innovation.* C, Mass., Robert Bentley, 1966. pp. 292. Deals with practical problems (in the U.S.A.).

MATHEMATICAL ASSOCIATION. *Mathematics Projects in British Secondary Schools.* L, Bell, 1968. pp. 38.

MILES, M. B. (ed.) *Innovation in Education.* NY, Teachers College P, 1964. pp. 689. Encyclopedia for forward-thinkers.

NATIONAL UNION OF TEACHERS. *The Curriculum of the Secondary School.* L, Evans, 1952. pp. 140. How to get rid of 'subjects' as chopped off segments of separate 'disciplines'? Dated as a document, but the question remains.

NISBET, S. *Purpose in the Curriculum.* U of LP, 1957. pp. 192. Accepting school subjects as given, sets out a framework of twelve objectives grouped under the headings of 'Adjustment to Environment' and 'Personal Growth', then analyses various subjects to see how far these objectives are fulfilled.

NUFFIELD FOUNDATION SCIENCE TEACHING PROJECT. *Physics: Teachers' Guide I–V.* L, Longman, 1966.

—— *Biology: Teachers' Guide I–V.* L, Longman, 1966.

—— *Chemistry: The Sample Scheme Stages I and II.* L, Longman, 1966.

OETTINGER, A. G. *Run, Computer, Run.* C, Mass., Harvard UP, 1969. pp. 303. Witty exposure of the mythology of innovation by an educational technologist whose verdict is that the impossible takes a good deal longer than the enthusiasts like to pretend.

ORGANIZATION FOR ECONOMIC COOPERATION AND DEVELOPMENT. *Curriculum Improvement and Educational Development.* Paris, OECD, 1966. pp. 79. Sees curriculum development as an integral and continuing part of educational policy making and planning; finds a piecemeal approach to the several disciplines no longer adequate; urges member countries to set up 'appropriate national permanent mechanisms' to deal with the problem.

PASSOW, A. H. (ed.) *Curriculum Crossroads.* NY, Teachers College P, 1962. pp. 123.

PELLEGRIN, R. J. *An Analysis of Sources and Processes of Innovation in Education.* U of Oregon, Center for Advanced Study of Educational Administration, 1966. A searching study of the type which needs replication in the U.K.

PLATT, W. J. *Research for Educational Planning.* Paris, UNESCO, International Institute for Educational Planning, 1970. pp. 67. Notes on emergent needs.

RICHARDSON, E. *The Environment of Learning.* L, Nelson, 1967. pp. 247. Secondary school curriculum in the context of its social setting.

RICHMOND, W. K. *The Teaching Revolution.* L, Methuen, 1967. pp. 220. Reviews organizational, curricular and methodological characteristics of the new pedagogy.

—— *The School Curriculum.* L, Methuen, 1971. pp. 279. Examines the strategies of innovation adopted in the U.S.A., France, Sweden, England and Scotland; adduces basic principles for curriculum renewal.

ROGERS, V. *The Social Studies in English Education.* L, Heinemann Educ., 1968. pp. 190. Critical review of current practices in the teaching of history, geography and the social sciences in primary and secondary schools.

ROMISZOWSKI, A. J. (ed.) *The Systems Approach to Education and Training.* L, Kogan Page, 1970. pp. 95. Models and modules galore; interesting paper by Gordon Pask on 'Practical Applications of Cybernetics to the Design of Training Systems'; also one by M. W. Neill on 'A Systems Approach to Course Planning at the Open University'.

ROSSI, P. H. and BIDDLE, B. J. (eds.) *The New Media and Education.* Chicago, Aldine, 1966. pp. 417.

SCHOOLS COUNCIL. *Working Paper No. 2: Raising the School Leaving Age.* L, HMSO, 1965. pp. 34.

—— *Working Paper No. 5: Sixth Form Curriculum and Examinations.* L, HMSO, 1966. pp. 38.

—— *Working Paper No. 8: French in the Primary School.* L, HMSO, 1966. pp. 84.

—— *The New Curriculum.* L, HMSO, 1967. pp. 86.

—— *Working Paper No. 11: Society and the Young School Leaver.* L, HMSO, 1967. pp. 84.

—— *Working Paper No. 14: Mathematics for the Majority.* L, HMSO, 1967. pp. 45.

—— *Humanities for the Young School Leaver: An Approach through Classics*; L, HMSO, 1967, pp. 30. *An Approach through English*; L, HMSO, 1968, pp. 14. *An Approach through History*; L, Evans/ Methuen Educ., 1969, pp. 48

—— *The First Three Years 1964–7.* L, HMSO, 1968. pp. 35.

—— *Technology and the Schools.* L, HMSO, 1968. pp. 35.

—— *Mathematics in Primary Schools.* L, HMSO, 1969. pp. 165.

SHANKS, M. *The Innovators: The Economics of Technology.* Harmondsworth, Penguin Books, 1967. pp. 302.

SHAPLIN, J. T. and OLDS, H. F. (eds.) *Team Teaching.* NY, Harper & Row, 1964. pp. 430. Outlines methods of re-deploying staff to make better use of differing teacher skills and more flexible grouping of pupils. See also LOVELL and FREEMAN (above).

SMITH, B. O., STANLEY, W. O. and SHORES, T. H. *Fundamentals of Curriculum Development.* Rev. ed. NY, World Books, 1957. pp. 685. Lays down five criteria for the selection of content:
1 Is the subject matter significant to an organized field of knowledge?
2 Does the subject matter stand the test of survival?
3 Is the subject matter useful?
4 Is the subject matter interesting to the learner?
5 Does the subject matter contribute to the growth and development of a democratic society?

SMITH, R. I. *Men and Societies.* L, Heinemann Educ., 1968. pp. 248. Appraisals of the implications of curriculum developments in the humanities and social sciences.

TABA, H. *Curriculum in Intergroup Relations.* Washington, D.C., American Council on Education, 1949. pp. 168.

TABA, H. *Curriculum Development: Theory and Practice.* NY, Harcourt, Brace & World, 1962. pp. 529. A standard American work; suggests that curriculum problems cannot properly be explored on the general level at all, but must be subject to experimental determination.

TAYLOR, L. C. (ed.) *Experiments in Education at Sevenoaks.* L, Constable Young Books, 1965. pp. 128. No turgid stuff here, one of the most attractive books in the literature; imaginative recounting of six sets of activities in a grammar school: art, new mathematics, creative English, technical workshop, voluntary social service and international relations. Worth half a dozen books on curriculum theory.

—— *Resources for Learning.* Harmondsworth, Penguin Books, 1971. pp. 277.

TAYLOR, W. *Heading for Change: Management for Innovation in the Secondary School.* Cardiff, Harlech TV, 1969. pp. 144. In-tray simulation for the management of innovations in large secondary schools.

TRICKER, R. A. R. *The Contribution of Science to Education.* L, Mills & Boon, 1967. pp. 154.

TYLER, R. W. *Basic Principles of Curriculum and Instruction.* U of Chicago P, 1950, 1969. pp. 83. Another standard American work, strong on assessment.

TYLER, R. W. *et al.* (eds.) *Perspectives of Curriculum Evaluation.* American Educational Research Association Monograph. Chicago, Rand McNally, 1967. pp. 102.

WHEELER, D. K. *Curriculum Process.* U of LP, 1967. pp. 320. Strongly influenced by TABA (see above); sees curriculum planning as five-phased: 1 Selection of aims, goals and objectives; 2 Selection of learning experiences; 3 Selection of content: 4 Integration of learning experiences and content; 5 Evaluation. Highly generalized and involved.

WOOTON, W. *SMSG: The Making of a Curriculum.* New Haven, Conn., Yale UP, 1965. pp. 182. The story of the School Mathematics Study Group, interesting as a case study in the logistics of curriculum development.

4 Educational Psychology

It is an illusion to suppose that the doubts and uncertainties which characterize philosophy of education and educational theory can be left behind once we enter the field of the social sciences. 'A great problem facing the student of educational psychology is the difficulty of deciding exactly what it is', says Stones (*Readings in Educational Psychology*, 1970). This difficulty, moreover, is by no means confined to beginners. For the majority of students, rightly or wrongly, educational psychology defines itself as that branch of psychology which is designed to help teachers (*a*) to understand the learner's development and the learning process, (*b*) to acquire an informed background for techniques of classroom instruction and educational methods generally. Loose as it is, such a definition is indicative of the vast scope and complexity of the field. Just where, and how, educational psychology can safely take off from general psychology remains a matter for debate. On the whole, academic opinion is inclined to think that a thorough grounding in general psychology (including physiology) is essential. It is hardly surprising, therefore, that many students fail to see the relevance of some course offerings, and that as regards the practical applications in the classroom their expectations are frequently disappointed. As they see it, the field lacks structure. *Their* objectives are not always the same as those of their teachers.

Analysis of textbooks quickly reveals wide variations in the elements included. A further difficulty is that of deciding the purposes and levels for which the study of educational psychology is undertaken. Clearly, it means different things to the layman, the non-graduate teacher, the B.Ed., M.Ed. or Ph.D. candidate, the clinical worker and the laboratory researcher.

Although it is customary to speak of psychology as a 'discipline', one of several from which the study of education draws its data, the fact is that it shades off here into the domain of physiology, there of linguistics, there of ethology, of sociology and of other so-called 'disciplines'. The differences in interest, method and approach between psychologists like Freud and B. F. Skinner, say, are if anything more profound than those which give rise to disagreement between educationists.

Twenty-five years ago psychology provided the main component for empirical studies in education, virtually the only one. Latterly its monopoly has been increasingly challenged by the ascendant claims of sociology. The intervening years have seen some significant changes not only in its leading personnel but also in the dogmas and doctrines cherished by an earlier generation of psychologists. In 1945 the cult of intelligence testing was at its height and the approved psychometric techniques were those typified by Sir Godfrey Thomson's book *The Factoral Analysis of Human Abilities* (5th ed. University of London Press, 1951). Spearman's '*g* plus *s*' formula was still the accepted model. That intelligence was innate and normally distributed was held to be proved, as was the constancy of the IQ.

Quantum mutatus ab illo . . . While it is not denied that intelligence can, in some sense, be measured, the conclusion now reached is that the constancy of the IQ is contradicted by the facts and that the normal distribution of intelligence is to be regarded, at best, as a 'not unreasonable assumption' (Lunzer, *Development in Learning*, 1968). The view that intelligence is a manifestation of learned behaviour and can be acquired (*Newsom Report*, 1963: cited under Educational Theory, p. 50), if still controversial, has gained ground steadily during the last twenty years, thanks largely to the evidence adduced by investigations into the effects of social class, linguistic and other environmental influences.

On this issue British educational psychologists remain somewhat undecided – and divided. While it would be unfair to accuse them of dragging their heels over the perennial Nature–Nurture controversy (now seen to be a pseudo-problem unless it is treated in terms of interaction between genetic and environmental factors), the tendency has been to remain cautiously conservative. The position of Sir Cyril Burt, doyen of British educational psychologists, remains essentially the same as it was in the pre-war era. P. E. Vernon (1950, 1960, 1969) was among the first to raise doubts about the widespread use of standardized intelligence tests. Earlier still, W. J. H. Sprott had confessed (in the second edition of his *General Psychology*, 1948) to having serious second thoughts on the score of innate intelligence, a change which he acknowledged as being due to reading Margaret Mead.

But if the cultural anthropologists and sociologists have had the better of the interdisciplinary exchanges to date, British educational psychologists by and large have been reluctant to abandon the fixed positions which they occupied during the heyday of intelligence-testing. S. Wiseman's *Education and Environment* (1964) speaks with two voices, neither of which is prepared to make more than grudging concessions to the environmentalist argument. Even H. J. Butcher's *Human Intelligence* (1968), which so admirably summarizes the mass of research findings from anthropological, sociological and cybernetic as well as psychological investigations, is so eclectic as to give the impression of being non-committal. It seems, indeed, that British educational psychology is constrained by an ideological and cultural climate of opinion, which has the effect of confirming it in its liking for pessimistic and deterministic interpretations. Not for it the bold assertion that 'any subject can be taught in some intellectually honest form to any child at any stage of development'!

Mention of Bruner's well-known hypothesis is itself a reminder of the fact that the study of educational psychology in Britain is to some extent overshadowed by American influences (incidentally, it is also a reminder of the fact that the study is still at the formative stage of development, seeing that Bruner's serious interest in educational psychology can be said to date from the mid-1950s). Thus, it would be hard to find a college of education student who had never heard of Skinner, say, but relatively easy to find quite a few who are unable to name the leading authorities on the home front. Many British students seem to find authors like R. M. Gagné and D. P. Ausubel more to their taste than the prescribed reading of home-produced textbooks. This preference can perhaps be explained by a lucidity of exposition and elegance of style which are all too often sadly lacking in the terminological prose of the typical British textbook. Any American dominance, however, is more obviously attributable to the economics of publishing and the advantages of the enormous American market for works of this kind – after all, there are well over two thousand institutions of higher learning in the U.S.A. For this reason alone the transatlantic traffic in educational books of all kinds tends to be one way – west to east. This explains why it is highly exceptional to find any reference to the work of British psychologists, educational or otherwise, in the U.S.A., where even the ideas of so eminent a figure as Jean Piaget remained more or less unknown, or at least unrecognized, until the publication of A. L. Baldwin's *Behavior and Development in Childhood* as recently as 1955. Against this, most British students in colleges of education and university departments of education are familiar with the experiment carried out by R. White and R. Lippitt on 'Authoritarian', '*laissez-faire*' and 'Democratic' social climates in the classroom (reported in D. Cartwright and A. F. Zander (eds.) *Group Dynamics*, 1952). It goes without saying that American students, for their part, are almost invariably unacquainted with similar investigations carried out in Britain.

The example chosen might be taken as one indication of the emergence of educational psychology as a genuinely international study. Recently the American influence has been offset by Continental ones, first and most strongly, of course, by the continuous and prolific output of studies of child development from Piaget and his associates, secondly by some notable contributions from the U.S.S.R. Brian Simon's *Psychology in the Soviet Union* (1957) represents an important landmark. In particular, the writings of Vygotsky, Luria and Yudovich have reinforced the growing interest in the dynamic relationship between language and learning.

In all this, nevertheless, it is difficult to resist the conclusion that British educational psychology has been slow to respond to the expansive mood of the second half of the twentieth century. It is not simply that the last two decades have seen few outstanding personalities, no Triton among the minnows, nor that most of the significant initiatives have come from abroad. If British educational psychology is open to criticism, it is certainly not on the grounds of lack of expertise or thoroughness; it is, rather, that in insisting on these very qualities its influence has been restricted, even restrictive.

Granted, educational psychology the world over has long been preoccupied with cognitive learning to the neglect of the affective aspects. Among the reasons for this, Chazan (in H. J. Butcher (ed.), *Educational Research in Britain*, 1968) mentions 'the lack of measuring instruments, the failure to establish an acceptable theoretical framework within which research can be carried out, and the complexities of the study of emotional developments, which is not easily amenable to laboratory experiment'. As he points out, such investigations that have been attempted so far have been more or less exclusively concerned with 'difficult', subnormal or handicapped children. It is arguable that one possible reason for the lack of suitable measuring instruments has been the official attitude adopted by the British Psychological Society whose *Psychological Tests: A Statement* (1966) laid it down 'that the term "test" should be restricted to assessment techniques yielding ratings or scores derived from procedures clearly described in the test manual and based on adequate standardization data'. The intention behind this ruling, which was to exclude the possibility of research findings being contaminated by subjective bias, may have been sound, but for all that its effects can now be seen to have been restrictive.

In fact, such breakthroughs as have been achieved since 1945 have been initiated by investigators, not least Piaget, who made little or no use of standardized tests. Piaget's work has been, and in places still is, criticized on the grounds of inadequate sampling, faulty experimental design and lack of statistical validation. Getzels and Jackson's *Creativity and Intelligence* (1962), one of the few books that have stimulated new lines of inquiry during the period concerned, has likewise been subjected to rough treatment by British reviewers to whom open-ended tests are anathema. 'Yet in spite of this, this approach has done more to show the qualitative differences in children's thinking at different age levels than standardized tests have', say J. D. Nisbet and N. J. Entwistle in *Educational Research Methods* (1970). The truth seems to be that any attempt to shake free from the stranglehold of 'official' policies for research is likely to be frowned on as ill conceived by psychologists of the old school – and equally likely to be welcomed by the rank and file of students and teachers. The successes achieved in child development, in creativity (and for that matter in programmed learning) are proof enough that an unconventional approach pays handsome dividends.

By comparison, British educational psychology must be reckoned unadventurous; meticulous rather than original, stolid rather than exciting. On the developmental side much useful work has been done by researchers like Lovell, Lunzer and Peel in replicating experiments originally carried out in Geneva with a view to confirming, modifying or rejecting the conclusions arrived at by Piaget. On the whole, the latter's theory that the order of succession in the stages of the child's mental growth is constant, and that none of these stages can be skipped, is now generally accepted; on the other hand, the actual onset of each of the various stages is seen to depend to a great extent on environmental circumstances. If the British contribution in the field of developmental psychology has been more modest than spectacular, therefore, at least it earns credit for demonstrating that there is no warrant for simply waiting until the child spontaneously reaches the appropriate level of assimilating any new body of knowledge. To begin with, the concepts of maturation and readiness were widely misunderstood, a pretext for all manner of slap-happy abuses in the schools. Indirect as it may have been, the pay-off from patient, consolidatory research in developmental psychology has strongly influenced policy-making in the primary school as the *Plowden Report* (1967: cited under Educational Theory, p. 50) and the Scottish Education Department's memorandum on *Primary Education in Scotland* (1965: cited under Educational Administration, p. 153) testify. More directly, it has helped to enlighten methods of teaching through such studies as R. Goldman's *Readiness for Religion* (1965: cited under Educational Theory, p. 56) and Z. P. Dienes's *An Experimental Study of Mathematics Learning* (1964), to name only two of the more illustrious examples.

But if developmental psychology has been busy consolidating its advances so has behaviourism. On the one hand there is the emphasis on motivation, backed by an impressive literature on child study; on the other the insistence on the need for specifying learning objectives in behavioural terms, which finds its support in the work of psychologists like B. F. Skinner and R. M. Gagné.

Like educational theory, educational psychology wears a Janus face. The alternations in professional opinion concerning the meshing of heredity with upbringing are nicely illustrated in N. Pastore's *The Nature-Nurture Controversy* (1965), which summarizes its seesawing from Francis Galton to J. B. Watson. Judging by the record, it seems that every psychologist that is born alive is either a little developmentalist or else a little environmentalist. Is there any point in telling students that the Nature-Nurture controversy is dead and that the time is long overdue when it should be given a decent burial when at every turn it shows itself to be very much alive and kicking? Kicking, not simply because Black pamphleteers in Britain (and A. R. Jensen in the U.S.A.) never tire in their efforts to revive it, but because educational psychology itself is torn by a kind of civil war over this issue. If the developmental school of thought represents a late twentieth-century version of Froebel's 'making the inner outer', the behaviourist school can be seen as an updating of Herbartian pedagogy. H. Entwistle's *Child-centred Education* (1970: cited under Educational Theory, p. 51) is a vindication of the first position, R. M. Gagné's *The Conditions of Learning* (1965) and D. P. Ausubel's *Educational Psychology: A Cognitive View* (1968) put the case for the other.

To be sure, psychologists are not to be blamed for failing to pull the chestnuts out of the educational and philosophical fire. Even so, there must be some sympathy for the view that educational psychology has not succeeded in providing the kind of practical assistance which students and teachers are entitled to expect. The difficulty of deciding exactly what educational psychology involves could hardly have arisen if those engaged in the field had paid sufficient attention to its 'structure' and 'sequence', to 'task analysis', to the learner's 'predispositions' ('entry

behaviour' in the jargon of the programmers), above all to the clarifica-
tion of 'objectives'. Great play is made of these in contemporary
courses: very little in the design of the courses themselves. As a result,
thinks N. L. Gage (in E. Stones (ed.) *Readings in Educational Psychology*, 1970), 'the educational psychologist has not been giving
prospective teachers enough of the kind of training they need. Most of the
first course in educational psychology is concerned with the characteristics of learning and the learner, with the learner's adjustment, with
the learner's growth and development and with measurement and
evaluation of the learner. It is not sufficiently focused on methods of
teaching or how teachers should behave.'

In the event, some of the components normally included in the field
of education – assessment for one, research methods for another – owe
their place more to the accident of history than to any better reason
and may be thought to belong more appropriately to purely *educational*
studies. It just happened that from Binet on mental testing began in the
ranks of psychologists and as the work extended testing came to be
thought of as peculiarly *their* business. Similarly in the case of experimental techniques. So long as psychology enjoyed its virtual monopoly
in the empirical study of education its arbitrament was rarely questioned:
it was only when rival social sciences vied for equal recognition that its
overlordship came to seem irksome. At the moment, educational
research is still in the process of shaking itself free from the shackles which
have tended to make it seem something of a barren exercise. Action
research, case studies, participant observation and other techniques
are no longer quite so suspect in academic circles as they were a few
years ago and point to the emergence of more realistic, go-getting
concepts of research *and* development. Michael Young's *Innovation
and Research in Education* (1967) reflects the change of attitude which
has taken place, stressing the urgent need for the investigation of
problems at the rock face rather than in the laboratory. While the
importance of 'pure' research is nowhere denied, the policy of the main
funding agencies today, e.g. the Schools Council, is to commission
research projects on the understanding that the findings will be *used*.

From one point of view, then, the scope of educational psychology
may be said to have widened. Significantly, the latest texts include
chapters on creativity, programmed learning, attitude scales, curriculum development, data processing and other topics which were formerly
excluded from its frames of reference. Between them, R. H. Thouless's
Map of Educational Research (1969) and H. J. Butcher's *Educational*

Research in Britain (1968, 1970) give a synoptic view of this broad and varied landscape. Both compilations, it will be noted, are the work of educational psychologists, which suggests that they, rather than educationists or sociologists, are still firmly in command.

In another sense, however, it is arguable that the old supremacy of educational psychology has been lost once and for all. Certainly, it is becoming increasingly difficult to distinguish its territory from that of other social sciences. How, for instance, is one to identify so influential a research worker as Basil Bernstein – as an educational psychologist, as a sociologist, as an authority on linguistics or what else? In any case, it is too early to see educational psychology in anything like its true perspective.

Histories of psychology do not normally play much of a part in courses for students training to become teachers. It might be better if they did. The following works of reference will be found useful in this connection:

BORING, E. G. *A History of Experimental Psychology*. 2nd ed. NY, Appleton-Century-Crofts, 1957 (first pub. 1929). pp. 777. Five-star, indispensable; exhaustive review of the physiological background.

BRETT, G. S. *History of Psychology* (ed. PETERS, R. S.). Rev. ed. L, Allen & Unwin, 1962. pp. 778. Shortened version of a three-volume classic; philosophical counterpart of BORING.

EVANS, E. G. S. *Modern Educational Psychology*. L, Routledge, 1969. pp. 120. Concise historical introduction; reviews progress of studies in child development, theories of personality formation, learning theories, mental testing and measurement.

FLUGEL, J. C. *A Hundred Years of Psychology*. L, Duckworth, 1951. pp. 424. Rather dated.

HEARNSHAW, L. S. *A Short History of British Psychology 1840–1940*. L, Methuen, 1964. pp. 331.

KANTOR, J. R. *The Scientific Evolution of Psychology*. Chicago, Principia P. Vol. 1, 1963, pp. 387. Vol. 2, 1969, pp. 427.

WATSON, R. I. *The Great Psychologists*. 2nd ed. Philadelphia, Lippincott, 1968. pp. 613.

WOODWORTH, R. S. and SHEEHAN, M. R. *Contemporary Schools of Psychology*. L, Methuen, 1956. pp. 480. Some of them no longer contemporary!

Bibliography

For the sake of convenience this is classified under the headings of:

1 The Nature of Human Abilities and Individual Differences

1.1 THE CONCEPT OF INTELLIGENCE

This section has been kept short deliberately. Most of the earlier titles dating from the period when intelligence testing was the rage have been omitted.

BUTCHER, H. J. *Human Intelligence: Its Nature and Assessment.* L, Methuen, 1968. pp. 344. By far the best summary of the research literature; sees intelligence as 'a quintessentially high-level skill at the summit of a hierarchy of intellectual skills'.

GUILFORD, J. P. *The Nature of Human Intelligence.* NY, McGraw-Hill, 1967. pp. 538. Develops a three-dimensional structure of the intellect model.

HUNT, J. MCV. *Intelligence and Experience.* NY, Ronald P, 1961. pp. 416. Influential American study stressing interaction between genetic and environmental variables.

HUSÉN, T. 'The effect of school structure upon utilization of ability', *in* SWIFT, D. F. (ed.) *Basic Readings in the Sociology of Education.* L, Routledge, 1970. pp. 301. Swedish evidence showing how the school as an organization affects pupils' performance.

INHELDER, B. and PIAGET, J. *The Growth of Logical Thinking from Childhood to Adolescence*. L, Routledge, 1958. pp. 356. Stages of genetic evolution in the individual.

MAXWELL, J. *The Level and Trend of National Intelligence*. U of LP, 1961. pp. 77. Scottish survey of the type not likely to be repeated.

MURPHY, G. *Human Potentialities*. L, Allen & Unwin, 1960. pp. 340.

—— *Freeing Intelligence through Teaching*. NY, Harper & Row, 1961. pp. 64.

PASTORE, N. *The Nature-Nurture Controversy*. NY, Columbia U, King's Crown P, 1949. pp. 213. Record of personal bias from Galton to the behaviourists.

PIAGET, J. *The Psychology of Intelligence*. L, Routledge, 1950. pp. 182. Key text.

SPROTT, W. J. H. *General Psychology*. 2nd ed. L, Longmans Green, 1948 (first pub. 1937). pp. 467.

VERNON, P. E. *Intelligence and Attainment Tests*. U of LP, 1960. pp. 207.

—— *The Structure of Human Abilities*. 2nd ed. L, Methuen, 1963 (first pub. 1950). pp. 208.

—— *Intelligence and Cultural Environment*. L, Methuen, 1969. pp. 272. Dates and titles reflect the gradual change of viewpoint in one of Britain's leading educational psychologists.

WISEMAN, S. *Education and Environment*. Manchester UP, 1964. pp. 224.

—— (ed.) *Intelligence and Ability*. Harmondsworth, Penguin Books, 1967. pp. 368.

1.2 LANGUAGE AND THOUGHT

The ways in which the structure of language affects modes of perception and thought, especially in the early years of life, are the concern of educationists as well as of students of psycholinguistics. Accordingly, this list includes a number of important works not normally classified under the heading of educational psychology.

BERNSTEIN, B. 'Social class and linguistic development', *in* HALSEY, A. H., FLOUD, J. and ANDERSON, A. (eds.) *Education, Economy and Society*. NY, Free P, 1961. pp. 625. One of several important papers by the same author on a theory of social learning; outlines 'restricted' and 'elaborated' codes.

BROWN, R. *Words and Things*. 3rd ed. NY, Free Press, 1963. pp. 398. Readable introduction; good section on phonetic symbolism.

CARROLL, J. B. *Language and Thought.* Englewood Cliffs, Prentice-Hall, 1964. pp. 118.

CHOMSKY, N. *Language and Mind.* NY, Harcourt, Brace & World, 1968. pp. 88. A breakthrough? Hypothesis is that language learning is only possible because humans have an inborn 'code' for generative grammar. Seminal study.

DE CECCO, J. P. (ed.) *The Psychology of Language, Thought and Instruction.* NY, Holt, Rinehart & Winston, 1967, pp. 446. A good reader. Contains Chomsky's masterly review of Skinner's *Verbal Behavior* – one of the most efficient demolition jobs in the literature.

—— *The Psychology of Learning and Instruction: Educational Psychology.* Englewood Cliffs, Prentice-Hall, 1968. pp. 800.

HAYAKAWA, S. I. *Language in Thought and Action.* NY, Harcourt, Brace & World, 1939, 1949. pp. 307. One of the older and racier American texts.

HERRIOT, P. *An Introduction to the Psychology of Language.* L, Methuen, 1970. pp. 198.

LURIA, A. R. *The Role of Speech in the Regulation of Normal and Abnormal Behaviour.* O, Pergamon P, 1961. pp. 100.

LURIA, A. R. and YUDOVICH, I. I. *Speech and Development of Mental Processes in the Child.* L, Staples P, 1959. pp. 126.

LYONS, J. *Chomsky.* L, Fontana Books, 1970. pp. 120. Lucid exposition of the basic ideas of this leading American authority.

MILLER, G. A. *Language and Communication.* NY, McGraw-Hill, 1951. pp. 298. Standard textbook, slightly dated.

OPIE, I. and OPIE, P. *The Lore and Language of School Children.* L, OUP, 1959. pp. 417. Fascinating study of the natural history of the oral transmission of children's rhymes, games, etc.

PIAGET, J. *The Language and Thought of the Child.* 3rd ed. L, Routledge, 1948. pp. 246.

POSTMAN, L. and KEPPEL, G. (eds.) *Verbal Learning and Memory.* Harmondsworth, Penguin Books, 1969. pp. 501. Selected readings.

SAPIR, E. *Language.* L, Rupert Hart-Davis, 1963. pp. 242. Near-classic, American.

SAPORTA, S. *Psycholinguistics: A Book of Readings.* NY, Holt, Rinehart & Winston, 1961. pp. 551.

SIMON, B. (ed.) *Psychology in the Soviet Union.* L, Routledge, 1957. pp. 305.

SKINNER, B. F. *Verbal Behavior.* NY, Appleton-Century-Crofts, 1957. pp. 478. Behaviourist interpretation, unsubtle.

STONES, E. (ed.) *Readings in Educational Psychology.* L, Methuen, 1970. pp. 478. Section 2 ('Thinking, Language and Learning') contains important papers by Carroll, Sapir, Luria, Vigotsky, Piaget.

WATTS, A. F. *The Language and Mental Development of Children.* L, Harrap, 1948. pp. 354. Handy textbook in its day, now superseded.

WHORF, B. L. *Language, Thought and Reality.* C, Mass., MITP/Wiley, 1956. pp. 278. Once-in-a-blue-moon book by insurance man (disciple of Sapir) with a flair for writing which makes it compulsive reading.

1.3 CREATIVITY

The extensive literature which has grown up around so-called creativity (one of those terms that is capable of meaning all things to all men) may be said to date from Guilford's 1950 address, more obviously perhaps from Getzels and Jackson's reported research in 1962. The growing interest in it can be partly attributed to a reaction against the limitations and *longueurs* of conventional intelligence testing.

BARRON, F. X. *Creativity and Personal Freedom.* L, Van Nostrand, 1968. pp. 322. Philosophical discussion of freedom and necessity, the need for transcendental experience.

BUTCHER, H. J. *Human Intelligence: Its Nature and Assessment.* L, Methuen, 1968. pp. 344. Chapter 4 reviews research literature on creativity.

FOSS, B. M. *New Horizons in Psychology.* Harmondsworth, Penguin Books, 1966. pp. 448. Brief notice.

GETZELS, J. W. and JACKSON, P. W. *Creativity and Intelligence.* NY, Wiley, 1962. pp. 293. Seminal study, still the best starting point for anyone venturing into this chancy field of research. See the appendix for the battery of tests and instructions for scoring.

GHISELIN, B. (ed.) *The Creative Process.* CUP, 1952. pp. 259.

GUILFORD, J. P. 'Creativity'. *American Psychologist,* vol. 5, 1950, pp. 444–54. But see HELSON and BEVAN (below).

HELSON, H. and BEVAN, W. *Contemporary Approaches to Psychology.* L, Van Nostrand, 1967 pp. 596. Section on 'Some theoretical views of creativity' by J. P. Guilford.

HUDSON, L. *Contrary Imaginations.* L, Methuen, 1966. pp. 181. One of the livelier British contributions; a study of convergent and divergent frames of mind in the Getzels and Jackson manner.

KNEELER, G. F. *The Art and Science of Creativity.* NY, Holt, Rinehart & Winston, 1965. pp. 106. Popular textbook.

KOESTLER, A. *The Act of Creation.* L, Hutchinson, 1964. pp. 751. Higher criticism.

TAYLOR, C. W. and BARRON, F. *Scientific Creativity: Its Recognition and Development.* NY, Wiley, 1963. pp. 419.

TAYLOR, C. W. and HOLLAND, T. (eds.) *Creativity: Progress and Potential.* NY, McGraw-Hill, 1964. pp. 241.

TERMAN, L. M. and ODEN, M. H. *The Gifted Child Grows Up.* Genetic Studies in Genius 4. Stanford UP, 1947. pp. 448.

—— *The Gifted Group at Mid-Life.* Genetic Studies in Genius 5. Stanford UP, 1959. pp. 187. Longitudinal studies of exceptionally able children.

TORRANCE, E. P. *Guiding Creative Talent.* Englewood Cliffs, Prentice-Hall, 1962. pp. 278.

—— *Education and the Creative Potential.* Minneapolis, U of Minnesota P, 1963. pp. 167.

—— *Rewarding Creative Behavior.* Englewood Cliffs, Prentice-Hall, 1965. pp. 353.

WERTHEIMER, M. (ed.) *Productive Thinking.* NY, Harper & Row, 1959. pp. 302.

2 Child Development and the Growth of Personality

If this section appears to be dominated by the work of Jean Piaget, the explanation is simple. The spate of commentaries on his voluminous writings continues to increase and now amounts to a light industry.

ALLPORT, G. W. *Pattern and Growth in Personality.* NY, Holt, Rinehart & Winston, 1961. pp. 593. Standard work.

BALDWIN, A. L. *Behavior and Development in Childhood.* NY, Dryden P, 1955. pp. 619.

—— *Theories of Child Development.* NY, Wiley, 1967. pp. 618. Evaluations and critiques of Lewin, Freud, Piaget, etc.; substantial study, well regarded.

BEARD, R. *An Outline of Piaget's Developmental Psychology for Students and Teachers.* L, Routledge, 1969. pp. 128.

BLUM, G. S. *Psychoanalytic Theories of Personality.* NY, McGraw-Hill, 1953. pp. 219. Side by side examination of rival and conflicting theories; strongly recommended.

BOYLE, D. G. *A Students' Guide to Piaget.* O, Pergamon P, 1969. pp. 176. Still there's more to follow.

BREASLEY, M. and HITCHFIELD, E. *A Teacher's Guide to Reading Piaget*. L, Routledge, 1969. pp. 171.

CATTELL, R. B. *The Scientific Analysis of Personality*. Harmondsworth, Penguin Books, 1965. pp. 400.

EYSENCK, H. J. *The Structure of Human Personality*. 3rd ed. L, Methuen, 1970. pp. 496.

FLAVELL, J. H. *The Developmental Psychology of Jean Piaget*. L, Van Nostrand, 1963. pp. 472. Difficult, but still the best exposition for those who feel unable to tackle the genuine article.

FURTH, H. G. *Piaget for Teachers*. Englewood Cliffs, Prentice-Hall, 1968. pp. 163.

—— *Piaget and Knowledge*. Englewood Cliffs, Prentice-Hall, 1969. pp. 270. Sound discussion of Piaget's theory of genetic epistemology.

GESELL, A. *The First Five Years of Life*. 4th ed. L, Methuen, 1966. pp. 408.

GESELL, A. and ILG, F. *The Child from Five to Ten*. L, Hamish Hamilton, 1946. pp. 475.

GINSBURG, H. and OPPER, S. *Piaget's Theory of Intellectual Development: An Introduction*. Englewood Cliffs, Prentice-Hall, 1969. pp. 237.

GUILFORD, J. P. *Personality*. NY, McGraw-Hill, 1959. pp. 562.

HOLLOWAY, G. E. T. *An Introduction to 'The Child's Conception of Geometry'*. L, Routledge, 1967. pp. 71.

—— *An Introduction to 'The Child's Conception of Space'*. L, Routledge, 1967. pp 77.
Further aspects of Piaget's work.

ISAACS, N. *The Growth of Understanding in the Young Child*. L, Ward Lock, 1961. pp. 41.

JERSILD, A. T. *The Psychology of Adolescence*. 2nd ed. NY, Macmillan, 1963. pp. 438.

LANGER, J. *Theories of Development*. NY, Holt, Rinehart & Winston, 1969. pp. 191. Examines three types of developmental theory: (*a*) behaviourist, (*b*) self-activity, (*c*) psychoanalytic; finds the concept of interaction common to all three and speculates on the possibility of an overarching theory, which will be at once descriptive and explanatory. A study of some distinction.

LIPSITT, L. P. and REESE, H. W. *Advances in Child Development and Behavior*, vol. 4. NY, Academic P, 1969. pp. 333.

LUNZER, E. A. and MORRIS, J. F. *Development in Learning*. L, Staples P. 3 vols: 1 *The Regulation of Behaviour*, 1968, pp. 416; 2 *Development in Human Learning*, 1968, pp. 487; 3 *Contexts of Education*, 1969, pp. 312. First-class throughout, the best British source book. Vol. 1 deals with fundamental problems of human psychology. Vol. 2 examines the ways in which children learn and how their powers mature. Vol. 3 is intended to serve as a comprehensive introduction to educational psychology.

MACFARLAND, H. S. N. *Human Learning: A Developmental Analysis*. L, Routledge, 1969. pp. 128. Very concise.

MAIER, H. *Three Theories of Child Development*. NY, Harper & Row, 1965. pp. 314. Related to American counselling procedures.

MUSSEN, P. H. *Carmichael's Manual of Child Psychology*. 3rd ed. NY, Wiley, 1970. 2 vols. pp. 1519 and 872. Encyclopedic; contains first-rate chapter by Piaget on Piaget.

MUSSEN, P. H., CONGER, J. J. and KAGAN, J. *Child Development and Personality*. 3rd ed. NY, Harper & Row, 1969. pp. 795.

—— (eds.) *Readings in Child Development and Personality*. NY, Harper & Row, 1965. pp. 480.

NASH, J. *Developmental Psychology*. Englewood Cliffs, Prentice-Hall, 1970. pp. 583. Canadian textbook, systematic, encyclopedic, sound. Markedly psychobiological approach.

NEWSON, J. and NEWSON, E. *Patterns of Infant Care in an Urban Community*. Harmondsworth, Penguin Books, 1969. pp. 286. Celebrated study of family life and folk ways in Nottinghamshire.

—— *Four Years Old in an Urban Community*. Harmondsworth, Penguin Books, 1970. pp. 570. And its sequel.

PEEL, E. A. *The Pupil's Thinking*. L, Oldbourne, 1960. pp. 200.

PIAGET, J. *The Child's Conception of the World*. L, Routledge, 1929. pp. 397. Animism, artificialism, etc.

PIAGET, J. and INHELDER, B. *The Psychology of the Child*. L, Routledge, 1969. pp. 173. The genuine article for once. A review of the master's life work.

RICHMOND, P. G. *An Introduction to Piaget*. L, Routledge, 1970. pp. 120. Still they come!

SIGEL, I. E. and HOOPER, F. H. (eds.) *Logical Thinking in Children*. NY, Holt, Rinehart & Winston, 1968. pp. 538. Textbook summarizing research findings on Piagetian theory.

STONE, L. J. and CHURCH, J. Childhood and Adolescence. NY, Random House, 1966. pp. 456.

TANNER, J. M. *Education and Physical Growth*. U of LP, 1961. pp. 144. Notable study of the secular trend towards earlier physical maturity.

WALL, W. D. *The Adolescent Child*. L, Methuen, 1948. pp. 206. Good in its day but teenage culture has left it high and dry.

WILLIAMS, N. *Child Development*. L, Heinemann Educ., 1970. pp. 110.

WINNICOTT, D. W. *The Child, the Family and the Outside World*. Harmondsworth, Penguin Books, 1964. pp. 240.

—— *The Family and Individual Development*. L, Tavistock, 1965. pp. 181.

VALENTINE, C. W. *The Normal Child and some of his Abnormalities*. Harmondsworth, Penguin Books, 1967. pp. 288.

3 The Learning Process

3.1 THEORIES OF LEARNING

According to Hill (1964), 'Learning theory summarizes a large amount of knowledge about the laws of learning in a small space.' The immediate retort must be that it does nothing of the kind. As Wiseman remarks, 'The literature here is enormous. To find one's way round the mass of publications, to pick out the significant contributions, is far from easy. But the teacher finds himself bewildered and frustrated, not so much by the volume of the work, but by the fact that the experiments conducted, the problems attacked, the theories advanced, seem to him to have little or no relevance to his own problems. The subjects of the experiments are not children, but rats and pigeons, dogs and dolphins.' (In W. R. Niblett (ed.) *How and Why do We Learn?*, 1965.)

It is as well to recognize at the outset that a good deal of what passes for 'learning theory' is not even remotely connected with human learning or with classroom practice. Hilgard (1964) distinguishes between (*a*) pure research and (*b*) technological research and development. At one extreme, for example, we have the learning theorist who is only interested in the conditioning of flatworms, at the other the writer of textbooks on methods of teaching specialist subjects. Hilgard's Step 1 (i.e. research on learning that has no regard for its educational applications – animal studies, physiological and biochemical investigations, etc.) may be a necessary preliminary to Step 3 (i.e. research that is more directly relevant because the subjects are school children and the material learned is school subject matter or skill), but in the existing state of the art there is something to be said for the view that the applications of learning theory have not been conspicuously successful or helpful. Step 3, in other words, represents a consummation devoutly to be wished.

AUSUBEL, D. P. *The Psychology of Meaningful Verbal Learning.* NY, Grune & Stratton, 1963. pp. 255.
—— *Educational Psychology: A Cognitive View.* NY, Holt, Rinehart & Winston, 1968. pp. 685.
AUSUBEL, D. P. and ROBINSON, F. G. *School Learning: An Introduction to Educational Psychology.* NY, Holt, Rinehart & Winston, 1969. pp. 691. Popular textbook incorporating Ausbel's Neo-Herbartian approach to problems of teaching.
FRANDSEN, A. N. *Educational Psychology.* 2nd ed. NY, McGraw-Hill, 1967. pp. 694. Popular textbook.
GAGNÉ, R. M. *The Conditions of Learning.* NY, Holt, Rinehart & Winston, 1965. pp. 308. Key text; sees cognitive learning as a hierarchical structure with problem-solving at the apex and each level dependent on the one immediately beneath it.
HILGARD, E. R. and BOWER, G. H. *Theories of Learning.* NY, Appleton-Century-Crofts, 1966. pp. 661. Standard work.
HILGARD, E. R. (ed.) *Theories of Learning and Instruction.* Chicago, National Society for the Study of Education, 1964. pp. 430. Comprehensive review.
HILL, W. F. *Learning: A Survey of Psychological Interpretations.* L, Methuen University Paperbacks, 1964. pp. 240. Concise.
HOLLAND, J. and SKINNER, B. F. *The Analysis of Behavior.* NY, McGraw-Hill, 1961. pp. 400. Serves a dual purpose as an introduction to (*a*) operant conditioning and (*b*) programmed learning.
LUNZER, E. A. and MORRIS, J. F. (eds.) *Development in Learning:* 1 *The Regulation of Behaviour.* L, Staples P, 1968. pp. 392. Excellent review of main theories of learning; criticizes S-R behaviourism and propounds an eclectic view.
MELTON, A. W. (ed.) *Categories of Human Learning.* NY, Academic P, 1964. pp. 356. Papers and discussions on main theories from classical conditioning to problem-solving; envisages a taxonomy of human learning.
MORRIS, R. *The Quality of Learning.* L, Methuen, 1951. pp. 120. Bright essay on the education of dull children.
NIBLETT, W. R. (ed.) *How and Why do We Learn?* L, Faber, 1965. pp. 196. A readable symposium.
SKINNER, B. F. *Science and Human Behavior.* NY, Macmillan, 1953. pp. 461.
SPENCE, K. W. *Behavior Theory and Conditioning.* New Haven, Conn., Yale UP, 1956. pp. 262. Decidedly Step 1; for advanced students.

3.2 LEARNING AND TEACHING

ALLEN, D. W. and RYAN, K. *Microteaching*. Reading, Mass., Addison-Wesley, 1969. pp. 151. Outlines new training technique which provides a controlled setting for practice by students and in-service teachers.

BRUNER, J. S. *The Process of Education*. C, Mass., Harvard UP, 1960. pp. 97.

—— *Toward a Theory of Instruction*. C, Mass., Belknap P, 1966. pp. 176. See under Educational Theory.

BURSTON, W. H. and THOMPSON, D. (eds.) *Studies in the Nature and Teaching of History*. L, Routledge, 1967. pp. 195.

CLAYTON, T. E. *Teaching and Learning*. Englewood Cliffs, Prentice-Hall, 1965. pp. 177.

CRONBACH, L. J. *Educational Psychology*. 2nd ed. NY, Harcourt, Brace & World, 1963. pp. 706. This has been a standard text but it may be less popular now.

DIENES, Z. P. *An Experimental Study of Mathematics-Learning*. L, Hutchinson, 1964. pp. 207.

—— *Building up Mathematics*. 2nd ed. L, Hutchinson, 1964. pp. 157. Two important studies involving the use of structured learning materials.

FLANDERS, N. A. *Analyzing Teacher Behavior*. NY, Addison-Wesley, 1970. pp. 448. Summarizes research on teacher–pupil interaction.

GOLDMAN, R. *Readiness for Religion*. L, Routledge, 1965. pp. 238. Highly influential Piagetian approach.

LOVELL, K. *Educational Psychology and Children*. U of LP, 1969. pp. 320.

MAXWELL, J. *Pupil and Teacher: An Introduction to Educational Psychology*. L, Harrap, 1969. pp. 288.

PEEL, E. A. *The Psychological Basis of Education*. Edinburgh, Oliver & Boyd, 1956. pp. 303.

SIMON, B. and SIMON, J. (eds.) *Educational Psychology in the Soviet Union*. L, Routledge, 1963. pp. 290.

STONES, E. *Learning and Teaching: A Programmed Introduction*. NY, Wiley, 1968. pp. 124. Linear programmed text for students of educational psychology.

—— *An Introduction to Educational Psychology*. L, Methuen, 1966. pp. 424. Comprehensive textbook, widely used.

THYNE, J. M. *The Psychology of Learning and Techniques of Teaching*. New ed. U of LP, 1968. pp. 288. Idiosyncratic textbook; useful chapters on teaching for transfer.

3.3 DISABILITIES IN LEARNING

The legion of handicapped children – autistic, spastic, brain-damaged, subnormal, blind, deaf, paraplegic, dyslexic, retarded, deprived, etc. – are the subjects of a vast and varied literature. Varied because each form of disability calls for specialist treatment and sympathetic insight. Since space does not allow of anything like a representative bibliography here, the reader is advised to consult the excellent one compiled by D. J. Thomas, *A Guide to the Literature of Special Education* (Liverpool UP, 1968; pp. 88).

BRUCE, V. R. *Awakening the Slower Mind.* O, Pergamon P, 1969. pp. 244. Wide-ranging survey with its heart in the right place.

CASHDAN, A. 'Handicaps in learning', *in* LUNZER, E. A. and MORRIS, J. F. (eds.) *Development in Learning,* vol. 3 (see section 2 above). A good survey.

CHAZAN, M. *Compensatory Education.* L, Schools Council Occasional Publications 1, 1968. pp. 64.

GULLIFORD, R. *Backwardness and Educational Failure.* L, NFER/U of Swansea, 1969. pp. 110.

HIGHFIELD, M. E. *The Young School Failure.* Edinburgh, Oliver & Boyd, 1949. pp. 127.

LACK, A. *The Teaching of Language to Deaf Children.* L, OUP, 1955. pp. 380.

LEVINSON, A. *The Mentally Retarded Child.* L, Allen & Unwin, 1955. pp. 128.

LEWIS, H. N. *Deprived Children.* L, OUP, 1954. pp. 163.

LINDSAY, Z. *Arts for Spastics.* L, Mills & Boon, 1966. pp. 71.

PRINGLE, M. L. KELLMER (ed.) *Deprivation and Education.* L, Longmans, 1965. pp. 307. Research papers and case studies of children who are (*a*) in care, (*b*) rejected or (*c*) underprivileged.

WILLIAMS, A. A. *Basic Subjects for the Slow Learner.* L, Methuen Educ., 1970. pp. 256. Literacy and numeracy for backward pupils.

WILSON, H. *Delinquency and Child Neglect.* L, Allen & Unwin for the Sir Halley Stewart Trust, 1962. pp. 195.

4 Social Psychology and Mental Health

If not altogether discredited, the concept of mental health is not as popular as it was twenty years ago. Moreover, interest in the social aspects of learning has to a large extent been transferred to the sociology of education (see pp. 121–43).

ARGYLE, M. *Psychology and Social Problems*. L, Methuen, 1964. pp. 224.

—— *The Psychology of Interpersonal Behaviour*. Harmondsworth, Penguin Books, 1967. pp. 224.

DOUGLAS, J. W. B. *The Home and the School*. L, Panther, 1969. pp. 224. Based on a nationwide survey; brings together and interprets a mass of evidence relating to family size, social class, home background, parental care, attitudes to school, and their effects in pupils' performance.

ERIKSON, E. H. *Childhood and Society*. NY, Norton, 1950. Harmondsworth, Penguin Books, 1969. pp. 432. Notable work by eminent Neo-Freudian ego psychologist.

FLEMING, C. M. (ed.) *Studies in the Social Psychology of Adolescence*. L, Routledge, 1951. pp. 266. Dated.

FRASER, E. *Home Environment and the School*. U of LP, 1959. pp. 85. Exemplary Scottish study.

GUSKIN, A. E. and GUSKIN, S. L. *A Social Psychology of Education*. Reading, Mass., Addison-Wesley, 1969. pp. 212. Educational problems viewed in interpersonal terms.

HARDING, D. W. *Social Psychology and Individual Values*. L, Hutchinson, 1966. pp. 184. A little masterpiece; highly recommended.

JAHODA, M. (ed.) *International Concepts of Mental Health*. NY, Basic Books, 1958. pp. 136.

KRECH, D. and CRUTCHFIELD, R. S. *Theory and Problems of Social Psychology*. L, Tavistock, 1953. pp. 639.

WALL, W. D. *Education and Mental Health*. Paris, UNESCO, 1955. pp. 347. Very good in its day.

WILSON, J. *Education and the Concept of Mental Health*. L, Routledge, 1969. pp. 96.

5 Mental Testing

The scope of psychological testing is steadily widening and its techniques becoming more refined in the process. Only a small sample of representative works is given here. Fuller bibliographies are to be found in ANASTASI (1961) and CRONBACH (1964).

ANASTASI, A. *Psychological Testing*. 2nd ed. NY, Collier-Macmillan, 1961. pp. 657. A–Z coverage.

ANSTEY, E. *Psychological Tests*. L, Nelson, 1966. pp. 300. Mainly methodological; sound on basic concepts of reliability, validity, etc.

BRITISH PSYCHOLOGICAL SOCIETY. *Psychological Tests: A Statement.* L, BPS, 1966. pp. 4.
BURT, SIR C. *Mental and Scholastic Tests.* 4th ed. L, Staples P, 1962. pp. 551. Used to be the standard work.
CRONBACH, L. J. *Essentials of Psychological Testing.* NY, Harper & Row, 1960. pp. 650. Standard work.
EVANS, K. M. *Sociometry and Education.* L, Routledge, 1962. pp. 149. A good introduction.
—— *Attitudes and Interests in Education.* L, Routledge, 1965. pp. 168.
JACKSON, S. *A Teacher's Guide to Tests.* L, Longmans, 1967. pp. 176.
NATIONAL FOUNDATION FOR EDUCATIONAL RESEARCH. *Test Agency Catalogue.* Slough and L, NFER/Newnes, 1969. pp. 98.
VERNON, P. E. *The Measurement of Abilities.* 2nd ed. U of LP, 1956. pp. 276.
—— *Personality Assessment.* L, Methuen, 1964. pp. 333. A critical survey.

6 Educational Assessment

The point has already been made that assessment is not, strictly speaking, the business of educational psychology. In fact, the growing interest in methods of assessment other than those relied on in conventional essay-type and end-of-course examinations has received most of its impetus from developments in curriculum study (see pp. 60–71) and educational technology (see pp. 190–206).

BORMUTH, J. R. *On the Theory of Achievement Test Items.* U of Chicago P, 1969. pp. 163. Penetrating; emphasizes the need for an operational relationship between instruction and the construction of valid test items.
DAVIS, F. B. *Educational Measurements and Their Interpretation.* Belmont, Calif., Wadsworth, 1964. pp. 422. A highly statistical textbook for advanced students.
EBEL, R. L. *Measuring Educational Achievement.* Englewood Cliffs, Prentice-Hall, 1965. pp. 481. Standard work.
EGGLESTON, J. F. and KERR, J. F. *Studies in Assessment.* L, English UP, 1970. pp. 256. Interesting case studies of new techniques in action.
GRONLUND, N. E. (ed.) *Readings in Measurement and Evaluation: Education and Psychology.* NY, Macmillan, 1968. pp. 416.

LAUWERYS, J. A. and SCANLON, D. G. (eds.) *World Year Book of Education 1969: Examinations* L, Evans, 1969. pp. 416. Source book.

MACINTOSH, D. M., WALKER, D. A. and MACKAY, D. *The Scaling of Teachers' Marks and Estimates.* New ed. Edinburgh, Oliver & Boyd, 1962 (first pub. 1949). pp. 182.

MACINTOSH, H. G. and MORRISON, R. B. *Objective Testing.* U of LP, 1969. pp. 112. A useful introduction to a technique which is rapidly coming to the fore; types of item, item analysis, construction, administration and scoring of tests explained.

MEHRENS, W. A. and EBEL, R. L. (eds.) *Principles of Educational and Psychological Measurement.* Chicago, Rand McNally, 1967. pp. 438. A good reader: measurement theory, scaling, norms, reliability, validity, item analysis, etc.

PIDGEON, D. and YATES, A. *An Introduction to Educational Measurement.* L, Routledge, 1969. pp. 126. Authoritative.

SCHOOLS COUNCIL. *An Introduction to Objective-type Examinations.* CSE Examinations Bulletin No. 4. L, HMSO, 1964. pp. 20.

—— *School-based Examinations.* CSE Examinations Bulletin No. 5. L, HMSO, 1965. pp. 29.

—— *Multiple Marking of English Compositions.* CSE Examinations Bulletin No. 12. L, HMSO, 1966. pp. 50.

THORNDIKE, R. L. and HAGEN, E. P. *Measurement and Evaluation in Psychology and Education.* NY, Wiley, 1969. pp. 714.

TYLER, R. W. (ed.) *National Society for the Study of Education 68th Year Book*, Part 2: 'Educational Evaluation: New Roles and Means'. U of Chicago P, 1969. pp. 540. Up-to-date overview of developments in the field of assessment.

WISEMAN, S. (ed.) *Examinations and English Education.* Manchester UP, 1961. pp. 208.

7 Experimental Methods and Research

As things are, research-mindedness can hardly be called the hallmark of the teaching profession. Hitherto, the bulk of educational research has been conducted at the higher degree level – much of it motivated by the desire for some kind of academic award – with the result that few of its findings were fed back into the schools and that most of them were unintelligible to the average student and practitioner. With more and more people engaged in it, and at different levels, educational research is no longer quite so esoteric or so far removed from everyday problems as it used to be. At the same time, many students feel the need for guidance in research methods which otherwise strike them as being mysterious and difficult. How to choose a topic for investigation? Where to find the relevant literature on the topic one has in mind? How to interpret the findings of other investigators? How to design a project of one's own? How to report such a project? Answers to all these questions are to be found in the following:

BLACKWELL, A. M. (ed.) *A List of Researches in Education and Educational Psychology 1918–1948.* Slough and L, NFER/Newnes, 1951. pp. 173. *Supplement 1: 1952–3,* 1954, pp. 57. *Supplement 2: 1953–4,* 1956, pp. 62. For subsequent lists see under NATIONAL FOUNDATION FOR EDUCATIONAL RESEARCH (below).

BORG, W. R. *Educational Research, An Introduction.* L, Longmans, 1963. pp. 418.

BUTCHER, H. J. *Sampling in Educational Research.* Manchester UP, 1966. pp. 29.

—— *Educational Research in Britain.* U of LP, 1968. pp. 408.

BUTCHER, H. J. and PONT, H. B. (eds.) *Educational Research in Britain 2.* U of LP, 1970. pp. 298.

Two indispensable works of references (a third volume is planned for 1972).

CAMPBELL, D. T. and STANLEY, J. C. *Experimental and Quasi-Experimental Designs for Research.* 4th ed. Chicago, Rand McNally, 1969. pp. 84. Strongly recommended for number-blind students.

CANE, B. and SCHROEDER, C. *The Teacher and Research.* Slough, NFER, 1970. pp. 130. A study of teachers' priorities and opinions on educational research and development.

CARTWRIGHT, D. and ZANDER, A. F. (eds.) *Group Dynamics: Research and Theory.* 3rd ed. L, Tavistock, 1968 (first pub. 1952). pp. 592.

EVANS, K. M. *Planning Small-scale Research.* Slough, NFER, 1968. pp. 89. A practical guide for teachers and students.

FOSKETT, D. J. *How to Find Out: Educational Research.* O, Pergamon P, 1965. pp. 132. For beginners.

FOX, D. J. *The Research Process in Education.* NY, Holt, Rinehart & Winston, 1969. pp. 758.

GAGE, N. L. *Handbook of Research on Teaching.* Chicago, Rand McNally, 1963. pp. 1218. Mine of information.

HARRIS, C. W. *Encyclopedia of Educational Research.* NY, Macmillan, 1960. pp. 1564. Monumental record.

KERLINGER, F. *Foundations of Behavioural Research.* NY, Holt, Rinehart & Winston, 1964. pp. 739. A first rate book on research techniques.

LEWIS, D. G. *Experimental Design in Education.* U of LP, 1968. pp. 192. Assumes a measure of statistical competence.

LOVELL, K. and LAWSON, K. S. *Understanding Research in Education.* U of LP, 1970. pp. 164. A useful introduction.

NATIONAL FOUNDATION FOR EDUCATIONAL RESEARCH. *Current Researches in Education and Educational Psychology 1959–60.* Slough, NFER, 1961. pp. 180. Continues series, published annually, begun by Mrs Blackwell, listing all postgraduate theses accepted by British universities.

NISBET, J. D. and ENTWISTLE, N. J. *Educational Research Methods.* U of LP, 1970. pp. 192. A model of lucid exposition; strongly recommended.

OSGOOD, C. E. *Method and Theory in Experimental Psychology.* L, OUP, 1953. pp. 800. Typical American textbook.

THOULESS, R. H. *Map of Educational Research.* Slough, NFER, 1969. pp. 332. A major work of reference.

TRAVERS, R. M. W. *An Introduction to Educational Research.* L, Collier-Macmillan, 1969. pp. 512.

WISEMAN, S. *Reporting Research in Education.* Manchester UP, 1952. pp. 23. Advice on the layout of theses.

YOUNG, M. *Innovation and Research in Education.* L, Routledge, 1965. pp. 216. Urges the need for a more realistic approach to the investigation of practical problems, research *and* development, as distinct from 'pure' research.

8 Statistical Methods

When it comes to grasping statistical concepts many students seem to suffer from a blind spot. Yet statistical methods are now *de rigueur* in all the social sciences. For the totally innumerate, unfortunately, there is no easy way out, though it is to be regretted that in this sector there are so few books which go out of their way to remove an all-too-common mental block – and none of the calibre of CAMPBELL and STANLEY (see above).

FERGUSON, G. *Statistical Analysis in Psychology and Education.* 2nd ed. NY, McGraw-Hill, 1966. pp. 446. Advanced.

GOTKIN, L. G. and GOLDSTEIN, L. S. *Descriptive Statistics.* NY,

Wiley, 1964. 2 vols. pp. 255 and 229. A programmed text which helps overcome the statistics barrier.

GUILFORD, J. P. *Fundamental Statistics in Psychology and Education.* NY, McGraw-Hill, 1965. pp. 605. A standard text in many departments.

HAYS, W. L. *Statistics for Psychologists.* NY, Holt, Rinehart & Winston, 1963. pp. 719. Fairly advanced.

KING, W. H. *Statistics in Education.* L, Macmillan, 1970. pp. 188. Fairly elementary.

LEWIS, D. G. *Statistical Methods in Education.* U of LP, 1970. pp. 200. Given a reasonable mathematical background, as reliable an introduction as any; next best thing to a do-it-yourself kit.

LORD, F. M. and NOVICK, M. R. *Statistical Theories of Mental Test Scores.* Reading, Mass., Addison-Wesley, 1968. pp. 568. Very advanced; the book to end all books (and most students) on the subject.

5 History of Education

An age of technology is supposedly forward-looking, more interested in projections for the future than in interpretations of the past. Faced with a choice between the twin mottoes which grace the portals of the U.S. Office of Archives in Washington, D.C. – 'What is past is prologue' and 'Study history' – it is more inclined to accept the former, an adage which can easily be twisted into meaning much the same as Henry Ford's 'History is bunk'.

Supposedly, that is. The extraordinary fact is that the demand for histories of education of one sort or other – and the variety is enormous – far from drying up, appears to be increasing. One indication of the buoyancy of the market is the constant reissuing of works by authors whose reputations were established at, or before, the turn of the century – scholars like S. S. Laurie, Foster Watson, R. L. Archer and J. W. Adamson; not to mention the reappearance in facsimile editions of much older and forgotten works like Sir Thomas Bernard's *Of the Education of the Poor* (1809), J. A. St John's *The Education of the People* (1858) and O. Walker's *Of Education* (1673). A more obvious indication is the steady spate of brand-new publications: roughly half of all books in the literature of education fall into some kind of historical category.

That the history of education was a well cultivated field long before 1945 goes without saying. Indeed, some of the early studies, H. Rashdall's *Universities of Europe in the Middle Ages* (1895) for one, were so monumental as to leave the impression that little was to be gained by trying to improve upon them. The same might be said of J. K. Freeman's *Schools of Hellas* (1905) and Aubrey Gwynn's *Roman Education from Cicero to Quintilian* (1926), both of which represent the fruits of classical scholarship at its serene best. It is at any rate significant that the last twenty-five years have seen precious few studies of education in the ancient world or the Middle Ages by British writers.

In his able review of the literature (in J. W. Tibble (ed.) *The Study of Education*, 1966) Brian Simon makes the point that the history of education impinges on so many fields of activity that it is difficult to decide where it begins and ends. Parish pump affairs or the rise and fall

97

of civilizations, what happened last year or the march of time from 3000 B.C. to the present day, great men and small-fry – all is grist to the historian's mill. How to classify, let alone cope with, this prodigious and sprawling literature? As Arnold Toynbee asks: 'How, then, are our educational institutions to convey this overwhelming massive heritage of knowledge to a puny and ephemeral human mind?' The solution he proposes, unfortunately, is not one that is likely to recommend itself to organizers of courses on the history of education in British colleges and university departments of education: 'Let our students survey the history of all mankind all over the planet since the age when man's pre-human ancestors first became human; but at the same time let them scrutinize the history of some local short-lived tribe or parish' (in E. D. Myers, *Education in the Perspective of History*, 1960). Shortage of time rules it out as a practical possibility.

Prospective teachers are the main consumers of histories of education and hence an important influence on the ways in which the economic laws of supply and demand operate. In recent years there has undoubtedly been a decline in the number of courses of the world survey type (often satirized as Cook's tours from Plato to Dewey), with the result that encyclopedic accounts, so well typified by W. Boyd's *The History of Western Education* (1921, 9th ed. 1969), are no longer favoured. This is not the case in the U.S.A. where such courses continue to flourish and where the reliance on a single comprehensive textbook tends to be heavier than it is in this country. A glance at the opening section of the following bibliography is enough to show the extent of the American monopoly of the genre. In Britain, it appears, the state of the market is not conducive to a broad canvas treatment. It is true that there is a trend towards courses advertising themselves as 'History of Educational Thought', but to date their emergence has not been accompanied either by a systematic attempt to trace the movement of ideas or by any notable revival of interest in the 'Great Educators' as they used to be called. Monographs on the latter are too often sketchy affairs and some of the big names, e.g. Herbart, are missing altogether.

In Brian Simon's judgement it is with the social functions of education that the historian should be principally concerned, yet little has been done to investigate the changing nature of educational theory and practice and a definitive history of the curriculum is still awaited.* It

* But see the History of Education Society's symposium *The Changing Curriculum* (Methuen, 1971, pp. 106), which represents a notable contribution to such a work.

may be that the contempt for historicism, so forcibly expressed in Popper's *The Open Society and its Enemies* (1945), has had something to do with this apparent neglect, though, judging by the number of adulatory biographies of minor Victorian worthies, this cannot be the main reason for it.

On the credit side it can be said that there is now available a wide selection of source materials for the study of the history of education both in the form of facsimile editions and anthologies of key documents, e.g. J. S. Maclure's *Educational Documents, England and Wales, 1816-1967* (2nd ed. 1968) and D. W. Sylvester's *Educational Documents 800-1816* (1970). The same cannot be said of British source books for the study of major works in the development of educational thought: most of them tend to be bitty and present extracts which are too snippetty to be meaty. Here again, the American 'heavies', expensive as they are, are a better purchase, besides reflecting a more informed background of scholarship.

Of all the changes that have taken place in the British approach to the history of education in recent years, none is more striking than the growing hold of parochial-mindedness upon it. Not only has it given up any pretence of surveying the world scene, but in concentrating its attention on 'some local short-lived tribe' it appears to have lost interest in anything that happened before 1800. Seeing that the national system is so recent in its origins, it is not really surprising that three out of every four books produced since 1945 deal with English education during the nineteenth century, though it may be thought that this preoccupation with the formative period of the system has had the effect of limiting the field and, which is worse, narrowing the concepts of history and education alike. This narcissism (for a discussion of its side effects see the section on comparative education) needs correction.

Moreover the 'patch' treatment seems to be getting patchier. The periods covered are becoming progressively shorter, the volumes slimmer and flimsier. No doubt because the nineteenth-century ground has been covered so often before most authors feel that the most they can do is to fill up the gaps, most of them small ones. Thus Eaglesham's *From School Board to Local Education Authority* (1956) illuminates the clash of personalities and policies in the late 1890s; Rich's *The Education Act 1870* (1970) trains the spotlight on a single year; Maclure's *One Hundred Years of London Education* (1970) on a single city. Instead of the wide international sweep and a time span of millennia, British historians of education for the most part now opt for the local scene and a time span of a decade or less. Recent history, too, claims a greater share of their attention than ever before; no matter how trivial the incident, its topicality is often enough a guarantee that a book on the subject will appear within a twelvemonth. In terms of Toynbeean 'challenge and response', this retreat from the grand manner may well be symptomatic of a Little England frame of mind in contemporary scholarship. Yet another change which cannot pass unnoticed is the growing preference for sociological interpretations of nineteenth–twentieth century developments. If courses on the history of education in many teacher training establishments have been gradually edged out in order to make room for the teaching of sociology of education the effects can be seen in the attempts now being made to merge the two 'disciplines' in a literary form, which as often as not merits description as a bastard growth in so far as the outcome is neither good history nor sound sociology. Granted, there are studies which deserve to be excepted from this general indictment – Olive Banks's *Parity and Prestige in English Secondary Education* (1955) and Harold Silver's *The Concept of Popular Education* (1965), to name only two. Of some of the others, the less said the better: in so far as the social aspects need emphasizing one cannot help feeling that most sociologists would be better employed in minding their own business.

For genuine distinction, certainly, the prize must go to the professional historians. The sorry truth is that most histories of education are bread and butter affairs, matter of fact in their content, plain to the point of prosiness in their styles of presentation. In the past, too, they have tended to be the stamping ground for the less than illustrious members of the academic community who go by the name of 'educationists'. The steady contraction of the range of British contributions to this field may have been accompanied by a rising level of competence but it can hardly be said to have stimulated the average student's sense of history, let alone given depth and breadth to his studies. The rare exceptions, and the ones that prove the rule, are authors like W. H. G. Armytage who contrive to scintillate while at the same time displaying immense erudition. It is interesting to note that Armytage's seemingly lightweight monograph, *The French Influence on English Education* (1968), one of a remarkable, if unequal, quartet, runs to a mere 114 pages yet lists well over 300 references in its guide to further reading. No treatment could be further removed from that of the conventional textbook. *Four Hundred Years of English Education* (1964) by the same author packs more imaginative insight into a footnote than most

pedestrian historians can summon up in a whole chapter: light as a
soufflé yet somehow suffering from that same *mal du siècle* which
afflicts all British historians of education today and renders them
incapable of producing anything more sizeable than a tantalizingly
brilliant sketch.

Rather more solid fare is provided in Kenneth Charlton's *Education
in Renaissance England* (1963) and, on a more specialized topic,
A. Beales's *Education Under Penalty 1547–1689* (1963), two works which
earn honourable mention for meticulous scholarship and for turning
their attention to developments in the pre-industrial era. No less
meritorious on both counts is Joan Simon's *Education and Society in
Tudor England* (1966).

So long as the teaching of history of education in the colleges and
university departments responsible for the training of teachers remains
tied hand and foot to nineteenth–twentieth century developments in
the national system, the market for books that step outside normal
course requirements (to be brutally frank, the kind of books that do not
help students to pass examinations) is bound to be small. As it is, the
shelves of most university libraries are stacked with historical theses
which never see print because publishers cannot afford the risk, in
many cases the certainty, of serious financial loss. Scotland, Ireland
and Wales (which suffers from being lumped together with England
for administrative purposes) are particularly hard hit in this respect.

Broadly speaking, this leaves us with two main classes of books about
the history of education: (1) the run of the mill ones, which comply with
the known requirements of teacher training courses and cater for them
accordingly; (2) books by historians, which are intended mainly for
historians. Seeing that the teaching of the subjects in the colleges and
university departments of education is restricted in scope and rarely
rises above a modest level, it follows that 'quality' studies are more or
less confined to the second category. For elegance of style and sophisticated scholarship the latter are the ones that give delight and hurt not.
Few works of fiction, for example, tell a more absorbing story or centre
on so eccentric a character as R. J. White's *Dr Bentley: A Study
in Academic Scarlet* (1965) – emphatically *not* the kind of book which
finds its way into every college library. On the other hand, piddling
accounts of student unrest on this or that campus command ready sales
and are consumed with relish by all and sundry. By contrast, works of
more lasting fibre, say D. Newsome's *Godliness and Good Learning*
(1961) or T. W. Bamford's *The Rise of the Public Schools* (1967) are

easily overlooked. At the moment S. Rothblatt's *The Revolution of the Dons* (1968) and H. Kearney's *Scholars and Gentlemen* (1970) are causing something of a stir in academic circles and it is to be hoped that sooner rather than later this influence will filter through the more humdrum levels where at present potboiling is the common practice. In the meantime, the mass of students training to become teachers continues to wade through a mass of prescribed reading, much of it sadly inferior stuff, nearly all of which is devoted to one aspect – not a very creditable one, either – of the recent social history of This England. Cynics may conclude that this is because learning to become scholars and gentlemen no longer figures among the objectives of the courses they are expected to follow.

Bibliography

Brian Simon's guide to the literature (in TIBBLE, J. W. (ed.) *The Study of Education*. L, Routledge, 1966. pp. 240) is as reliable and concise as any for general purposes. For specialist topics, the following bibliographies are available:

1 HIGSON, C. W. J. (ed.) *Sources for the History of Education*. L, Library Association, 1967. pp. 196. Classified in sections: (A) Books published in the fifteenth to seventeenth centuries; (B) Books published 1701–1800; (C) Books published 1801–1870; (D) Textbooks and children's books 1801–1870; (E) Government publications up to 1918. All in all, an invaluable research tool.

2 GOSDEN, P. H. J. H. *Educational Administration in England and Wales: A Bibliographical Guide*. Leeds UP, 1967. pp. 55. See in particular sections A, B, C, H and I.

3 CHRISTOPHERS, A. *An Index to Nineteenth Century British Educational Biography*. U of L (mimeographed). Lists 450 titles published before 1962.

4 FINES, J. *The Teaching of History in the United Kingdom: A Select Bibliography* L, Historical Association, 1969. pp. 56.

5 WALLIS, P. J. *Histories of Old Schools*. U of Newcastle-upon-Tyne Dept of Education, 1966. pp. 98. A revised list for England and Wales; arranged by counties.

6 POWELL, J. P. (ed.) *Universities and University Education: A Select Bibliography*. Slough, NFER, 1966. pp. 51. Sections 3.4 to 3.5 inclusive are mainly historical.

7 ARGLES, M. and VAUGHAN, J. E. *British Government Publications*

Concerning Education. Liverpool U, Institute of Education, 1966. pp. 24.

Updating of existing bibliographies is best done by consulting the *British Education Index* (published by the Library Association – three issues per annum) and the *Annual Educational Bibliography,* published by the International Bureau of Education, Geneva.

Note: A complete bibliography of the history of education in Scotland compiled on behalf of the Scottish Council for Research in Education is now available, published by the University of London Press (1971). The History of Education Society is also preparing its own bibliography.

Shortage of space has imposed a certain arbitrariness in selecting titles for inclusion in a list which otherwise might easily have been extended to fill this book – and several others. It has also restricted annotation to the tersest commentary. The layout adopted is as follows:

1 General histories of education
2 Education in the ancient world
3 National histories of education (other than British)
4 Histories of educational thought
    4.1 Readers
    4.2 Histories
5 Studies of the Great Educators and biographies
    5.1 Ancient world
    5.2 Medieval
    5.3 Renaissance and Reformation
    5.4 Eighteenth century
    5.5 Nineteenth century
    5.6 Twentieth century
6 History of education in Britain
    6.1 General
    6.2 England and Wales
        6.2.1 Source books
        6.2.2 Textbooks and general
        6.2.3 Medieval
        6.2.4 Renaissance and Reformation
        6.2.5 Eighteenth century
        6.2.6 Nineteenth century
        6.2.7 Twentieth century
        6.2.8 Church and state
    6.3 Progressive schools

1 General Histories of Education

BOYD, W. *The History of Western Education*. Revised and enlarged by E. J. KING. L, Black, 1921, 9th ed. 1969. pp. 491. Born 1921 and still going strong; the sole British survivor in this category and a worthy one.

BRUBACHER, J. S. *A History of the Problems of Education*. NY, McGraw-Hill, 1947. pp. 688.

BUTTS, R. F. *A Cultural History of Western Education*. 2nd ed. NY, McGraw-Hill, 1955. pp. 645.

COLE, L. *A History of Education*. NY, Holt, Rinehart & Winston, 1966. pp. 700. Socrates to Montessori.

GILLETT, M. *A History of Education: Thought and Practice*. NY, McGraw-Hill, 1966. pp. 443.

GOOD, H. G. and TELLER, J. D. *A History of Western Education*. 3rd ed. NY, Macmillan, 1969. pp. 630.

JARMAN, T. L. *Landmarks in the History of Education*. 2nd ed. L, Murray, 1963. pp. 325.

MEYER, A. E. *An Educational History of the Western World*. NY, McGraw-Hill, 1965. pp. 516.

MYERS, E. D. *Education in the Perspective of History*. L, Longmans, 1960. pp. 388. Interesting concluding chapter by Arnold Toynbee, whose influence is apparent throughout.

POUNDS, R. L. *The Development of Education in Western Culture*. NY, Appleton-Century-Crofts, 1968. pp. 307.

THOMPSON, M. M. *An Outline of the History of Education*. 3rd ed. NY, Barnes & Noble, 1951. pp. 159.

ULICH, R. R. *A History of Religious Education.* U of LP, 1908. pp. 312.
Documents and interpretations of the Judaeo-Christian tradition.

2 Education in the Ancient World

BECK, F. A. G. *Greek Education 450–350 B.C.* L, Methuen, 1964.
pp. 384.

CASTLE, E. B. *Ancient Education and Today.* Harmondsworth, Penguin
Books, 1961. pp. 224. A good introduction.

FREEMAN, K. J. *Schools of Hellas.* L, Macmillan, 1907. pp. 299.

GWYNN, A. *Roman Education from Cicero to Quintilian.* O, Clarendon P,
1926. pp. 260.

JAEGER, W. *Paideia: The Ideals of Greek Culture.* Tr. G. HIGHET. O,
Blackwell, 1939–45. 3 vols. pp. 510, 442 and 374. Peerless! Volumes
2 and 3 of this incomparable work of classical scholarship deal with
the Periclean and Hellenistic periods.

—— *Early Christianity and Greek Paideia.* L, OUP, 1962. pp. 160.

MARROU, H. I. *A History of Education in Antiquity.* Tr. G. LAMB. L,
Sheed & Ward, 1956. pp. 466. A major work of reference.

MOOKERJI, R. K. *Ancient Indian Education.* L, Macmillan, 1951.
pp. 655.

WOODY, T. *Life and Education in Early Societies.* NY, Macmillan, 1949.
pp. 825.

3 National Histories of Education (other than British)

AUSTIN, A. G. *Australian Education 1788–1900.* Melbourne, Pitman,
1961. pp. 282. Traces the evolution of the public system from the
colonial period.

CREMIN, L. A. *Transformation of the School.* NY, Knopf, 1961. pp. 387.
Progressivism in American education 1876–1957.

DORE, R. P. *Education in Tokugawa Japan.* L, Routledge, 1965. pp. 336.
Samurai tradition in the seventeenth to eighteenth centuries.

FOGARTY, R. *Catholic Education in Australia.* Melbourne UP, 1959.
2 vols. pp. 257 and 567.

KATZ, J. *Elementary Education in Canada.* NY, McGraw-Hill, 1961.
pp. 306.

MEYER, A. E. *An Educational History of the American People.* NY,
McGraw-Hill, 1957. pp. 489.

PHILLIPS, C. E. *Development of Education in Canada.* Ontario, Gage,
1957. pp. 626.

4 Histories of Educational Thought

4.1 READERS

BASKIN, W. (ed.) *Classics in Education.* NY, Philosophical Library, 1966. pp. 728. Anthology of key passages from the writings of the world's great thinkers on education, ancient and modern.

COHEN, A. and GARNER, N. (eds) *Readings in the History of Educational Thought.* U of LP, 1967. pp. 272. Short extracts grouped on a topic basis.

LAWRENCE, E. (ed.) *Origins and Growth of Modern Education.* Harmondsworth, Penguin Books, 1970. pp. 400. Short extracts, including some unusual ones, with linking commentary.

ULICH, R. R. (ed.) *Three Thousand Years of Educational Wisdom.* C, Mass., Harvard UP, 1954. pp. 668. The best available selection from great documents.

4.2 HISTORIES

COHEN, B. *Educational Thought: An Introduction.* L, Macmillan, 1969. pp. 110. Mercifully brief.

CURTIS, S. J. and BOULTWOOD, M. E. A. *A Short History of Educational Ideas.* 4th ed. L, U Tutorial P, 1968. pp. 639. A factual handbook.

MAYER, F. *A History of Educational Thought.* Columbus, Ohio, Merrill, 1960. pp. 494.

PRICE, K. *Education and Philosophical Thought.* Boston, Mass., Allyn & Bacon, 1962. pp. 511. Attempts an analytic approach to speculative theories: Socrates to J. S. Mill. Recommended for advanced study.

RUSK, R. R. *The Doctrines of the Great Educators.* L, St Martins P, 1969 (first pub. Macmillan, 1918). pp. 356. An old favourite and hardy perennial; individual studies from Plato and Quintilian to Dewey and Whitehead.

ULICH, R. R. *History of Educational Thought.* Rev. ed. NY, American Book Co., 1968. pp. 452. An excellent companion for the author's *Three Thousand Years of Educational Wisdom* (see section 4.1 above).

5 Studies of the Great Educators and Biographies

5.1 ANCIENT WORLD

BLACK, R. S. *Plato's Life and Thought.* L, Kegan Paul, 1949. pp. 200.

BOYD, W. *Plato's 'Republic' for Today.* L, Heinemann Educ., 1962. pp. 224. A sound introduction.

JAEGER, W. *Aristotle.* Tr. R. RICHARDSON. L, OUP, 1962 (first pub. 1934). pp. 475. Fundamentals of the history of his development.

NETTLESHIP, R. L. *The Theory of Education in Plato's 'Republic'*. L, OUP, 1935. pp. 155. An old-timer from as far back as 1880.

POPPER, K. R. *The Open Society and Its Enemies*. Vol. 1: *The Spell of Plato*. L, Routledge, 1945. pp. 268.

RICHMOND, W. K. *Socrates and the Western World*. L, Redman, 1954. pp. 214.

WINN, C. and JACKS, M. L. *Aristotle: His Thought and its Relevance Today*. L, Methuen, 1967. pp. 114. Slight.

5.2 MEDIEVAL

DUCKETT, E. S. *Alcuin, Friend of Charlemagne*. Hamden, Conn., Archon Books, 1965. pp. 339.

—— *Anglo-Saxon Saints and Scholars*. Hamden, Conn., Archon Books, 1967. pp. 485.

HOWIE, G. *Educational Theory and Practice in Saint Augustine*. L, Routledge, 1969. pp. 348.

All three above are exemplary works of scholarship, the more welcome for throwing more light on the Dark Ages.

5.3 RENAISSANCE AND REFORMATION

AXTELL, J. L. (ed.) *John Locke: Educational Writings*. CUP, 1968. pp. 442.

CROWTHER, J. G. *Francis Bacon, The First Statesman of Science*. L, Cresset P, 1960. pp. 362.

FARRINGTON, B. *Francis Bacon, Philosopher of Industrial Science*. NY, Collier Books, 1961. pp. 157.

GANSS, G. E. *Saint Ignatius' Idea of a Jesuit University*. Milwaukee, Marquette UP, 1956. pp. 368.

HUIZINGA, J. *Erasmus of Rotterdam*. Tr. F. HOPMAN. L, Phaidon P, 1952. pp. 266. Appraisal of the life and work of the great Renaissance humanist by a distinguished scholar and philosopher.

JEFFREYS, M. V. C. *John Locke: Prophet of Common Sense*. L, Methuen, 1967. pp. 120.

TURNBULL, G. H. *Hartlib, Dury and Comenius*. Liverpool UP, 1947. pp. 477. Gleanings from Hartlib's papers.

WATSON, F. (ed.) *Tudor School Boy Life: The Dialogues of Juan Luis Vives*. L, Cass, reprinted 1970 (first pub. 1908). pp. 247.

WEBSTER, C. (ed.) *Samuel Hartlib and the Advancement of Learning*. CUP, 1969. pp. 220. Puritanism and the Scientific Revolution in seventeenth century England.

WHITE, R. J. *Dr Bentley: A Study in Academic Scarlet.* L, Eyre & Spottiswoode, 1965. pp. 304. Masterly portrait of a rascally, despotic Master of Trinity.

5.4 EIGHTEENTH CENTURY

BARNARD, H. C. (ed.) *Fénelon on Education.* CUP, 1966. pp. 152. Includes translation of 'Treatise on the Education of Girls'.

BEST, J. H. (ed.) *Benjamin Franklin on Education.* NY, Columbia U, Teachers College P, 1962. pp. 174.

BOYD, W. *Émile for Today.* L, Heinemann Educ., 1956. pp. 204.

CLAYDON, L. F. *Rousseau on Education.* NY, Collier-Macmillan, 1969. pp. 147.

CUMMING, I. *Helvetius.* L, Routledge, 1955. pp. 260. His life and place in the history of educational thought.

DOBINSON, C. H. *Jean-Jacques Rousseau: His Thought and its Relevance Today.* L, Methuen, 1969. pp. 146. Chatty, discursive.

HEAFFORD, M. *Pestalozzi: His Thought and its Relevance Today.* L, Methuen, 1967. pp. 100.

SILBER, K. *Pestalozzi: The Man and His Work.* L, Routledge, 1960. pp. 352.

ZELDIN, D. *The Educational Ideas of Charles Fourier, 1772–1837.* L, Cass, 1969. pp. 167. Fascinating account of an eccentric visionary and little-known *philosophe.*

5.5 NINETEENTH CENTURY

ALEXANDER, E. *Matthew Arnold and John Stuart Mill.* L, Routledge, 1965. pp. 313.

BAMFORD, T. W. *Thomas Arnold.* L, Cresset P, 1960. pp. 232. Definitive biography of a great Victorian headmaster.

—— *Thomas Arnold on Education.* CUP, 1970. pp. 182. Selections from his writings, sermons, letters.

BIBBY, C. *T. H. Huxley.* L, Watts, 1959. pp. 330.

BURSTON, W. H. (ed.) *J. S. Mill on Education.* CUP, 1969. pp. 204.

CONNELL, W. F. *The Educational Thought and Influence of Matthew Arnold.* L, Routledge, 1950. pp. 304.

DILKE, C. W. *Dr Moberly's Mint-Mark: A Study of Winchester College.* L, Heinemann, 1965. pp. 180.

FODEN, F. *Philip Magnus.* L, Valentine, Mitchell, 1970. pp. 298. First Director of the City and Guilds of London Institute.

HARRISON, J. F. C. *Robert Owen and the Owenites in Britain and*

America. L, Routledge, 1969. pp. 392. The quest for the new moral world.

KELLY, T. *George Birkbeck*. Liverpool UP, 1957 pp. 380.

LILLEY, I. M. (ed.) *Friedrich Froebel: Selected Writings*. CUP, 1967. pp. 180. A selection from his writings.

LINDHARDT, P. G. *Grundtvig: An Introduction*. L, SPCK, 1952. pp. 144. Ideas of the guiding spirit of the Danish Folk High School movement.

LOW-BEER, A. *Herbert Spencer*. NY, Collier-Macmillan, 1969. pp. 162. A new look at one of the most neglected men in English and world education.

SILVER, H. (ed.) *Robert Owen on Education*. CUP, 1969. pp. 240. Good introduction with selections from Owen's writings.

SIMONS, D. *Georg Kerschensteiner: His Thought and its Relevance Today*. L, Methuen, 1966. pp. 152. Life, work and ideas of influential German thinker who championed the cause of vocational-industrial training as the basis for general education.

SMITH, P. and SUMMERFIELD, G. *Matthew Arnold and the Education of the New Order*. CUP, 1969. pp. 259.

5.6 TWENTIETH CENTURY

ANNAN, N. *Roxburgh of Stowe*. L, Longmans, 1965. pp. 228. Quality study of a staid, rather uninspiring subject.

ARCHAMBAULT, R. D. (ed.) *Dewey on Education*. NY, Random House, 1966. pp. 235. Appraisals, including one by J. S. Bruner.

BANTOCK, G. H. *T. S. Eliot and Education*. L, Faber, 1970. pp. 116. Sympathetic study of literary intellectualism.

GARDNER, D. E. M. *Susan Isaacs*. L, Methuen Educ., 1969. pp. 192.

LOWNDES, G. A. N. *Margaret McMillan*. L, Museum P, 1960. pp. 110. The children's champion.

MITCHELL, F. W. *Sir Fred Clarke: Master Teacher 1880–1952*. L, Longmans, 1967. pp. 254. Life, work and papers of the leading figure in British education in the immediate post-war years.

PARK, J. *Bertrand Russell on Education*. L, Allen & Unwin, 1965. pp. 147.

PERRY, L. (ed.) *Bertrand Russell, A. S. Neill, Homer Lane, W. H. Kilpatrick*. NY, Collier-Macmillan, 1967. pp. 160. Accounts of four progressive educators.

STANDING, E. M. *Maria Montessori: Her Life and Work*. L, Hollis & Carter, 1957. pp. 354.

WILLS, W. D. *Homer Lane.* L, Allen & Unwin, 1966. pp. 275. Filial biography of a wayward genius, founder of the Little Commonwealth.

WIRTH, A. C. *John Dewey as Educator.* NY, Wiley, 1966. pp. 322.

6 History of Education in Britain

6.1 GENERAL

CURTIS, S. J. *History of Education in Great Britain.* L, U Tutorial P, 1948. pp. 407.

—— *Education in Britain since 1900.* L, Dakers, 1952. pp. 317. Like the former, an honest-to-goodness factual record.

OSBORNE, G. S. *Scottish and English Schools.* L, Longmans, 1966. pp. 351. A comparative survey of the past fifty years.

SMITH, W. O. L. *Education in Great Britain.* L, OUP, 1949. pp. 200.

WILLIAMS, R. *Culture and Society 1780–1950.* L, Chatto & Windus, 1961. pp. 370.

—— *The Long Revolution.* Harmondsworth, Penguin, 1965. pp. 400. Two notable studies of the evolution of the first industrial nation.

6.2 ENGLAND AND WALES

6.2.1 *Source Books*

MACLURE, J. S. *Educational Documents, England and Wales, 1816–1967.* 2nd ed. L, Methuen, 1968. pp. 323. Selected extracts with introduction and linking commentary. Recommended.

SEABORNE, M. *Education.* L, Studio Vista, 1966. pp. 208. Attractive picture book (220 illustrations).

SYLVESTER, D. W. *Educational Documents 800–1816.* L, Methuen, 1970. pp. 290. Complement to MACLURE (above). Recommended.

6.2.2 *Textbooks and General*

ADAMSON, J. W. *English Education 1789 to 1902.* CUP, reprinted 1964. pp. 520.

ARMYTAGE, W. H. G. *Heavens Below.* L, Routledge, 1961. pp. 464. Utopian experiments in England 1560–1960.

—— *The American Influence on English Education.* L, Routledge, 1967. pp. 118.

—— *The French Influence on English Education.* L, Routledge, 1968. pp. 114.

—— *The German Influence on English Education.* L, Routledge, 1969. pp. 141.

ARMYTAGE, W. H. G. *The Russian Influence on English Education*. L, Routledge, 1969. pp. 151. Least successful of this *tour de force* quartet.

—— *Four Hundred Years of English Education*. 2nd ed. CUP, 1970 (first pub. 1964). pp. 353.

BARNARD, H. C. *A Short History of English Education 1760–1944*. U of LP, 1947. pp. 400.

—— *A History of English Education from 1760*. 2nd ed. U of LP, 1961. pp. 364.

CURTIS, S. J. and BOULTWOOD, M. E. A. *An Introductory History of English Education Since 1800*. 4th ed. L, U Tutorial P, 1966. pp. 456.

DENT, H. C. *1870–1970: Century of Growth in English Education*. L, Longmans, 1970. pp. 182.

GOSDEN, P. H. J. H. *The Development of Educational Administration in England and Wales*. O, Blackwell, 1966. pp. 228. Strongly recommended.

JUDGES, A. V. (ed.) *Pioneers of English Education*. L, Faber, 1952. pp. 251.

LOWNDES, G. A. N. *The Silent Social Revolution 1895–1965*. L, OUP, 1969. pp. 350. Revised version of a minor classic originally published in 1937.

MORRISH, I. *Education Since 1800*. L, Allen & Unwin, 1970. pp. 244.

STURT, M. *The Education of the People*. L, Routledge, 1967. pp. 432. Plain, unvarnished record of the rise of the elementary school system in the nineteenth century.

6.2.3 *Medieval*

ADAMSON, J. W. *The Illiterate Anglo-Saxon*. CUP, 1946. pp. 168. A connoisseur's piece.

KNOWLES, D. D. *The Religious Orders in England*. CUP. 3 vols: 1, 1948, pp. 348; 2, 1955, pp. 407; 3, 1959, pp. 522. A major source.

LAWSON, J. *Medieval Education and the Reformation*. L, Routledge, 1967. pp. 115. Flimsy.

RICKERT, E. *Chaucer's World*. L, OUP, 1948. pp. 478. Useful background reading.

6.2.4 *Renaissance and Reformation*

BEALES, A. C. F. *Education Under Penalty: English Catholic Education from the Reformation to the Fall of James II*. L, Athlone P, 1963. pp. 307. Hideous plight of English R.C.s in an age of persecution and martyrdom.

CHARLTON, K. *Education in Renaissance England.* L, Routledge, 1965. pp. 312. Scholarly and readable.

KEARNEY, H. *Scholars and Gentlemen.* L, Faber, 1970. pp. 214. Universities and society in pre-industrial Britain 1500–1700. Strongly recommended.

LAURIE, S. S. *Studies in the History of Educational Opinion from the Renaissance.* L, Cass, reprinted 1968. pp. 261. Not confined to England; fine essays on Sir Thomas Elyot, Ascham, Bacon, Milton, Locke.

SIMON, J. *Education and Society in Tudor England.* CUP, 1966. pp. 452. Notable study.

VINCENT, W. A. L. *The State and School Education 1640–1660.* L, SPCK, 1950. pp. 156.

—— *The Grammar Schools: Their Continuing Tradition 1660–1714.* L, John Murray, 1969. pp. 297.

WATSON, F. *The English Grammar Schools to 1660.* L, Cass, reprinted 1968 (first pub. 1908). pp. 548. Their curriculum and practice.

—— *The Old Grammar Schools.* L, Cass, reprinted 1968 (first pub. 1916). pp. 150.

6.2.5 *Eighteenth Century*

BARNARD, H. C. *Education and the French Revolution.* CUP, 1969, pp. 268.

HANS, N. *New Trends in Education in the Eighteenth Century.* L, Routledge, 1951 pp. 278.

JONES, M. G. *The Charity School Movement.* L, Cass, reprinted 1964. pp. 446. A study of eighteenth-century Puritanism in action.

NEUBURG, V. E. (ed.) *Eighteenth Century Education: Selected Sources 1718–92.* L, Woburn P, 1969. From the writings of Bishop Butler, F. Fox, Mrs Trimmer, etc.

SMITH, J. W. A. *The Birth of Modern Education.* L, Independent P, 1955. pp. 332 The Dissenting Academies.

WORDSWORTH, C. *Scholae Academicae.* L, Cass, reprinted 1968 (first pub. 1877). pp. 435. Some account of the studies in the English universities in the eighteenth century.

6.2.6 *Nineteenth Century*

ALTICK, R. D. *The English Common Reader.* U of Chicago P, 1957. pp. 430. A social history of the mass reading public.

ARCHER, R. L. *Secondary Education in the Nineteenth Century.* L, Cass, reprinted 1966 (first pub. 1921). pp. 363.

BERNARD, SIR T. *Of The Education of the Poor.* L, Woburn P, 1970 (first pub. 1809). Facsimile edition.

COLLINS, P. A. W. *Dickens and Education.* L, Macmillan, 1963. pp. 262.

GOSDEN, P. H. J. H. *The Development of Educational Administration in England and Wales.* O, Blackwell, 1966. pp. 228.

JOHNSON, M. *Derbyshire Village Schools in the Nineteenth Century.* Newton Abbot, David & Charles, 1970. pp. 224.

LEESE, J. *Personalities and Power in English Education.* L, Arnold, 1950. pp. 334.

MACLURE, J. S. *One Hundred Years of London Education.* L, Allen Lane, 1970. pp. 207.

RICH, E. E. *The Education Act 1870.* L, Longmans, 1970. pp. 124.

ST JOHN, J. A. *The Education of the People.* L, Woburn P, reprinted 1970 (first pub. 1858). Facsimile edition.

SELLMAN, R. R. *Devon Village Schools in the 19th Century.* Newton Abbot, David & Charles, 1968. pp. 171.

SILVER, H. *The Concept of Popular Education.* L, MacGibbon & Kee, 1965. pp. 288. Very good on the first half of the nineteenth century. Recommended.

SIMON, B. *Studies in the History of Education 1780–1870.* L, Lawrence & Wishart, 1960. pp. 375.

—— *Education and the Labour Movement 1870–1918.* L, Lawrence & Wishart, 1965. pp. 372.

WARDLE, D. *English Popular Education 1780–1970.* CUP, 1970. pp. 182. Concise social history; thematical.

6.2.7 *Twentieth Century*

BANKS, O. *Parity and Prestige in English Secondary Education.* L, Routledge, 1955. pp. 272. Sociological analysis. Recommended.

BERNBAUM, G. *Social Change and the Schools 1918–1944.* L, Routledge, 1967. pp. 120.

DENT, H. C. *Change in English Education: A Historical Survey.* U of LP, 1952. pp. 120.

—— *Growth in English Education 1946–52.* L, Routledge, 1955. pp. 220.

EAGLESHAM, E. J. R. *From School Board to Local Education Authority.* L, Routledge, 1956. pp. 220. Next-best-thing to a whodunnit; intrigues and infighting culminating in the Cockerton Judgment and the 1902 Education Act.

—— *The Foundations of 20th Century Education in England.* L, Routledge, 1967. pp. 155.

EDWARDS, A. D. *The Changing Sixth Form in the 20th Century.* L, Routledge, 1970. pp. 115.

EYKEN, W. VAN DER and TURNER, B. *Adventures in Education.* L, Allen Lane, 1969. pp. 190. Out of the way studies in recent local history.

MUSGRAVE, P. W. *Society and Education in England since 1800.* L, Methuen, 1968. pp. 152.

PARKINSON, M. *The Labour Party and the Organization of Secondary Education 1918–1965.* L, Routledge, 1970. pp. 139.

RUBINSTEIN, D. and SIMON, B. *The Evolution of the Comprehensive School 1926–1966.* L, Routledge, 1969. pp. 113.

6.2.8 *Church and State*

BAGLEY, J. J. and BAGLEY, A. J. *The State and Education in England and Wales 1833–1968.* L, Macmillan, 1969. pp. 88.

BROTHERS, J. *Church and School.* Liverpool UP, 1964. pp. 180. A study of the impact of education on religion.

BURGESS, H. J. *Enterprise in Education.* L, SPCK, 1958. pp. 256. Church of England voluntaryism to 1870.

CRUICKSHANK, M. *Church and State in English Education.* L, Macmillan, 1963. pp. 200.

DUNN, W. K. *What Happened to Religious Education?* Baltimore, Johns Hopkins UP, 1958. pp. 346. It's a good question. Inserted here as affording interesting comparison with developments in the U.S.A.

HISTORY OF EDUCATION SOCIETY. *Studies in the Government and Control of Education Since 1860.* L, Methuen, 1970. pp. 96.

HULME, A. *School in Church and State.* L, Society of St Paul, 1960. pp. 212. Outlines the work of the Catholic Church and its legal position.

KAZAMIAS, A. M. *Politics, Society and Secondary Education in England.* U Park, Pennsylvania State UP, 1966. pp. 382.

MCLEISH, J. *Evangelical Religion and Popular Education: A Modern Interpretation.* L, Methuen, 1969. pp. 192. Wales eighteenth century, England nineteenth century.

MATHEWS, H. F. *Methodism and the Education of the People 1791–1851.* L, Epworth P, 1949. pp. 215.

MURPHY, J. *The Religious Problem in English Education.* Liverpool UP, 1959. pp. 287.

—— *Church, State and Schools in Britain 1800–1970.* L, Routledge, 1971. pp. 152.

NEWSOME, D. *Godliness and Good Learning.* L, John Murray, 1961. pp. 291. Ideals of Victorian Christianity. Strongly recommended.

PRITCHARD, F. C. *Methodist Secondary Education.* L, Epworth P, 1949. pp. 352.

SACKS, B. *The Religious Issue in the State Schools of England and Wales 1902-14.* Albuquerque, U of New Mexico P, 1961. pp. 292.

6.3 PROGRESSIVE SCHOOLS

Note: By a curious quirk of convention, so-called progressive schools in Britain are treated as if they occurred solely in the independent sector of the education system.

BOYD, W. and RAWSON, W. *The Story of the New Education.* L, Heinemann, 1965. pp. 202.

CHILD, H. A. T. (ed.) *The Independent Progressive School.* L, Hutchinson, 1962. pp. 167.

SELLECK, R. J. W. *The New Education 1870-1914.* L, Pitman, 1968. pp. 374. The English Background 1870-1914. Detailed account of reform movement by Australian scholar.

SKIDELSKY, R. *English Progressive Schools.* Harmondsworth, Penguin Books, 1969. pp. 272.

STEWART, W. A. C., and MCCANN, W. P. *The Educational Innovators.* L, Macmillan. *Vol. 1: 1750-1880,* 1967, pp. 396. *Vol. 2: Progressive Schools 1880-1967,* 1968, pp. 370. Fully documented accounts of some of the less conventional public and private schools and their headmasters.

6.4 INDEPENDENT SCHOOLS

Note: For histories of individual schools, see the bibliography by P. J. WALLIS (p. 102 above), also W. A. L. VINCENT (see section 6.2.4).

BAMFORD, T. W. *The Rise of the Public Schools.* L, Nelson, 1967. pp. 349. A major study.

BISHOP, T. J. H. and WILKINSON, R. *Winchester and the Public School Elite.* L, Faber, 1967. pp. 263. A sociological analysis.

OGILVIE, V. *The English Public School.* L, Batsford, 1957. pp. 228.

6.5 UNIVERSITIES

ARMYTAGE, W. H. G. *Civic Universities* L, Benn, 1955. pp. 328.

ASHBY, SIR E. *Technology and the Academics.* L, Macmillan, 1958, pp. 118.

BERDAHL, R. O. *British Universities and the State*. Berkeley, U of California. P, 1959. pp. 229.

DENT, H. C. *Universities in Transition*. L, Cohen & West, 1961. pp. 176.

KNELLER, G. F. *Higher Learning in Britain*. Berkeley, U of California P, 1955. pp. 301.

ROBERTS, S. C. *British Universities*. L, Collins, 1947. pp. 47.

ROTHBLATT, S. *The Revolution of the Dons*. L, Faber, 1968. pp. 320.

SILVER, H. and TEAGUE, S. J. *The History of British Universities 1800–1969 excluding Oxford and Cambridge: A Bibliography*. L, Society of Research into Higher Education, 1970. pp. 264.

WINSTANLEY, D. A. *Later Victorian Cambridge*. CUP, 1948. pp. 380.

6.6 TECHNICAL EDUCATION

ARGLES, M. *South Kensington to Robbins*. L, Longmans, 1964. pp. 178. A concise introduction.

ARMYTAGE, W. H. G. *The Rise of the Technocrats*. L, Routledge, 1965. pp. 448.

—— *A Social History of Engineering*. L, Faber, 1966. pp. 378.

ARTZ, F. B. *The Development of Technical Education in France 1500–1850*. C, Mass., MITP, 1966. pp. 274. Inserted here for comparison with developments abroad.

BELL, Q. *The Schools of Design*. L, Routledge, 1963. pp. 290.

COMBER, N. M. *Agricultural Education in Great Britain*. L, British Council, 1948. pp. 28.

EDWARDS, K. H. R. *The Secondary Technical School*. U of LP, 1960. pp. 206.

VENABLES, P. F. R. *Technical Education*. L, Bell, 1955. pp. 645.

6.7 FURTHER AND ADULT EDUCATION

HARRISON, J. F. C. *A History of the Working Men's College 1854–1954*. L, Routledge, 1954. pp. 215.

—— *Learning and Living 1790–1960: A Study in the History of the English Adult Education Movement*. L, Routledge, 1961. pp. 420.

HUDSON, J. W. *The History of Adult Education*. L, Woburn P, 1969 (facsimile of 1st ed. 1851). pp. 238.

KELLY, T. *A History of Adult Education in Great Britain*. Liverpool UP, 1962. pp. 352.

LIEPMANN, K. *Apprenticeship: An Inquiry into its Adequacy Under Modern Conditions*. L, Routledge, 1960. pp. 204.

PEERS, R. *Adult Education: A Comparative Survey.* L, Routledge, 1959. pp. 398.

POLE, T. *A History of the Origin and Progress of Adult Schools.* L, Woburn P, 1968 (facsimile of 2nd ed. 1816). pp. 128.

RAYBOULD, S. G. *The English Universities and Adult Education.* L, Workers' Educational Association, 1951. pp. 169.

—— (ed.) *Trends in English Adult Education.* L, Heinemann, 1959. pp. 258.

—— *University Extramural Education in England 1945–62.* L, Michael Joseph, 1964. pp. 207.

STOCKS, M. *The Workers' Educational Association: The First Fifty Years.* L, Allen & Unwin, 1953. pp. 157.

TYLECOTE, M. *The Mechanics' Institutes of Lancashire and Yorkshire Before 1851.* Manchester UP, 1957. pp. 343.

6.8 TEACHING PROFESSION

BALLARD, M. *The Story of Teaching.* L, Longmans Young Books, 1969. pp. 104. Suitable for school use.

CASTLE, E. B. *The Teacher.* L, OUP, 1970. pp. 246. His changing role through the ages.

MANZER, R. *Teachers and Politics.* Manchester UP, 1970. pp. 164. The NUT as a pressure group.

RICH, R. W. *The Teacher in a Planned Society.* U of LP, 1950. pp. 120.

TROPP, A. *The School Teachers.* L, Heinemann, 1957. pp. 286. The growth of the teaching profession in England and Wales from 1800 to the present day.

6.9 CURRICULUM

ABRAMS, P. *The Origins of British Sociology.* U of Chicago P, 1969. pp. 304.

BISHOP, G. D. *Physics Teaching in England from Early Times up to 1850.* L, PRM Publishers, 1961. pp. 199.

BOLGAR, R. R. *The Classical Heritage and its Beneficiaries.* CUP, 1954. pp. 592. Erudite study of the influence of Latin and Greek on European civilization and culture.

CARDWELL, D. S. L. *The Organization of Science in England.* L, Heinemann Educ., 1957. pp. 216.

CARLINE, R. *Draw They Must.* L, Arnold, 1968. pp. 325. A history of the teaching and examining of art from the Renaissance to the present day. Not confined to Britain.

CHANCELLOR, V. E. *History for their Masters.* Bath, Adams & Dart, 1970. pp. 153. Systematic analysis of the content and ideology of nineteenth-century textbooks used in the teaching of history.

CLARKE, M. L. *Classical Education in Britain 1500–1900.* CUP, 1959. pp. 233.

COTGROVE, S. F. *Technical Education and Social Change.* L, Allen & Unwin, 1958. pp. 221.

GOSDEN, P. H. J. H. (ed.) *How They Were Taught.* O, Blackwell, 1969. pp. 299. Anthology of contemporary accounts of learning and teaching in England 1800–1950.

MUIR, P. *English Children's Books 1600–1900.* L, Batsford, 1954. pp. 256.

OGILVIE, R. M. *Latin and Greek.* L, Routledge, 1964. pp. 196. Influence of the Classics in English life and affairs from 1600 to 1918.

PALMER, D. J. *The Rise of English Studies.* L, OUP, 1965. pp. 202. The story of the Oxford English School.

RODERICK, G. W. *The Emergence of a Scientific Society in England 1800–1965.* L, Macmillan, 1967. pp. 112.

WATSON, F. *The Beginnings of the Teaching of Modern Subjects in England.* L, 1909. pp. 555.

6.10 H.M. INSPECTORATE

BALL, N. *Her Majesty's Inspectorate 1839–49.* Edinburgh, Oliver & Boyd, 1965. pp. 268. Its origins under the guidance of Dr Kay.

EDMONDS, E. L. *The School Inspector.* L, Routledge, 1962. pp. 202.

6.11 PHYSICAL EDUCATION

MCINTOSH, P. C. *Physical Education in England Since 1800.* 2nd ed. L, Bell, 1968. pp. 320.

6.12 EDUCATION OF WOMEN

KAMM, J. *Hope Deferred.* L, Methuen, 1965. pp. 344.

6.13 HANDICAPPED CHILDREN

PRITCHARD, D. G. *Education and the Handicapped 1760–1960.* L, Routledge, 1963. pp. 258.

6.14 EDUCATIONAL TECHNOLOGY

SAETTLER, P. *A History of Instructional Technology.* NY, McGraw-Hill, 1968. pp. 399.

6.15 SCOTLAND

BAIN, A. *Education in Stirlingshire from the Reformation to the Act of 1872.* U of LP/Scottish Council for Research in Education, 1965. pp. 300.

BONE, T. (ed.) *Studies in the History of Scottish Education 1872–1939.* U of LP/SCRE, 1967. pp. 317.

—— *School Inspection in Scotland 1840–1966.* U of LP/SCRE, 1968. pp. 276.

BOYD, W. *Education in Ayrshire Through Seven Centuries.* U of LP/SCRE, 1961. pp. 237.

DAVIE, G. E. *The Democratic Intellect.* Edinburgh UP, 1962. pp. 352. Scotland and her universities in the nineteenth century.

KNOX, H. M. *Two Hundred and Fifty Years of Scottish Education 1696–1946.* Edinburgh, Oliver & Boyd, 1953. pp. 254.

LAW, A. *Education in Edinburgh in the Eighteenth Century.* U of LP/SCRE, 1965. pp. 239.

OSBORNE, G. S. *Change in Scottish Education.* L, Longmans, 1968. pp. 192.

SCOTLAND, J. *The History of Scottish Education.* U of LP, 1970. 2 vols: 1 *From the Beginning to 1872,* pp. 385; 2 *From 1872 to the Present Day,* pp. 294.

SIMPSON, I. J. *Education in Aberdeenshire before 1872.* U of LP/SCRE, 1947. pp. 229.

Note: The Scottish Council for Research in Education originally planned a series of county histories covering the whole country. This plan has now been discontinued.

It should be added that some of the best works are only partly concerned with education – e.g.:

SAUNDERS, L. J. *Scottish Democracy 1815–1840.* Edinburgh, Oliver & Boyd, 1950. pp. 444.

SMOUT, T. C. *A History of the Scottish People 1560–1830.* L, Collins. 1969. pp. 576.

6.16 IRELAND

AKENSON, D. A. *The Irish Education Experiment.* L, Routledge, 1970. pp. 440. Traces the development of a national system in the nineteenth century.

ATKINSON, N. *Irish Education.* Dublin, Figgis, 1969. pp. 256. A history of educational institutions.

DOWLING, P. J. *The Hedge Schools of Ireland*. Cork, Mercier P, 1968. pp. 126.

MCELLIGOT, T. J. *Education in Ireland*. Dublin, Institute of Public Administration, 1966. pp. 201. Contains extensive bibliography.

6 *Sociology of Education*

Despite the efforts of its Victorian progenitors, any formal study of the sociology of education suffered a period of arrested development in Britain during the early decades of the twentieth century and got off to a relatively late start. As if making up for lost time, it has gained ground steadily since the end of the Second World War when the writings of Karl Mannheim and Sir Fred Clarke helped to bring about a revival. Still up and coming, the sociology of education is now very much in the ascendant and, as the monthly spate of fresh publications indicates, this must be reckoned the fastest growing sector in the entire field of educational studies. Reviewing its rise and progress, no one can fail to be impressed by its boom-town growth (twenty-five years ago a country lane and a few straggling cottages, today the Great Wen) but its effects on the ideology and modes of thinking about education are no less impressive and certainly more far reaching. The extent of the change in outlook which has occurred can be exemplified in a number of ways. In the first place, the habit of thinking contextually, i.e. in terms of the interaction of external influences and constraints, has led to traditional notions about innate ability being radically revised. Again, it has shifted the focus of attention from the content of the curriculum to the conditions of learning. Above all, it has tended to shift the centre of interest from the individual and his problems to those of the collective: whereas in 1945 the term 'adolescent' conjured up the mental image of a pimply youth, by 1970 the phenomenon was conceptualized as 'the generation gap'.

In the U.S.A., whence most of the seminal theories and supportive techniques have come, interest in the sociology of education developed earlier and on a much more massive scale. Whereas Britain had to wait until 1955 for a reliable, home-produced textbook for students, at least twenty-five such American works were published between 1916 and 1932, one of which (Willard Waller, *The Sociology of Teaching*, New York, Wiley, 1932) is still in use. How far this popular interest in the social sciences was generated by the cultural climate of the 'melting pot of nations' and how far it was necessitated by the sheer scale and organizational complexities of the world's most advanced industrial economy is itself a sociological question, one which is better left open for the moment. Academically, that interest was fed from many sources: from cultural anthropology (Malinowski, Ruth Benedict, Margaret Mead), from political economy (Max Weber), from institutional economics (Thorstein Veblen) and latterly from industrial psychology (G. Homans) and management studies (A. Etzioni *et al.*). Each of these has contributed its quota to a family of theories and techniques ranging from group dynamics and sociometry to role theory, organization theory and, if only putatively, general systems theory. In view of the claims of sociology to rank as a distinct discipline, of which more anon, it is as well to recognize both its hybrid origins and its recent emergence.

Even at the height of the current vogue it is possible to detect undertones of uncertainty about the nature, scope and purpose of the sociology of education, as if sociology and education were uncomfortable bedfellows. Marriage or misalliance? Is there not, for instance, a doctrinaire touchiness in the insistence on calling it the sociology of education? After all, no one sees anything wrong in speaking of educational psychology. What's in a name?

A great deal, say the purists. The kind of educational sociology that found its way into university and college courses formerly was too often unsystematic and, worse still, implicated in moral commitments. In the U.S.A. these two faults are thought to have been the cause of the study's falling into disrepute in the 1940s. In so far as sociology defines itself as the study of all forms of human association, it must do everything possible to remain neutral, unadulterated by any trace of personal bias. If it can never be entirely value-free, it cannot allow itself to be swayed by moral considerations. Only in this way can sociology perfect a genuinely scientific methodology and establish a sound theoretical framework – so the argument runs: whatever it does it must never take sides.

Some of the leading British investigations, e.g. Mays (1962) and Jackson and Marsden (1962), have been criticized for doing just that, allowing their personal convictions to distort experimental design and prejudice their results. Even so scrupulous a study as that of Floud, Halsey and Martin (1957) has not entirely escaped the accusation of being leftist in sympathies. By comparison with the gritty reporting of *Education and the Working Class* and the unashamedly crusading spirit displayed in many a passage of *Education and the Urban Child*, the research papers which now meet with academic approval make aseptic reading – colourless, bleak stuff the average student may well conclude.

The right of the educational sociologist to declare his personal commitment has been defended by Elvin (1965), but in general the argument in favour of intellectual discipline has prevailed and the practice is frowned upon, to say the least.

Nevertheless, the fact remains that the relationship between the 'science' of sociology and the 'art' of education *is* an uneasy one. It involves an issue which has been discussed off and on ever since Durkheim's little treatise on *The Rules of Sociological Method* made its appearance in 1895 (translation by Solovay and Muella, Glencoe, Ill., Free Press, 1950). Although these rules have subsequently been modified (see, for example, Max Weber's *The Methodology of the Social Sciences*, trans. Shils and Finch, Glencoe, Ill., Free Press, 1941; also Gunnar Myrdal's *Value in Social Theory*, London, Routledge, 1958), the dilemma arising from the separation of the social sciences from philosophy has persisted and the central issue remains unresolved. On the whole, sociologists have endeavoured to follow Durkheim's advice: 'Treat social facts as *things*'. His classical study, *Suicide*, has served as their primary model. Significantly, it had nothing whatever to do with the existential despair of the life-sick individuals who provided its data. As a science, sociology's interests are strictly supra-personal: it is concerned not with people but with cohorts, age groups, subcultures, institutions, organization, networks, systems, structures, functions. While it suits the purposes of demographic accounting, however, the equation of social facts as *things* raises peculiar difficulties for the educationist.

In *The Educational Implications of Social and Economic Change* (London, HMSO, 1967), W. J. H. Sprott asks, 'What *is* society?', and confesses that the only honest answer is 'a figment of the imagination' – figment in the sense that no one has ever seen, or can hope to see, an actual society. This is not to deny any reality to the mind models which each of us has of the society in which we live, simply to acknowledge that these internalized models are by definition abstract and conceptual. As happens in the case of language, the further up the ladder of abstraction we ascend the further removed from concrete realities we are and the more highly speculative our theories become. Thus, structural-functional analysis of the Talcott Parsons type yields a systems theory which is so highly theoretical that, as MacKenzie (1967) says, it is incapable of practical application. To put it crudely, in systems engineering the theory works because it is dealing with *things*, i.e. with physical components which are amenable to measurement and manipulation. In conceptual systems the theory itself may still hold good, but because its analyses are independent of, or at any rate far removed from, the decisions that have to be taken at the lower levels, the theory remains for the most part an intellectual exercise.

For the politician, the planner and the administrator, faced with decision-making problems affecting the lives of millions, a certain detachment may be desirable and an informed theoretical background is essential. But as Hodgkin (1970) points out, 'As we move down the scale, from large groups to small, we are moving away from the level of objective social sciences, where statistics and general rules may be important, to a level where we must be deeply involved and, for a while, must diminish our objectivity.'

This raises the question of the part to be played by the sociology of education in the training of teachers and social workers. It is to be feared that many of the courses at present proliferating in university departments of education and colleges of education are prompted more by eagerness to clamber aboard a bandwagon than by any clearer definition of objectives, and that some of them may turn out to be as arid and pointless as those they have displaced. In this connection W. Taylor (in J. W. Tibble (ed.) *The Study of Education,* 1966: cited under Educational Theory, p. 55) takes Garforth (1962) to task for advocating a topic and project approach: 'The language and sociological manner of thinking is not best acquired by a consideration of the literature of our contemporary moral concerns, by an exploration of the mass media, the social services or the leisure facilities of the neighbourhood', he affirms. Instead, he would prefer to see the students' attention to be concentrated on what he calls 'the structural contexts within which the genesis and nature of much problems and concerns can be appreciated, and without some knowledge of which no rational understanding of social process can be achieved'. He goes on: 'The justification for the inclusion of sociological studies in the course for intending teachers does not rest upon any observable link between the pursuit of such studies and the improvement of classroom technique and practice. Rather it is dependent upon the requirement that the teacher should first of all be capable of thinking logically and rationally about the whole range of social phenomena that he encounters in his personal and professional life. It is this rational intellect, the ability to sort out face and value judgment, the respect for evidence, the capacity for making valid generalizations, that has been valued, over and above a training in teaching method and classroom skill, by those responsible for appointing teachers in "superior" schools. . . .'

This line of reasoning is typical of the discipline-centred school of thought. Once can see what he means, of course, but unfortunately Taylor's argument is flatly contradicted by his own admissions, first that the time available in the initial training course is very limited, secondly and more seriously by his assertion that 'the type of high-level abstraction that is involved in a good deal of sociological theory is quite beyond the comprehension of most eighteen year olds – and even of the more mature postgraduates in university departments of education and fourth year B. Ed.s.'

This championing of the cause of rational intellect is all very fine, only we have heard it too often before and in very different connections – in defence of the retention of Classics, for example. If it means that the sociology of education earns its place by virtue of being a humane study with its own intrinsic worth, it is easy to think of others which have far better claims. The ability to sort out fact from value judgement is certainly not fostered by sociology alone: on the contrary, as we have seen, sociologists are still undecided as to what constitutes a 'fact' and what a 'value'. It seems pertinent to remark, too, that those institutions that enjoy the highest reputations as centres for the study of the social sciences are the very ones in which student protest has been most passionate, which scarcely bears out the belief that such studies fulfil the requirement of 'thinking logically and rationally about the whole range of social phenomena that he counters in his personal and professional life'. If anything, it would seem that the concentration on the impersonal aspects of learning, the imposed neutrality which characterizes all the social sciences (psychology possibly excepted), is in some way responsible for the emotively charged atmosphere of these institutions.* As for respect for evidence, the truth is that, to date, most of the evidence adduced by sociologists is either inconclusive, open to a variety of interpretations, or merely a ratification of common sense.

In short, the claim of sociology to be a distinctive 'discipline' with an established methodology of its own is at once premature and pretentious. The disputes which have arisen over the relationship between general psychology and educational psychology are, therefore, certain to

* Without comment:
'In Britain, as elsewhere, the student who takes up sociology, economics or political science finds he or she has to reject the conformist ideas and technocratic skills which his teachers seek to instil.' R. Blackburn, 'A brief guide to bourgeois ideology', *in* A. Cockburn and R. Blackburn (eds.) *Student Power* (Harmondsworth, Penguin Books, 1969).
'The hypocrisy of objectivity, of apoliticism, of the innocence of study, is much more flagrant in the social sciences than elsewhere, and must be exposed.' D. Cohn-Bendit *et al.*, 'Why sociologists ?', *in* Cockburn and Blackburn, op. cit.

recur sooner or later and more acutely in courses devoted to the sociology of education. More acutely because there is a fundamental disagreement between the perspectives and the rationale of the sociologist and
the educator. What 'makes sense' to the one, say, as role theory may
well seem rigmarole to the other. What the prospective and practising
teacher rightly looks for from sociology is much the same as what he
looks for from psychology – vocational guidance, nothing less, and in the
majority of cases nothing more. What is needed, then, might well be
called 'educational sociology' after all. To seek its furtherance by
appealing to its questionable benefits as an element in the general
education of teachers and to its even more questionable side effects in
promoting the 'rational intellect' is to ask for trouble. It assumes the
existence of a well-defined structure in a field of knowledge which is
still to be adequately mapped; and it means introducing the study at
a symbolic level for which the rank and file of students are not ready;
in other words, in ignoring the preconditions of learning, it misses out
the enactive stage, or, as Whitehead called it, the Stage of Romance.

As a result, most students do not acquire the 'language' of sociology
so much as its jargon. They learn to talk glibly of 'isolates' and 'reject-
ees', to fiddle with sociograms in much the same way that young
children once used to make paper envelopes as part of their craft work,
to frame this or that type of questionnaire and memorize what so-and-so
has to say about the school as an organization, but at the end of the day
it is doubtful whether they are any wiser or better equipped to face
up to the problems of life as it is lived in the classroom than they were
at the beginning. In the hands of tyros, dabbling in systems theory all
too easily degenerates into the gentle art of drawing diagrams consisting
of empty 'boxes' connected by two-way arrows denoting something
which goes by the name of feedback. Simulation and gaming may
help – oddly enough, they have the blessing of the intellectual discip-
linarians who normally disapprove of any concession to play-way
methods – but in so far as they evoke an active response by dramatizing
the learning situation the reason, clearly, is that they are student-
centred rather than discipline-centred.

No one doubts, of course, that the numerous demographic, contextual
and case studies which are reported in the literature have helped to
bring about a more broad-minded approach by teachers to the mass of
average and below-average ability pupils, and enabled administrators
and heads of schools to gain deeper insight into the nature of shared
decision-making. If only indirectly, the sociology of education has shown

itself to be a potentially humane study. As the record shows, both in Britain and the U.S.A., it has been continuously preoccupied with two major themes: (1) the place of teenagers in modern industrial society, (2) inequalities of opportunity in the existing system of education. For the first, which concerns young people who are variously classed as maladjusted, unattached, delinquent, drop-outs, etc., see Wall (1948), Hollingshead (1949), Fleming (1951), Ferguson (1952), Wilkins (1955), Cohen (1955), Pearson (1958), Bandura (1959), Mays (1959), Wittenberg(1959), Coleman(1961), Veness (1962), Wall (1968). For the second, which includes a host of studies of the interaction of social class, family background, language and other influences on school performance, see Davis (1948), Nisbet (1953), Banks (1955), Floud *et al.* (1957), Fraser (1959), Dixon (1962), Mays (1962), Jackson and Marsden (1962), Wiseman (1964), Bernstein (1965), Musgrove (1966), Craft *et al.* (1967).

To be sure, these are by no means the only themes to emerge. Recently there have been some excellent studies of the institutional effects of schooling. See Taylor (1963), Holly (1963), Eggleston (1967), Hargreaves (1967), Shipman (1968), Lacey (1970). Some of these take a broad canvas, others narrow the focus of inquiry to particular schools. In addition, following Lieberman's influential lead (1956), the status and role of teachers have been scrutinized more closely than ever before. A still more recent departure, exemplified by Baron and Taylor (1969), seeks to apply the techniques of social science in educational administration.

As sociology launches out in new directions in the field of education, however, what cannot escape notice is the fact that the two major concerns which energized it during its formative period – the unruliness of the roaring boys in school and in the streets and the hullabaloo over the 11-plus examination and all that – were both matters of grave *public* concern. The same can hardly be said of some of the latest lines of investigation. Any gain in precision and neutrality has meant a loss in readability. Apart from Hoggart (1962), the British literature to date has failed to produce 'best-sellers' on a par with those by Whyte (1957), Galbraith (1960) and Riesman (1964) in the U.S.A. The inference is that it is so jealous of academic rectitude as to be short of ideas. The danger is that if current trends in sociological research are allowed to go unarrested, it will lose the common touch which it must retain if it is to be serviceable for educational theory and practice. Pessimists may even conclude that the faceless posture it has chosen to assume is a sign that it has already lost touch.

Anyone who feels daunted by the number of titles listed in the following bibliography can take comfort in the thought that he is not expected to consult them all and will be wiser not to try. Quite apart from potboilers (now coming thick and fast!) the literature is diffuse and largely repetitive. The beginner who wants a four-course meal might do worse than whet his appetite on a general introduction to sociology (Bottomore, 1963), followed by an up-to-date reader (Craft, 1970), a good textbook (Banks, 1968) and a practical guide to research methods (Mann, 1968).

Any student who has digested these will have no reason to complain.

Bibliography

This bibliography is arranged in chronological order to highlight developments in this rapidly growing field. A cursory inspection reveals just how meagre the British contribution was before the mid-1950s. It also reveals a number of recurrent themes, which have engaged the interest and attention of sociologists both in the U.S.A. and in Britain during the 1945–70 period.

Titles from general sociology have been included, in most cases without comment.

1946

REEVES, M. *Growing up in a Modern Society.* U of LP. pp. 126. Marks a significant turning point in the immediate post-war era in Britain in adopting a sociological approach to education.

WARNER, W. L., HAVIGHURST, R. J. and LOEB, M. B. *Who Shall Be Educated?* L, Routledge. pp. 180. Stimulating, provocative discussion of widespread and deep-rooted inequalities of opportunity in the American education system.

1947

WEBER, M. *The Theory of Social and Economic Organization.* NY, Free P; L, Wm Hodge. pp. 404.

1948

BROWN, F. J. *Educational Sociology.* L, Technical P. pp. 626. An

American textbook, typical of its period, one of the first to be used in Britain.

CLARKE, F. *Freedom in the Educative Society.* U of LP. pp. 104. A highly influential book by Nunn's successor as Director of the University of London's Institute of Education; argues that education (not to be identified with schooling) should be a supervised function of the social life as a whole: 'We educate *for* society and we also educate *by* society.'

DAVIS, A. *Social Class Influences upon Learning.* C. Mass., Harvard UP. pp. 110. Summarizes a Negro professor's extensive research into the effects of segregation in the schools. Allison Davis's work gave the lead which has been followed up in numerous American and British investigations into social class and related influences on pupils' performance in school.

JENNINGS, H. H. *Sociometry in Group Relations.* Washington, D.C., American Council on Education. pp. 85. An early American introduction to Moreno-type techniques.

WALL, W. D. *The Adolescent Child.* L, Methuen. pp. 206.

1949

DAVIS, K. *Human Society.* L, Macmillan. pp. 655. A well established American textbook, which discusses basic concepts; marks the changeover to a more rigorous, analytical methodology.

HOLLINGSHEAD, A. DE B. *Elmtown's Youth.* NY, Wiley. pp. 480. A classic social survey of young people's out-of-school activities in the Mid-west using methods of observation derived from cultural anthropology; one of the best examples of an American genre which has been copied elsewhere.

MERTON, R. K. *Social Theory and Social Structure.* NY, Free P. pp. 423.

1950

BALES, R. F. *Interaction Process Analysis.* Reading, Mass., Addison-Wesley. pp. 203. Highly technical introduction to a method of social investigation which is now widely used.

SEGAL, C. S. *Backward Children in the Making.* L, Muller. pp. 171. Early English study of the depressive effects of urban environment in north Kensington.

1951

FLEMING, C. M. (ed.) *Studies in the Social Psychology of Adolescence*. L, Routledge. pp. 266. Reflects the changing focus of attention on the adolescent as an individual to his relations with the peer group and the neighbourhood..

HOMANS, G. L. *The Human Group*. L, Routledge. pp. 484. A classic study of group dynamics; includes accounts of the famous Hawthorne experiments.

HUSÉN, T. 'The Influence of Schooling upon IQ'. *Theoria*, XVII. A distinguished Swedish educationist's appraisal of the falsity of the doctrine of the 'constancy of IQ' and the 'pool of ability' myth.

PARSONS, T. *The Social System*. NY, Free P. pp. 575. An exposition of structural-functional analysis and general systems theory.

1952

FERGUSON, T. *The Young Delinquent in his Social Setting*. L, OUP. pp. 158. Title speaks for itself.

1953

LEWIS, M. M. *The Importance of Illiteracy*. L, Harrap. pp. 188.

MORENO, J. L. *Who Shall Survive?* Boston, Mass., Beacon P. pp. 763.

NISBET, J. D. *Family Environment: A Direct Effect of Family Size on Intelligence*. Occasional Papers on Eugenics. L, Cassel. pp. 51. An early Scottish study of the influence of home background.

OTTAWAY, A. K. C. *Education and Society: An Introduction to the Sociology of Education*. L, Routledge (rev. ed. 1962). pp. 182. The first reputable textbook by a British author.

1954

AUSUBEL, D. P. *The Theory and Problems of Adolescent Development*. NY, Grune & Stratton. pp. 580.

GLASS, D. V. (ed.) *Social Mobility in Britain*. L, Routledge. pp. 412. Demonstrates the important part played by education in deciding upward and downward mobility; draws attention to the split level of social status created by a system of selective grammar and non-selective secondary schools.

1955

BANKS, O. *Parity and Prestige in English Secondary Education.* U of LP. pp. 262. Analyses the dysfunctions produced by the development of elementary and grammar schools as separate systems in the nineteenth and early twentieth centuries; contrasts the 'sponsored mobility' in Direct Grant and Independent schools with the 'contest mobility' in the maintained sector.

BROOKOVER, W. A. *et al. A Sociology of Education.* NY, American Book Co. pp. 436. According to Banks (1968), 'the first effort in more than a quarter of a century to examine the school system from a consistently sociological rather than an "applied education" frame of reference'.

COHEN, A. K. *Delinquent Boys: The Culture of the Gang.* NY, Free P. pp. 202. One of a long line of American studies of adolescent aggression dating back to Thrasher's *The Gang: A Study of 1313 Groups in Chicago* (1936) and beyond.

GORER, G. *Exploring English Character.* L, Cresset P. pp. 328. A gifted amateur's attempt to survey the folkways of a modern industrial society in the Ruth Benedict–Margaret Mead manner.

MEAD, M. and WOLFENSTEIN, M. *Childhood in Contemporary Cultures.* U of Chicago P. pp. 474. A worldwide picture of child-rearing practices, etc., in different cultures.

OESER, O. A. *Teacher, Pupil and Task.* L, Tavistock. pp. 196. An Australian's book for prospective teachers, which has proved to be very popular; includes simple accounts of how to devise and use sociograms, etc.

SPINDLER, G. D. *Education and Anthropology.* Stanford UP. pp. 302. See KNELLER (1965), below.

SPROTT, W. J. H. *Sociology.* L, Hutchinson. pp. 192.

WILKINS, L. T. *The Adolescent in Britain,* London: Social Survey. L, Central Office of Information.

1956

DURKHEIM, E. *Education and Sociology.* Tr. and Introduction S. D. FOX. NY, Free P. pp. 163.

KLEIN, J. *The Study of Groups.* L, Routledge. pp. 200.

LIEBERMAN, M. *Education as a Profession.* Englewood Cliffs, Prentice-Hall. pp. 540. An authoritative and influential study of the status and roles of teachers in American society and their influence as an organized pressure group.

MANNHEIM, K. *Essays on the Sociology of Culture*. L, Routledge. pp. 253.

1957

FLOUD, J., HALSEY, A. H. and MARTIN, F. M. *Social Class and Educational Opportunity*. L, Heinemann. pp. 152. Almost certainly the most influential piece of reported team research in Britain during the period, based on an analysis of the results of the 11-plus examination in south-west Hertfordshire and Middlesbrough. A study in the ecology of educational opportunity, it showed that in both areas middle-class parents were more interested in their children's progress than parents from working-class backgrounds – the 'achievement syndrome'. On the other hand, physical environment (housing, income, etc.) was seen to be less important an influence in the more affluent south-west Herts area than in Middlesbrough where the successful pupils at each social level were distinguished by the relative material prosperity of their homes.

Now out of print, but far from being outdated, this work provided the initial evidence and helped to pave the way for the series of major official reports (*Crowther, Newsom, Robbins*) which were soon to follow.

MANNHEIM, K. *Systematic Sociology*. L, Routledge. pp. 169.

TROPP, A. *The School Teachers*. L, Heinemann. pp. 286. A study of the British situation with special reference to the NUT (for a detailed follow-up, see MANZER (1970), below).

WHYTE, W. H. *The Organization Man*. L, Cape. pp. 430.

YOUNG, M. D. and WILLMOTT, P. *Family and Kinship in East London*. L, Routledge. pp. 232. A social survey, typical of many carried out by the Institute of Community Studies.

1958

BRIM, O. C. *Sociology and the Field of Education*. Beverly Hills, Calif., Sage. pp. 93.

MARCH, J. G. *Handbook of Organizations*. NY, Wiley. pp. 262.

PEARSON, G. H. J. *Adolescence and the Conflict of Generations*. NY, Norton. pp. 186. This title, together with those by BANDURA,

MAYS and WITTENBURG (see under 1959), reflects the growing preoccupation with the phenomenon of the 'generation gap', 'pupil protest' and the tendency on the part of the young to reject adult authority in any shape or form.

SPROTT, W. J. H. *Human Groups*. Harmondsworth, Penguin Books. pp. 219. Strongly influenced by HOMANS (1951), above.

WEBER, M. *The Protestant Ethic and the Spirit of Capitalism*. NY, Scribner. pp. 292.

1959

ABRAMS, M. A. *The Teenage Consumer*. L, London Press Exchange. Examines the links between the economics of affluence and the emergence of popular youth culture.

BANDURA, A. *Adolescent Aggression: A Study of the Influence of Child-training Practices and Family Interrelationships*. NY, Ronald P. pp. 475.

CENTRAL ADVISORY COUNCIL FOR EDUCATION (ENGLAND). *15 to 18 (The Crowther Report)*. L, HMSO. pp. 520. Marks a departure from pre-war official thinking as typified by the *Hadow, Spens* and *Norwood Reports* in being strongly influenced by demographic and sociological evidence.

COLLIER, K. G. *The Social Purposes of Education*. L, Routledge. pp. 236.

FRASER, E. *Home Environment and the School*. U of LP. pp. 83. An exemplary Scottish study, mainly psychological but with sociological implications.

MAYS, J. B. *On the Threshold of Delinquency*. Liverpool UP. pp. 243.

MITCHELL, G. D. *Sociology: The Study of Social Systems*. L, U Tutorial P. pp. 174.

SUMNER, W. G. *Folkways*. NY, Dover Publications. pp. 692.

WITTENBERG, R. M. *Adolescence and Discipline: A Mental Hygiene Primer*. NY, Association P. pp. 318.

1960

ELKIN, F. *The Child and Society: The Process of Socialization*. NY, Random House. pp. 121. A sound introduction.

GALBRAITH, J. K. *The Affluent Society*. Boston, Mass., Houghton Mifflin. pp. 368.

MORENO, J. L. *The Sociometry Reader*. NY, Free P. pp. 773.

1961

COLEMAN, J. S. *The Adolescent Society: The Social Life of the Teenager and its Impact on Education.* NY, Free P. pp. 368.

ETZIONI, A. *A Comparative Analysis of Complex Organizations.* NY, Free P. pp. 366. A reader; advanced management studies and applied organization theory.

HALMOS, P. *The Teaching of Sociology to Students of Education.* Keele U, Sociological Review Monograph No. 4. pp. 134. Considers aims, content and methods of courses for teacher trainees.

HALSEY, A. H. (ed.) *Ability and Educational Opportunity.* L, HMSO. pp. 212. International, interdisciplinary symposium centred on the various environmental factors – economic, social – affecting the learner's educability.

HALSEY, A. H. *et al.* (eds.) *Education, Economy and Society.* NY, Free P. pp. 625. Papers from American and British sources on a variety of topics – cost-effectiveness, manpower forecasting, etc., and an important contribution by Bernstein on the sociolinguistic aspects of learning.

HOGGART, R. *The Uses of Literacy.* Harmondsworth, Penguin Books. pp. 319. A popular apologia for working-class culture.

KLUCKHOHN, F. R. and STRODTBECK, F. L. *Variations in Value Orientations.* Chicago, Row, Peterson. pp. 437. Develops a model of human value systems based on five 'universal problems', each of which has three possible 'solutions':

Problems	Solutions		
Human nature	Evil	Mixture of good and evil	Good
Relationships between man and nature	Subjugation to nature	Harmony with nature	Mastery over nature
Evaluation of past, present and future time	Emphasis on the past	Emphasis on the present	Emphasis on the future
Evaluation of the meaning of activity	Emphasis on being	Emphasis on becoming (development)	Emphasis on doing
Social relationships	Individuality		Collectivity

The model, subsequently refined, has been widely used in the analysis of attitudes inherent in different cultures and subcultures.

1962

BELL, R. R. *The Sociology of Education.* Homewood, Ill., Dorsey P. pp. 368. A source book.

BREDEMEIER, H. C. and STEPHENSON, R. M. *The Analysis of Social Systems.* NY, Holt, Rinehart & Winston. pp. 411.

DIXON, S. *Some Aspects of School Life and Progress in a Comprehensive School in Relation to Pupils' Social Background.* U of LP. One of the first of a series of case studies of individual schools. See also HOLLY (1963), HARGREAVES (1967) and LACEY (1970).

EVANS, K. M. *Sociometry and Education.* L, Routledge. pp. 149. A reliable guide to the theory and practice of sociometric testing and assessment.

GARFORTH, F. W. *Education and Social Purpose.* L, Oldbourne. pp. 174. Favours a topic approach to contemporary issues in contemporary Britain; mass media, dehumanization in industry, the decline of religion, welfare-statism, etc.

HAVIGHURST, R. J. and BERNICE, L. *Society and Education.* 2nd ed. Boston, Mass., Allyn & Bacon. pp. 585. Education as a subsystem of society.

JACKSON, B. and MARSDEN, D. *Education and the Working Class.* L, Routledge (Penguin Books 1966). pp. 268. One of the most readable documents in the literature; forthright reporting (often verbatim) of the views expressed by parents and children in a West Riding industrial town. Sees the grammar school as an essentially middle-class institution in which 'scholarship boys' of lower-working-class origins are inevitably misfits because its ethos and rituals are foreign to them.

MANNHEIM, K. and STEWART, W. A. C. *An Introduction to the Sociology of Education.* L, Routledge. pp. 187. Swansong of a major thinker of the World War II era; based on Mannheim's manuscript notes, rewritten and reworked by one of his former students; seeks to hold the balance between the claims of individual freedom and creative initiative on the one hand, and those of subservience and conformity on the other. Philosophically interesting, but somewhat dated as regards method.

MAYS, J. B. *Education and the Urban Child.* Liverpool UP. pp. 208. Sympathetic portrait of deprivation in the Crown Street district slums; urges the need for all-round social reforms, a plea recognized in the *Plowden Report*'s designation of 'educational priority areas'.

VENESS, T. *School Leavers*. L, Methuen. pp. 252. Reveals the low levels of aspiration and expectation of the majority of secondary modern school pupils.

WEBER, M. *Basic Concepts in Sociology*. Tr. and Introduction H. P. SECHER. NY, Citadel P. pp. 123.

1963

BOTTOMORE, T. *Sociology: A Guide to Problems and Literature*. L, Unwin U Books. pp. 330.

CENTRAL ADVISORY COUNCIL FOR EDUCATION (ENGLAND). *Half Our Future (The Newsom Report)*. L, HMSO. pp. 299. The 'Newsom children', as they have come to be called, are those between the ages of 13 and 16 classed as being of average or less than average ability. The keynote of the report is expressed in the assertion that the kind of intelligence as measured in the tests so far applied is largely an acquired characteristic. Profiles of the Brown, Jones and Robinson pupils repay close study.

COMMITTEE ON HIGHER EDUCATION. *Higher Education (The Robbins Report)*. L, HMSO, Cmnd. 2154. pp. 335. Like Newsom, strongly sociological in outlook, insisting throughout that 'more means better'. Main recommendations have now been implemented but the numerous statistical tables, particularly those in Appendix One, are a veritable mine of information and must be considered essential reading.

HOLLY, D. N. *Social and Academic Selection in a London Comprehensive School*. U of LP.

LEWIN, K. *Field Theory in Social Science*. L, Tavistock. pp. 346. Lewin's social psychology sees the development of the individual in the context of external forces and constraints, which together constitute the life 'field'. His work represents an important change of outlook on the part of psychologists.

MUSGROVE, F. *The Migratory Élite*. L, Heinemann. pp. 192.

SPINDLER, G. D. (ed.) *Education in Culture: Anthropological Approaches*. NY, Holt, Rinehart & Winston. pp. 571. A good reader.

TAYLOR, W. *The Secondary Modern School*. L, Faber. pp. 254. Views the modern school in its developmental and social setting, evaluates its successes and failures, and concludes that it serves to depress the performance and aspirations of the majority of pupils. Exposes the 'parity of esteem' legend as barren and argues that there is no excuse for perpetuating the social inequalities induced by a tripartite system.

1964

ARGYLE, M. *Psychology and Social Problems*. L, Methuen. pp. 232.

DOUGLAS, J. W. B. *The Home and the School*. L, MacGibbon & Kee. pp. 190. A major landmark, based on a nationwide survey; brings together and interprets a mass of evidence relating to family size, social class, differences in the material background of the home, parental care, attitudes to school life, streaming of classes, etc., and their effects on pupils' performance.

ETZIONI, A. *Modern Organizations*. Englewood Cliffs, Prentice-Hall. pp. 120.

JACKSON, B. *Streaming: An Educational System in Miniature*. L, Routledge. pp. 156. Scathing indictment of a practice which is hard of dying, spiced with lurid quotes from parents and children whose life-style has allegedly been marred by it.

MCKINLEY, D. G. (ed.) *Social Class and Family Life*. NY, Free P. pp. 306. Contains article by Talcott Parsons on 'The school class as a social system'.

MAYS, J. B. *Growing up in the City*. NY, Wiley. pp. 225. A study of juvenile delinquency in an urban neighbourhood.

MUSGROVE, F. *Youth and the Social Order*. L, Routledge. pp. 160.

RIESMAN, D. *The Lonely Crowd*. New Haven, Conn., Yale UP. pp. 386.

SCHRAMM, W. (ed.) *The Effects of Television on Children and Adolescents*. Paris, UNESCO. pp. 54. Findings mostly inconclusive, as with Himmelweit's survey in Britain.

WEBER, M. *The Theory of Social and Economic Organization*. NY, Free P. pp. 436. A key text.

WILKINSON, R. *The Prefects*. L, OUP. pp. 243. Arguably the most brilliantly written book in this bibliography, a devasting critique (by an old Wykehamist) of the English Public Schools as the last resting places of a mandarin culture.

WISEMAN, S. *Education and the Environment*. Manchester UP. pp. 216.

1965

BERNSTEIN, B. 'A socio-linguistic approach to social learning', *in* GOULD, J. (ed.) *Penguin Survey of Social Sciences*. Harmondsworth,

Penguin Books. pp. 183. Summarizes Bernstein's seminal research into two different modes of speech: (*a*) a 'restricted code' (public language), (*b*) an 'elaborated code' (formal language). Broadly, the former is associated with low socio-economic groups, the latter with the middle class. Children accustomed to the restricted code are at a disadvantage in the formal learning situation, tend to be passive, poorly motivated and ill adapted to verbal reasoning.

BLYTH, W. A. L. *English Primary Education: A Sociological Description.* L, Routledge. 2 vols. pp. 226 and 158. Vol. 1 classifies nursery, infant and junior schools according to their social setting – inner ring, outer ring, rural, etc. – and examines the ways in which their organization, outlook and work are affected by that setting. Vol. 2 is mainly concerned with the social content of the curriculum and methods of teaching.

CORWIN, R. G. *A Sociology of Education.* NY, Appleton-Century-Crofts. pp. 454. Masterly textbook which examines the ways in which American schools function as complex bureaucratic organizations.

DONNISON, D. V. *Social Policy and Administration.* L, Allen & Unwin. pp. 270.

ELVIN, H. L. *Education and Contemporary Society.* L, Watts. pp. 220. Chapter 2 makes excellent sense, rightly refusing to be drawn into doctrinaire arguments as to whether the studies referred to are or are not sociological. One of the few outstanding contributions to educational theory in recent years.

HALLORAN, J. D. *The Effects of Mass Communication.* Leicester UP. pp. 84. With reference to television.

KLEIN, J. *Samples from English Cultures.* L, Routledge. 2 vols. pp. 435 and 436. Source materials illustrative of changing patterns of family life, child-rearing, etc.

KNELLER, G. F. *Educational Anthropology.* NY, Wiley. pp. 171. A short introduction which discusses the main theories and findings of cultural anthropology and their relevance to (mainly American) educational problems.

LAURIE, P. *Teenage Revolution.* L, Blond. pp. 158.

LOOMIS, C. P. and LOOMIS, Z. K. *Modern Social Theories.* L, Van Nostrand. pp. 800. Largely taken up with explication of advanced Parsonian concepts.

MAYS, J. B. *The Young Pretenders.* L, Michael Joseph. pp. 206.

MEAD, G. H. *On Social Psychology.* U of Chicago P. pp. 358. Posthumous work, mainly from transcripts, by one of the great pioneers of modern sociology.

MUSGRAVE, P. W. *The Sociology of Education*. L, Methuen. pp. 278. A lucid, comprehensive textbook, widely used.

PARSONS, T. (ed.) *Theories of Society*. L, Macmillan. 2 vols. pp. 1520.

1966

BIDDLE, B. J. and THOMAS, E. J. *Role Theory, Concepts and Research*. NY, Wiley. pp. 453. A standard work of reference.

BOTTOMORE, T. B. *Élites and Society*. Harmondsworth, Penguin Books. pp. 160.

ERIKSON, E. H. (ed.) *The Challenge of Youth*. NY, Doubleday. pp. 340.

GREEN, B. S. R. and JOHNS, E. A. *An Introduction to Sociology*. O, Pergamon P. pp. 159.

HERRIOT, R. E. and ST JOHN, N. H. *Social Class and the Urban School*. NY, Wiley. pp. 289. The impact of pupil background on teachers and principals. Reflects the need for new methods and approaches to counter indiscipline and indifference in the drop-out generation.

KALTON, G. *The Public Schools*. L, Longmans. pp. 173. An independent, factual survey of the independent sector of the English system of education.

MUSGROVE, F. *The Family, Education and Society*. L, Routledge. pp. 156. Vigorously written, drawing together all the threads of evidence on the theme of linking home and school.

RAISON, T. (ed.) *Youth in New Society*. L, Hart-Davis. pp. 197.

1967

ANDERSON, C. (ed.) *The Social Context of Educational Planning*. Paris, OECD. pp. 35.

BERNBAUM, G. *Social Change and the School 1918–1944*. L, Routledge. pp. 120. A short, rather slight monograph on developments in England between World Wars I and II.

CENTRAL ADVISORY COUNCIL FOR EDUCATION (ENGLAND). *Children and Their Primary Schools (The Plowden Report)*. Vol. 1: *Report*. L, HMSO. pp. 556. Chapter 3, 'The children and their environment', summarizes evidence from national surveys and the research literature.

CRAFT, M., RAYNOR, J. and COHEN, H. (eds.) *Linking Home and School*. L, Longmans. pp. 246. A good reader, which reproduces extracts from the work of leading British sociologists of education: Blyth, Klein, Mays, Bernstein, Young, Taylor, etc.

EGGLESTON, S. J. E. *The Social Context of the School*. L, Routledge. pp. 116. Careful exposition of the ways in which the school responds (or fails to respond) to its catchment area, the 'community context'.

HARGREAVES, D. *Social Relations in a Secondary School*. L, Routledge. pp. 226. A high quality contextual and case study of a secondary modern school; unravels the network of influences which give rise to pro-school and anti-school subcultures.

HUSÉN, T. 'The effect of school structure upon utilization of ability', in *Social Objectives in Educational Planning*. Paris, OECD. pp. 312. Repeats the arguments of his 1951 paper (see above) now impressively reinforced by evidence accumulated since Sweden's all-out adoption of the comprehensive school principle.

MABEY, R. *Class: A Symposium*. L, Blond. pp. 176.

MacKENZIE, W. J. M. *Politics and Social Science*. Harmondsworth, Penguin Books. pp. 432. Contains few references to education, but ranks as important background reading nevertheless, if only for its critique of Parsonian system theory.

MAYS, J. B. *The School in its Social Setting*. L, Longmans. pp. 94.

MORRISH, I. *Disciplines of Education*. L, Allen & Unwin. pp. 336. Has good chapters on Durkheim, G. H. Mead and Karl Mannheim, each accompanied by perceptive commentaries.

MUSGRAVE, P. W. *Technical Change, the Labour Force and Education*. O, Pergamon P. pp. 286.

RICHARDSON, J. E. *The Environment of Learning*. L, Nelson. pp. 247. Conflict and understanding in the secondary school.

1968

BANKS, O. *The Sociology of Education*. L, Batsford. pp. 224. To date the most scholarly British textbook in the field; includes a good deal of information from comparative education; synthesizes the main research findings and expounds the main theories while remaining eminently readable.

CLEGG, A. and MEGSON, B. *Children in Distress*. Harmondsworth, Penguin Books. pp. 176. Informal, highly sympathetic introduction to the problems of social deprivation.

GETZELS, J. W., LIPHAM, M. J. and CAMPBELL, R. F. *Educational Administration as a Social Process*. NY, Harper & Row. pp. 420. Theory, research, practice (see BARON and TAYLOR, 1969, below.)

GOODACRE, E. J. *Teachers and their Pupils' Home Background.* Slough, NFER. pp. 170.

LAMBERT, R. J. and MILLHAM, S. *The Hothouse Society.* L, Weidenfeld & Nicolson. pp. 400. Preliminary findings, none of them very startling, of a social survey of England's independent schools.

LAWTON, D. *Social Class, Language and Education.* L, Routledge. pp. 181.

MANN, P. H. *Methods of Sociological Inquiry.* O, Blackwell. pp. 195. An admirable handbook, chockful of invaluable advice on how to collect data, conduct surveys, administer tests, analyse and present results. Students of the sociology of education wishing to embark on investigations of their own might well begin here. Includes stimulating suggestions for further reading.

MITCHELL, G. D. (ed.) *A Dictionary of Sociology.* L, Routledge. pp. 224.

MUSGRAVE, P. W. *The School as an Organization.* L, Macmillan. pp. 104. Attempts a comparative analysis of the English and Scottish school systems: discusses overall structure, the role of the head and the assistant teacher, the school and the school class.

—— *Society and Education in England since 1800.* L, Methuen. pp. 152. A none-too-successful attempt to rake over ground that is already well covered by historians.

SHIPMAN, M. D. *The Sociology of the School.* L, Longmans. pp. 176. Contrasts the 'structural-functional' with the 'centre of conflict' model, sees them as co-existing and goes on to consider problems of order and discipline in the school in the light of recent organization theory (mainly Etzioni's).

SUGERMAN, B. *Sociology.* L, Heinemann Educ. pp. 98.

WALL, W. D. *Adolescents in School and Society.* Slough, NFER. pp. 136. A synthesis of research findings presented in non-technical style; deals with theories of adolescence, intelligence, learning and motivation, curriculum, vocational guidance, maladjustment, backwardness, delinquency, etc. Mainly psychological but with sociological overtones.

1969

BARON, G. and TAYLOR, W. *Educational Administration and the Social Sciences.* L, Athlone P. pp. 193. A notable symposium. Dust-cover claims that it 'marks a new development in the literature of education in England', a claim that is not altogether exaggerated, although a similar development had taken place at least ten years earlier in the U.S.A. The attempt to convert educational administration into a field of systematic study is nicely illustrated by explanatory chapters on systems theory, organization theory, cost effectiveness analysis, role theory and operational research.

HOYLE, E. *The Role of the Teacher.* L, Routledge, pp. 103.

KING, R. A. *Education.* L, Longmans. pp. 138. The contemporary scene in British education viewed from a sociological perspective; slight, neutral.

MUSGROVE, F. and TAYLOR, P. H. *Society and the Teacher's Role.* L, Routledge. pp. 104

SWIFT, D. F. *The Sociology of Education.* L, Routledge. pp. 121. Introductory analytical perspectives.

TAYLOR, G. and AYRES, N. *Born and Bred Unequal.* L, Longmans. pp. 132. Perceptive account of 'human ecology' in different regional environments.

TAYLOR, W. *Society and the Education of Teachers.* L, Faber. pp. 304.

WAKEFORD, J. *The Cloistered Elite.* L, Macmillan. pp. 272. A sociological analysis of the English public boarding school.

1970

ASHLEY, B. J., COHEN, H. S. and SLATTER, R. G. *An Introduction to the Sociology of Education.* L, Macmillan. pp. 160. Terse exposition (strongly influenced by Talcott Parsons) of basic concepts, the family and socialization, the teaching-learning process, classroom situation, etc.; intention is to provide framework for a foundation course, cutting out factual details.

CRAFT, M. (ed.) *Family, Class and Education: A Reader.* L, Longmans. pp. 269. And a very good one, too. Demographic, contextual and subcultural studies.

ENTWISTLE, H. *Education, Work and Leisure.* L, Routledge. pp. 128. Considers changing attitudes and values as industrial society moves towards an age of automation.

HODGKIN, R. A. *Reconnaissance on an Educational Frontier.* L, OUP. pp. 108.

LACEY, C. *Hightown Grammar.* Manchester UP. pp. 214. One of the most accomplished and convincing case studies yet reported, this time of a grammar school in an industrial town, viz. the North of England; elaborates a model showing how differentiation (i.e.

academic streaming) leads to polarization and the emergence of pro-school and anti-school subcultures.

LAMBERT, R., BULLOCK, R. and MILLHAM, S. *A Manual to the Sociology of the School.* L, Weidenfeld & Nicolson. pp. 348. Intended as a practical guide for research workers; outlines main theories and methodology.

LUNN, J. C. B. *Streaming in the Primary School.* Slough, NFER. pp. 508.

MANZER, R. *Teachers and Politics.* Manchester UP. pp. 164. An examination, based on a Ph.D. thesis, of the role of the NUT as a professional pressure group.

MUSGRAVE, P. W. (ed.) *Sociology, History and Education.* L, Methuen. pp. 293. Yet another reader, good in parts, which reproduces papers by sociologists using historical material.

SCHOFIELD, M. *Social Research.* L, Heinemann Educ. pp. 138. Handbook of techniques for social surveys.

SWIFT, D. F. (ed.) *Basic Readings in the Sociology of Education.* L, Routledge. pp. 301. Another reader with contributions from British and American sources. After defining the field, deals with the social animal (*sic*), the school, the social environment and social functions of education.

7 Educational Administration

1 The British System of Education

Until very recently the vast majority of books available under this heading could be classified as guides of one sort or another. That is to say their *raison d'être* was to help readers to understand how the system works and how it came into being. Their method was almost exclusively descriptive with, at most, a modicum of historical explanation. In view of the ramshackle nature of the English system of education during its formative period in the nineteenth century and the added complications arising from the expansion of its services in the twentieth, this prolific literature provides a necessary information service – and not only for overseas visitors who often find its idiosyncrasies baffling. Many a citizen, for that matter many an experienced teacher, would be hard put to unravel the intricacies of the legal, financial and administrative arrangements which have to be observed, say, in the maintenance of 'aided' and 'county' schools, or to define precisely the delegation of powers to its divisional executives by a local education authority. Indeed, nothing would be easier than to draw up a quiz based on the various Education Acts since 1944 which only professional administrators would be expected to take in their stride and which would leave everyone else guessing. In a democracy education may be everybody's business, but in Britain the grass roots are withered: unlike the U.S.A., the system does not allow of the electorate's direct choice of representatives for the handling of its educational affairs either at the level of the local or the central government. Ratepayers can vote for the councillor of their choice: they have no say in getting him on (or off) the authority's education committee. Similarly in the case of members of parliament. Again, the average parent is lamentably ignorant about his rights – though he is left in no doubt about his duties if he steps out of line – and apathetic when it comes to asserting them because he feels impotent in the face of officialdom.

On the whole, public opinion is satisfied that the arrangements are both fair and efficient, but the very fact that the machinery is so complicated means that there are many puzzled people. For them, if for no one else, factual accounts can be interesting enough. For students, particularly those training to become teachers, some acquaintance with the ways in which the system operates is essential: short of mugging up the facts there is no way of satisfying the examiners in most courses on educational administration! For the rest, the verdict can only be that most of the literature in Section 1 of this bibliography is not strictly concerned with administrative problems at all and must be characterized as competent, preoccupied with pettifogging details, largely uncritical and almost entirely dull. As guidebooks go, there is little to choose between them. The best digest is G. Baron's *A Bibliographical Guide to the English Educational System* (3rd ed. 1965): exhaustive, well annotated and interspersed with breezy discussions of classified topics.

2 Institutions

Things are not much better as regards books about the various types of institutions which form the component parts of the system, for here too the accounts tend to be mainly descriptive and historical. Two exceptions to the rule which deserve honourable mention are W. A. L. Blyth's *English Primary Education: A Sociological Description* (1965) and W. Taylor's *The Secondary Modern School* (1963). Books about the grammar school are too often blatantly partisan, sometimes to the point of being blinkered, while those dealing with the comprehensive school carry chips on their shoulders and are apt to resort to special pleading. As a study of that most English of all institutions, the Public School, Rupert Wilkinson's *The Prefects* (1963) shines like a good deed in a world of words that is not so much naughty as banal.

Following the *Robbins Report* (1963) there have been some lively exchanges in the field of higher education, a dialogue sharpened in its cut and thrust by the resurgence of student power. The teething troubles of the old foundations and the efforts now being made by some of the older ones to put their house in order, the uneasiness in academic circles at the prospect of the university losing its pride of place in the face of growing competition from the polytechnics, the blurring of the lines of demarcation between 'further' and 'higher' education – all this may not seem to be the stuff of educational administration but if it has a place it must be here.

This leaves the local education authorities, the Department of Education and Science itself (not forgetting the Scottish Education

Department) and the major political parties. From time to time the latter issue their own policy-making statements, but to date there have been singularly few studies – M. Parkinson's *The Labour Party and the Organization of Secondary Education 1918–65* (1970) is one – of the infighting and clash of interests and personalities involved in the process. Again, apart from one or two isolated, minor investigations of the methods of conducting business in local education authorities, the decision-making process at the local level has received very little attention. As for the goings-on inside the central corridors of power and the division of roles, functions and responsibilities between here-to-day-and-gone-tomorrow ministers and the permanent officials who serve them, who can tell? At the top of the Establishment, the researcher is usually left darkling. Politicians, like civil servants, do not write books about education while they are in office: anything they have to say frankly on the subject is reserved for their memoirs. That they are not unresponsive to organized presssure groups is shown by R. Manzer's *Teachers and Politics* (1970). In general, nevertheless, there is no resisting the conclusion that important policy decisions, like those for and against the adoption of a comprehensive principle for the organization of secondary schools, are taken on political rather than on educational grounds.

3 Politics, Management and Organization

Just as national area studies are a necessary first step in developing a methodology for comparative education (see pp. 163–82), so the kinds of book discussed in the first half of this introduction underline the need for a more systematic theory and practice of educational administration. As its title proclaims, *Educational Administration and the Social Sciences*, edited by G. Baron and W. Taylor (1969), heralds the dawn of a new era. There are two good reasons for thinking that from now on factual, descriptive accounts of the state system of education will give way to more sophisticated and searching analyses of the 'state' of the 'system'.

First, if it has done nothing more, the wave of student sit-ins, protests and unruly demonstrations has at least served as a reminder that education is, after all, a branch of politics. In the Aristotelian sense this has always been true. The cry 'Keep politics out of education' has never had a more forlorn ring than it has today. By rights, politics ought to rank alongside philosophy as a constituent element in the field of educational studies. Instead, it has been treated as if it were somehow taboo, inhibited, if not suppressed, by all manner of artificial embargoes, with the result that vital educational issues which call for plain speaking have been beclouded by double-talk. In these conditions, politics has had to be smuggled in by the side door, usually by way of economics and sociology; and now that this has happened it seems only a matter of time before it takes its rightful place. The confrontation between a minority of militant students and a handful of university authorities is no mere flash in the pan: it typifies the head-on clash between the claims of participatory democracy and the demands made by bureaucratic controls which threaten society at large. As Max Weber saw it, the bureaucratic administrator's authority depended upon his professional training and skills. So long as these skills were indispensable or in short supply his position was secure. But in an educated society more and more people begin to question the legitimacy of his right to tell them what and what not to do: they want to know more about the ways in which power is distributed, and the more they know the more inclined they are to insist that decision-making must be shared. The bureaucrat follows the rule book; they want to change the rules. In this situation, ways and means of managing conflict have to be found. To refuse to admit that these ways and means are not necessarily political because they do not coincide with our notions of party politics (which the militants are not alone in rejecting as irrelevant) is to miss the point. W. J. M. Mackenzie's erudite *Politics and Social Science* (1967), though somewhat diffuse and difficult to follow in places, puts the issues in their proper perspective and W. O. Lester Smith's *Government of Education* (1965) asks and answers some pertinent questions. So, more aggressively, do the leader-writers of the activist movement.

Second, the sheer size of the educational enterprise – bigger schools, bigger student enrolments, bigger costs, bigger everything – has forced planners to the conclusion that there is no alternative to the adoption of methods which have proved indispensable in the conduct of Big Business and in military operations. Lessons learned in the field of industrial relations and in scientific management may not be immediately applicable in educational administration but there is ready to hand a formidable array of theoretic techniques – organization theory, systems theory, communication theory, role theory, queueing theory, group dynamics, network analysis, operational research, cost-effectiveness analysis, work study, simulation and gaming – each of which has been tried out in a variety of contexts. No one pretends that, collectively, they add up to a panacea for the management of conflict situations. No one denies that, individually, their applications have achieved more than a limited success. Systems theory, for example, may help teachers to realize how the web of constraints inside and outside the classroom and the school is formed, but is a long way short of helping them to pull more strings than they can at present (for further discussion on this point see under Sociology of Education and Educational Technology). It may well be that a good deal of the prestige enjoyed by some of these techniques owes more to their novelty than to anything else. Even so, the spin-off from them has led to more experimental, imaginative methods of teaching.

More so than most academic studies, educational administration is wide open to the criticism that 'Those who can, do: those who can't, teach' (some systems theorists, one suspects, would be hard put to manage a bingo hall). This taunt has never had quite the same force in the U.S.A. where the multiplicity of small town, district and county school boards has resulted in the number of lucrative administrative posts being much greater than it is in Britain. Thanks to this – and the firm belief that leaders are made, not born – the American literature is well stocked with textbooks on the theory and practice of educational administration. Several American universities offer higher degrees which are geared to the practical training of school superintendents and State Department of Education officials. British universities, on the other hand, have resisted every attempt to convert them into 'service stations' and have been slow to come round to the view that a vocationally based doctorate for administrators is either feasible or desirable. The Master of Education remains an all-purpose, academic award, obtainable in places without candidates ever being introduced to the business of administration. In this, as in so many other respects, the British preference is still for the gifted amateur. In any case, the argument goes, the number of professional administrators needed to run the educational services in this country is bound to be small.

But the need for administrative skills is not confined to the offices of local and central government or to planning boards. There is a growing body of opinion which thinks that head teachers should be trained for the job. Team teaching and media usage have given greater plausibility to the idea of the assistant teacher as manager. Input-output analysis has turned the spotlight on the problems of assessing the teacher's effectiveness. Above all, the habit of thinking contextually is itself symptomatic of that widening of intellectual horizons in educational theory as a whole which has been referred to more than once in this survey. In short, as A. E. Etzioni puts it in *Modern Organization* (1964),

> Organizational analysis has broadened its concerns to include:
> 1 both formal and informal elements of the organization and their articulation,
> 2 the scope of informal groups and the relation between such groups inside and outside the organization,
> 3 both lower and higher ranks,
> 4 both social and material rewards and their effects on each other,
> 5 the interaction between the organization and its environment,
> 6 both work and non-work organizations.

Hitherto, the work of administration has been thought of as being largely routine, as a static process – a matter of implementing given policies and seeing that regulations were carried out. It is now being thought of in more dynamic terms. Although the idea of the school executive has been slow in taking root in Britain, where it is still regarded with a mixture of suspicion and downright hostility in many quarters, it has been gaining ground ever since Frederick Taylor introduced quantitative methods of 'scientific management' to the business world in 1910. Today, 'Management can be viewed as a broader activity than administration in that emphasis is placed on creative decision-making which is designed to alter the course of future events. Management further requires decision-making beyond initial acceptance of an objective. It is continually extending the boundaries of its system and improving itself within the boundaries, trying to achieve higher levels of efficiency effectiveness.' (H. W. Handy and K. M. Hussain, *Network Analysis for Educational Management*, 1969, p. 5)

Both in its aspirations and its strategies, this managerial revolution has much in common with educational technology (see pp. 190–206) and so-called curriculum development (see under Curriculum Study). Taylorism has been exposed as too crude an approach to work-study and the dehumanizing effects of similar approaches in education have been savagely criticized by writers like R. Callahan in *Education and the Cult of Efficiency* (1962) and G. H. Bantock in *Education in an Industrial Society* (1963). Great play has been made of the fact, which is undeniable, that many of the theories and analytical techniques which have been applied successfully in industry and commerce, where the objectives are clear cut, are not obviously transferable – and may be non-transferable – to educational problems. Nevertheless, certain broad guidelines have emerged and it is no accident that they are the same as those followed in programmed learning and in the design of curriculum projects. S. L. Optner summarizes them in *Systems Analysis for Business and Industrial Problem Solving* (1965):

1 The problem process must be flow-charted, showing at least the principal decision-making points.
2 Details of the principal decision process must be described.
3 The principal alternatives and how they were generated must be demonstrable.
4 The assumptions pertinent to each alternative must be clearly identified.
5 The criteria by which each alternative will be judged must be fully stated.
6 Detailed presentation of data, data relationships and the procedural steps by which such data were evaluated must be part of any solution.
7 The major alternative solutions and details to explain why other solutions were eliminated must be shown.

As a set of categorical imperatives it may be thought that this amounts to a late twentieth-century equivalent of the Cartesian method. *Faute de mieux*, nothing less will suffice in an age of technology.

Bibliography

In addition to Baron's all-purpose guide (section 1.1 below), students should consult P. H. J. H. Gosden's *Educational Administration in England and Woles: A Bibliographical Guide*, published by the University of Leeds Institute of Education, 1967. Fully annotated and exhaustive, this is arranged in the following sections:

A Historical, social and legal background
B Administrative agencies, central and local
C Inspection
D Consultative arrangements
E Finance
F Curriculum and examinations
G School building
H Further education

I   Universities
J   Bibliographies and periodicals

Two other guides to the literature are:

ARGLES, M. and VAUGHAN, J. E. *British Government Publications Concerning Education*. 3rd ed. U of Liverpool School of Education 1969. pp. 24.

KELLY, T. *A Select Bibliography of Adult Education in Great Britain*. 2nd ed. L, Nat. Inst. of Adult Education, 1962. pp. 96.

The list that follows is arranged under the headings of:

1 The British system of education
   1.1   England and Wales
   1.2   Scotland
2 Institutions
   2.1   Primary schools
   2.2   Secondary schools
   2.3   Secondary modern
   2.4   Secondary technical
   2.5   Secondary grammar
   2.6   Comprehensive secondary
   2.7   Independent schools
   2.8   Further education
   2.9   Higher education: general information
   2.10 Universities
3 Politics, management and organization

1 The British System of Education

1.1 ENGLAND AND WALES

ALEXANDER, W. P. *Education in England*. L, Newnes, 1954. pp. 128. The national system – how it works.

ALEXANDER, W. P. and BARRACLOUGH, F. *County and Voluntary Schools*. 4th ed. L, Councils and Educational P, 1967. pp. 109.

ARMFELT, R. *The Structure of English Education*. L, Routledge, 1955. pp. 207. Passable in its day, but that day is past.

BARON, G. *A Bibliographical Guide to the English Educational System*. 3rd ed. L, Athlone P, 1965. pp. 124. See introduction.

BURGESS, T. *A Guide to English Schools*. Harmondsworth, Penguin Books, 1964 (rev. ed. 1970). pp. 232. Fresh factual description.

DENT, H. C. *The Educational System of England and Wales*. U of LP, 1961 (rev. ed. 1970). pp. 238.

GOSDEN, P. H. J. H. *The Development of Educational Administration in England and Wales*. O, Blackwell, 1966. pp. 228. Scholarly historical account.

JAMES, W. *A Middle Class Parent's Guide to Education*. L, Hodder & Stoughton, 1964. pp. 128. For those who like to feel more equal than others.

LELLO, A. J. *The Official View on Education*. O, Pergamon P, 1964. pp. 143. Digests of all the major reports 1944 to 1963.

LOWNDES, G. A. N. *The English Educational System*. L, Hutchinson, 1960. pp. 160.

PEDLEY, F. H. *Guide to The Educational System in England and Wales*. O, Pergamon P, 1964. pp. 240.

1.2 SCOTLAND

HUNTER, S. L. *The Scottish Educational System*. O, Pergamon P, 1968. pp. 280.

OSBORNE, G. S. *Scottish and English Schools*. L, Longmans, 1966. pp. 368. A comparative survey of the past fifty years.

2 Institutions

2.1 PRIMARY SCHOOLS

ATKINSON, M. *Junior School Community*. 2nd ed. L, Longmans, 1962. pp. 198.

BLACKIE, J. E. *Inside the Primary School*. L, Dept of Education and Science/HMSO, 1967. pp. 148. But see this author's *Good Enough for the Children* (L, Faber, 1963, pp. 157) for a more personal interpretation.

BLYTH, W. A. L. *English Primary Education: A Sociological Description*. L, Routledge, 1965. 2 vols. pp. 224 and 160.

BROWN, M. and PRECIOUS, N. *The Integrated Day in the Primary School*. L, Ward Lock Educational, 1968. pp. 192.

CAMPBELL, F. *Eleven-Plus and All That*. L, Watts, 1956. pp. 212.

CENTRAL ADVISORY COUNCIL FOR EDUCATION (ENGLAND). *Children and Their Primary Schools (The Plowden Report)*. Vol. 1: *Report*. L, HMSO, 1967. pp. 556. The last of the major post-war official reports, which should have been the first

DANIEL, M. V. *Activity in Primary School*. O, Blackwell, 1947. pp. 310.

GARDNER, D. E. M. *The Education of Young Children.* L, Methuen, 1956. pp. 118. In the Susan Isaacs tradition.

GARDNER, D. E. M. and CASS, J. E. *The Role of the Teacher in the Infant and Nursery School.* O, Pergamon P, 1965. pp. 184.

MARSH, L. *Alongside the Child in the Primary School.* L, Black, 1970. pp. 154.

MARSHALL, S. *An Experiment in Education.* CUP, 1963. pp. 222. Sensitive story of a headmistress's experiences in a rural primary school.

RICHMOND, W. K. *Purpose in the Junior School.* L, Redman, 1949. pp. 221. Like DANIEL (above) belongs to the heyday of activity and experience.

SCOTTISH EDUCATION DEPARTMENT. *Primary Education in Scotland.* Edinburgh, HMSO, 1965. pp. 230. Official blessing for a more child-centred approach.

2.2 SECONDARY SCHOOLS

DENT, H. C. *Secondary Education for All.* L, Routledge, 1949. pp. 224. In the tripartite era, that was.

GROSS, R. E. (ed.) *British Secondary Education.* L, OUP, 1965. pp. 596.

PASSOW, A. H. *Secondary Education for All: The English Approach.* Columbus, Ohio State UP, 1961. pp. 290. A considered American appraisal.

2.3 SECONDARY MODERN

CENTRAL ADVISORY COUNCIL FOR EDUCATION (ENGLAND). *Half Our Future (The Newsom Report).* L, HMSO, 1963. pp. 299. Needs no gloss as the blueprint for a new deal for non-academic pupils.

CHAPMAN, J. V. *Your Secondary Modern Schools.* L, College of Preceptors, 1959. pp. 298.

DEMPSTER, J. J. B. *Education in the Secondary Modern School.* L. Methuen, 1947. pp. 75.

—— *Selection for Secondary Education: A Survey.* L, Methuen, 1954. pp. 136.

—— *Purpose in the Modern School.* L, Methuen, 1956. pp. 126.

KNEEBONE, R. M. T. *I Work in a Secondary Modern School.* L, Routledge, 1957. pp. 182. Sounds grim!

LOUKES, H. *Secondary Modern.* L, Harrap, 1956. pp. 128. The hungry sheep look up for moral and spiritual guidance and are not fed.

MACKENZIE, R. F. *State School*. Harmondsworth, Penguin Books, 1970. pp. 140. Ill-fated efforts of a progressive headmaster of a Scottish junior secondary school. See the same author's blistering outburst, *A Question of Living* (L, Collins, 1963. pp. 159).

TAYLOR, W. *The Secondary Modern School*. L, Faber, 1963. pp. 254. The book to end all books on this subject.

2.4 SECONDARY TECHNICAL

DOBINSON, C. H. *Technical Education for Adolescents*. L, Harrap, 1951. pp. 124.

EDWARDS, K. H. R. *The Secondary Technical School*. U of LP, 1966. pp. 206.

2.5 SECONDARY GRAMMAR

DAVIES, H. *Culture and the Grammar School*. L, Routledge, 1965. pp. 192. Middle of the road.

DAVIS, R. *The Grammar School*. Harmondsworth, Penguin Books, 1967. pp. 288. Right wing.

HUTCHINSON, M. and YOUNG, C. *Educating the Intelligent*. Harmondsworth, Penguin Books, 1969. pp. 240. Investment in human capital argument.

JACKSON, B. and MARSDEN, D. *Education and the Working Class*. L, Routledge, 1962. pp. 268. Left wing.

KING, R. *Values and Involvement in a Grammar School*. L, Routledge, 1969. pp. 216.

LACEY, C. *Hightown Grammar*. Manchester UP, 1970. pp. 214. Sound research study showing how pro- and anti-academic attitudes are formed in a school in which too many pupils chase too few rewards.

REE, H. *The Essential Grammar School*. L, Harrap, 1956. pp. 84. Main theme: There'll always be an England.

SKINNER, J. W. *School Stresses: The Grammar School Today and Tomorrow*. L, Epworth P, 1949. pp. 128.

STEVENS, F. *The New Inheritors: Some Questions about the Education of Intelligent 'First Generation' Children*. L, Hutchinson Educ., 1970. pp. 198. But no question about the propriety of early selection.

VERNON, P. E. (ed.) *Secondary School Selection*. L, Methuen, 1957. pp. 216. Raises quite a few questions regarding the reliability and validity of 11-plus procedures.

YATES, A. and PIDGEON, D. A. *Admission to Grammar Schools*. Slough and L, NFER/Newnes, 1957. pp. 256.

2.6 COMPREHENSIVE SECONDARY

BENN, C. and SIMON, B. *Half Way There.* Maidenhead, McGraw-Hill, 1970. pp. 421. Exhaustive review of developments.

BERG, L. *Risinghill: Death of a Comprehensive School.* Harmondsworth, Penguin Books, 1968. pp. 287. A sad business.

BURGESS, T. *Inside Comprehensive Schools.* L, Dept of Education and Science/HMSO, 1970. pp. 204. A plain man's guide, issued before the Conservative government took office.

COLE, R. *Comprehensive Schools.* L, Oldbourne, 1964. pp. 223.

CONANT, J. B. *The Comprehensive High School.* NY, McGraw-Hill, 1967. pp. 95. The American experience.

CONWAY, E. S. *Going Comprehensive: A Study of the Administration of Comprehensive Schools.* L, Harrap, 1970. pp. 173.

DIXON, C. W. *Society, Schools and Progress in Scandinavia.* O, Pergamon P, 1965. pp. 212.

FORD, J. *Social Class and the Comprehensive School.* L, Routledge, 1969. pp. 199. Indicates that ability-grouping and class stratification are just as likely to persist in non-selective as in selective schools.

HALSALL, E. *Becoming Comprehensive.* O, Pergamon P, 1970. pp. 286. Case histories of individual schools in a wide range of settings.

INCORPORATED ASSOCIATION OF ASSISTANT MASTERS. *Teaching in Comprehensive Schools: A Second Report.* CUP, 1967. pp. 176.

INNER LONDON EDUCATION AUTHORITY. *London Comprehensive Schools.* L, ILEA, 1966, 1967. pp. 144.

MASON, S. C. (ed.) *In Our Experience: The Changing Schools of Leicestershire.* L, Longmans, 1970. pp. 190. Evaluations of the well-known Leicestershire Plan.

MILLER, T. W. G. *Values in the Comprehensive School.* Edinburgh, Oliver & Boyd, 1961. pp. 118.

MONKS, T. G. *Comprehensive Education in England and Wales.* L, NFER, 1968. pp. 282. Examines overall structure, internal organization of schools, teaching force and deployment of staff, etc.

NATIONAL UNION OF TEACHERS. *Inside the Comprehensive School.* L, School Master Publishing Co, 1958. pp. 235.

PEDLEY, R. *Comprehensive Education: A New Approach.* L, Gollancz, 1956. pp. 204.

—— *The Comprehensive School.* 4th ed. Harmondsworth, Penguin Books, 1969. pp. 226. Still the most convincing presentation of the case, by a bonny fighter.

RUBINSTEIN, D. and SIMON, B. *The Evolution of the Comprehensive School 1926–1966.* L, Routledge, 1969. pp. 126.

2.7 INDEPENDENT SCHOOLS

CHEETHAM, A. and PARFIT, D. *Eton Microcosm.* L, Sidgwick & Jackson, 1964. pp. 198. One for the coffee table.

DANCY, J. *The Public Schools and the Future.* L, Faber, 1963. pp. 169. Earnest, capable, well documented apologia, justifies their retention on the evidence of solid achievements.

DEPARTMENT OF EDUCATION AND SCIENCE. *The Public Schools Commission: First Report.* L, HMSO, 1968. pp. 254. Less than startling.

GILKES, A. N. *Independent Education: In Defence of Public Schools.* L, Gollancz, 1957. pp. 112.

HOWARTH, T. E. B. *Culture, Anarchy and the Public School.* L, Cassell, 1969. pp. 112.

KALTON, G. *The Public Schools: A Factual Survey of Headmasters' Conference Schools in England and Wales.* L, Longmans, 1966. pp. 179.

LAMBERT, R. *The Hothouse Society.* L, Weidenfeld & Nicolson, 1968. pp. 408. Boarding school life as seen through the eyes of the inmates.

MASTERS, P. L. *Preparatory School Today: Some Facts and Inferences.* L, Black, 1966. pp. 127.

OLLERENSHAW, K. *The Girls' Schools.* L, Faber, 1967. pp. 236. The future of the public and other independent schools for girls in the context of state education.

SNOW, G. *The Public School in the New Age.* L, Bles, 1959. pp. 144. Some complacent thinking here.

WAKEFORD, J. *The Cloistered Elite.* L, Macmillan, 1969. pp. 272. A sociological analysis of the English public boarding school.

WEINBERG, I. *The English Public Schools: The Sociology of Elite Education.* NY, Atherton P, 1967. pp. 225. An American viewpoint.

WILKINSON, R. *The Prefects.* L, OUP, 1963. pp. 260. Gentlemanly power or mandarin impotence? Trenchant study, the best of the bunch.

WILSON, J. *Public Schools and Private Practice.* L, Allen & Unwin, 1962. pp. 141.

WOLFENDEN, J. F. *The Public Schools of Today.* U of LP, 1949. pp. 111. Now yesteryear.

2.8 FURTHER EDUCATION

PETERS, A. J. *British Further Education.* O, Pergamon P, 1967. pp. 388. A critical textbook.

VENABLES, P. F. R. *Technical Education.* L, Bell, 1955. pp. 660. A standard work.

2.9 HIGHER EDUCATION: GENERAL INFORMATION

ARNOLD, E. (ed.) *A Guide to English Courses in the Universities.* Compiled for the English Association. L, John Murray, 1965. pp. 258.

BRITISH COUNCIL. *Higher Education in the United Kingdom: A Handbook for Students from Overseas and their Advisers.* L, Longmans Green, for the British Council and the Association of Commonwealth Universities, 1948–70 (issued every two years).

PRIESTLEY, B. (ed.) *British Qualifications.* 2nd ed. L, Kogan Page, 1970. pp. 672. A comprehensive guide to educational, technical, professional and academic qualifications in Britain (including Eire).

WATTS, A. G. (ed.) *Which University?* L, Cornmarket P, 1964, 1965. pp. 395. A guide for school leavers, parents and careers advisers.

2.10 UNIVERSITIES

AITKEN, J. and BELOFF, M. *A Short Walk on the Campus.* L, Secker & Warburg, 1966. pp. 268. Hilarious reporting of college life in the U.S.A.

ASHBY, E. and ANDERSON, M. *The Rise of the Student Estate in Britain.* L, Macmillan, 1970. pp. 186. Traces the progress of organized student opinion, the NUS, etc.

BEARD, R. M. *Research into Teaching Methods in Higher Education.* Rev. ed. L, Society for Research into Higher Education, 1968. pp. 64.

—— *Teaching and Learning in Higher Education.* Harmondsworth, Penguin Books, 1970. pp. 222.

BELOFF, M. *The Plateglass Universities.* L, Secker & Warburg, 1968. pp. 208. Light-hearted tour of the new foundations.

BLACKSTONE, T., GALES, K., HADLY, R. and LEWIS, W. *Students in Conflict: LSE in 1967.* LSE Monograph 5. L, Weidenfeld & Nicolson, 1970. pp. 320. Social scientists' post mortem.

BROOK, G. L. *The Modern University.* L, André Deutsch, 1965. pp. 192. Sober review; interesting appendix on 'The organization of a modern university'.

BURGESS, T. and PRATT, J. *Policy and Practice: The Colleges of Advanced Technology.* L, Allen Lane, 1970. pp. 236.

CAINE, SIR S. *British Universities: Purpose and Prospects.* L, Bodley Head, 1969. pp. 272. Stocktaking account by a senior administrator, formerly Director of the London School of Economics.

COCKBURN, A. and BLACKBURN, R. (eds.) *Student Power.* Harmondsworth, Penguin Books, 1969. pp. 384. Militant activist viewpoints.

COMMITTEE ON HIGHER EDUCATION. *Higher Education (The Robbins Report).* Cmnd. 2154. L, HMSO, 1963. pp. 335. A memorable landmark, packed with information, full of wise saws, e.g. 'If there is to be talk of a pool of ability, it must be of a pool which surpasses the widow's cruse in the Old Testament, in that when more is taken for higher education in one generation more will tend to be available in the next.'

DAICHES, D. (ed.) *The Idea of a New University.* 2nd ed. L, André Deutsch, 1970. pp. 272. Brave new world of Sussex.

FURNEAUX, W. D. *The Chosen Few.* L, OUP, for Nuffield Foundation, 1961. pp. 272. University selection in Britain.

KNELLER, G. F. *Higher Learning in Britain.* Berkeley, U of California P, 1955. pp. 301. American overview of its ethos and functions.

LAWLOR, J. (ed.) *The New University.* L, Routledge, 1968. pp. 200.

LAYARD, R., KING, J. and MOSER, C. *The Impact of Robbins.* Harmondsworth, Penguin Books, 1969. pp. 160.

LAYTON, D. (ed.) *University Teaching in Transition.* Edinburgh, Oliver & Boyd, 1968. pp. 172.

MOUNTFORD, SIR J. *British Universities.* L, OUP, 1966. pp. 188.

NIBLETT, W. R. (ed.) *Higher Education: Demand and Response.* L, Tavistock, 1969. pp. 262. Anglo-American-Canadian symposium.

PERKIN, H. J. *New Universities in the United Kingdom: Case Studies on Innovation in Higher Education.* L, HMSO, 1969. pp. 250.

REEVES, M. (ed.) *Eighteen Plus: Unity and Diversity in Higher Education.* L, Faber, 1965. pp. 226.

ROBINSON, E. E. *The New Polytechnics – The People's Universities.* Harmondsworth, Penguin Books, 1968. pp. 264.

SLOMAN, A. E. *A University in the Making.* L, BBC, 1964. pp. 92. The Essex plan, now somewhat agley according to some of its critics.

SPENDER, S. *The Year of the Young Rebels.* L, Weidenfeld & Nicolson, 1969, pp. 186. 'Inside' reporting of student unrest in American, Continental and British universities.

UNIVERSITY GRANTS COMMITTEE. *University Teaching Methods (The Hale Report).* L, HMSO, 1964. pp. 173. Finds academics strangely incurious about the effectiveness of the methods they use, but draws the line at compulsory training for lecturers.

—— *Audio-Visual Aids in Higher Scientific Education (The Brynmor Jones Report).* L, HMSO, 1965. pp. 153.

UNWIN, D. (ed.) *Media and Methods.* Maidenhead, McGraw-Hill, 1969. pp. 219. Instructional technology in higher education.

3 Politics, Management and Organization

ACKOFF, R. L. and RIVETT, P. *A Manager's Guide to Operations Research.* NY, Wiley, 1963. pp. 107.

ARGYRIS, C. *Understanding Organizational Behaviour.* L, Tavistock, 1961. pp. 179.

ARMITAGE, P., SMITH, C. and ALPER, P. *Decision Models for Educational Planning.* L, Allen Lane, 1969. pp. 124.

BARON, G. and HOWELL, D. A. *School Management and Government.* Research Studies 6, Royal Commission on Local Government in England. L, HMSO, 1968. pp. 144.

BARON, G. and TAYLOR, W. (eds.) *Educational Administration and the Social Sciences.* L, Athlone P, 1969. pp. 192. The best all-round introduction to the latest concepts and theories of educational administration and their applications; down-to-earth exposition of elementary systems theory, organization theory, role theory, operational research, etc.

BIDDLE, B. J. and THOMAS, E. J. *Role Theory: Concepts and Research.* NY, Wiley, 1966. pp. 453.

BROWN, W. *Exploration in Management.* L, Heinemann, 1960. pp. 348.

BUCKLEY, W. *Modern Systems Research for the Behavioural Scientists.* Chicago, Aldine, 1968. pp. 525. A source book.

CALLAHAN, R. *Education and the Cult of Efficiency.* U of Chicago P, 1962. pp. 273.

CAMPBELL, R. F. and GREGG, R. T. (eds.) *Administrative Behavior in Education.* NY, Harper & Row, 1957. pp. 558.

CAMPBELL, R. F., CORBALLY, J. E. and RAMSEYER, J. A. *Introduction to Educational Administration.* Boston, Mass., Allyn & Bacon, 1958. pp. 434.

CARTWRIGHT, D. and ZANDER, A. (eds.) *Group Dynamics: Research and Theory.* 3rd ed. L, Tavistock, 1968. pp. 592.

LE—F*

COLADARCI, A. P. and GETZELS, J. W. *The Use of Theory in Educational Administration*. Stanford UP, 1955. pp. 28.

CULBERTSON, J. A. and HENCLEY, S. P. (eds.) *Preparing Administrators: New Perspectives*. Columbus, U Council for Educational Administration, 1962. pp. 173. Overall strategies for training school administrators.

DAVIES, T. I. *School Organisation*. O, Pergamon P, 1969. pp. 252. Problems of time-tabling.

DRUCKER, P. F. *The Practice of Management*. L, Heinemann, 1955. pp. 355. Highly influential, and readable.

ETZIONI, A. *A Comparative Analysis of Complex Organizations*. NY, Free P, 1961. pp. 366. For advanced students.

—— *Modern Organization*. Englewood Cliffs, Prentice-Hall, 1964. pp. 128. A concise introduction.

FLANDERS, N. A. *Analyzing Teaching Behavior*. Reading, Mass. Addison-Wesley, 1970. pp. 448. Technical study of interaction analysis in the classroom.

GETZELS, J. W., LIPHAM, J. M. and CAMPBELL, R. F. *Educational Administration as a Social Process*. NY, Harper & Row, 1968. pp. 420. Theory, research, practice.

GRIFFITHS, D. E. *Administrative Theory*. NY, Appleton-Century. Crofts, 1959. pp. 128.

HALPIN, A. W. (ed.) *Administrative Theory in Education*. NY, Macmillan, 1958. pp. 188. Includes paper by Talcott Parsons on 'Some ingredients for a general theory of formal organization'.

HANDY, H. W. and HUSSAIN, K. M. *Network Analysis for Educational Management*. Englewood Cliffs, Prentice-Hall, 1969. pp. 186. Outlines basic logic of Critical Path Method (CPM) and Program Evaluation Review Technique (PERT), then explains how they can be applied to curriculum development and research projects, etc. Bibliography.

HARRIS, C. W. (ed.) *Problems in Measuring Change*. Madison, U of Wisconsin P, 1963. pp. 259. Highly statistical.

HOYLE, E. *The Role of the Teacher*. L, Routledge, 1969. pp. 112. A sociological analysis.

HUGHES, M. G. (ed.) *Secondary School Administration: A Management Approach*. O, Pergamon P, 1970. pp. 245. For teachers and would-be heads of departments.

KATZ, D. and KAHN, R. L. *The Social Psychology of Organizations*. NY, Wiley, 1966. pp. 498.

KIBBEE, J. M. *et al. Management Games.* NY, Reinhold, 1961. pp. 347. Playway techniques for business executives.

LANE, W. R. (ed.) *Foundations of Educational Administration.* NY, Macmillan, 1967. pp. 433. A behavioural analysis.

LEWIS, L. J. and LOVERIDGE, A. J. *The Management of Education.* L, Pall Mall P, 1965. pp. 124. Advice for planners in developing countries.

LIKERT, R. *New Patterns of Management.* NY, McGraw-Hill, 1961. pp. 279.

MACKENZIE, W. J. M. *Politics and Social Science.* Harmondsworth Penguin Books, 1967. pp. 424.

MANZER, R. *Teachers and Politics.* Manchester UP, 1970. pp. 164.

MORPHET, E. L., JOHNS, R. L. and RELLER, T. L. *Educational Administration.* Englewood Cliffs, Prentice-Hall, 1959. pp. 556. Concepts, practices and issues.

MOSSON, T. M. (ed.) *Teaching the Process of Management.* L, Harrap, 1967. pp. 200.

MOUZELIS, N. P. *Organization and Bureaucracy.* L, Routledge, 1967. pp. 240. A sound introduction to the basic concepts of organization theory.

NATIONAL SOCIETY FOR THE STUDY OF EDUCATION. *63rd Yearbook (Part 2): Behavioural Science and Educational Administration.* U of Chicago P, 1964. pp. 348.

OPTNER, S. L. *Systems Analysis for Business and Industrial Problem Solving.* Englewood Cliffs, Prentice-Hall, 1965. pp. 116.

PARKINSON, M. *The Labour Party and the Organization of Secondary Education 1918-1965.* L, Routledge, 1970. pp. 139.

REVANS, R. W. *The Theory of Practice in Management.* L, Macdonald, 1966. pp. 167. Standard work.

ROMISZOWSKI, A. J. (ed.) *The Systems Approach to Education and Training.* L, Kogan Page, 1970. pp. 95.

SILVERMAN, D. *The Theory of Organisation.* L, Heinemann, 1970. pp. 246. A good introduction.

SMITH, W. O. L. *Government of Education.* Harmondsworth, Penguin Books, 1965. pp. 208.

STOLLER, D. S. *Operations Research: Process and Strategy.* Berkeley, California UP, 1966. pp. 160.

—— *Operations Analysis in the U.S. Office of Education.* Paris, OECD, 1967.

TANSLEY, P. J. and UNWIN, D. *Simulation and Gaming in Education.* L, Methuen Educ., 1969. pp. 112.

TAYLOR, G. (ed.) *The Teacher as Manager.* NCET Books for Schools, 1970. pp. 166.

TAYLOR, W. *Society and the Education of Teachers.* L, Faber, 1969. pp. 304.

—— *Heading for Change.* Cardiff, Harlech TV, 1969. pp. 144. In-tray simulations for the management of innovations in a large secondary school.

8 Comparative Education, Education in Developing Countries and Educational Planning

As an academic study, comparative education cannot be reckoned one of the major growth points during the 1945-70 period. While the volume of published work in this sector is by no means inconsiderable it is made to seem almost insignificant when set against the surging output of research papers, books and reports concerned with the various aspects of educational technology or the sociology of education. As everyone knows, sociology has come a long way since Herbert Spencer's day, but while there is no excuse for suggesting that comparative studies have remained more or less at a standstill since Matthew Arnold's, the advances have been a good deal slower and less spectacular. This is particularly true as regards methodology.

In the same way, and for the same reasons, that natural history may be taken as representing the first stage in the development of a scientific zoology, so area studies (i.e. factual, descriptive accounts of foreign systems) are a necessary preliminary to any systematic study of comparative education. In so far as the majority of introductory courses in teacher training establishments are content to remain at the 'nature study' level they serve a useful purpose, if only as a propaedeutic, but it is questionable whether they deserve the title of comparative education. This is not a criticism of those who organize and teach such courses: the truth of the matter is that the theoretical framework and the analytical techniques which, it is hoped, will eventually provide the basis for a genuinely scientific approach have yet to be fully worked out, and until they have been this branch of educational studies is bound to be more descriptive than explanatory. In any case, properly conceived, comparative education calls for a maturity of mind, the ability to cope with a wide array of evidence drawn from cultural, historical, demographic, economic, political and other sources as well as a background of first-hand experience from travel abroad which the average young student does not possess. On the other hand, there is widespread interest in the subject and students frequently ask why it does not occupy a more

163

prominent place, supposing it gets any place at all, in teacher training courses. One reason is that many lecturers feel diffident and ill equipped when it comes to catering for what is undoubtedly a genuine demand. For discussions of the as-yet unresolved problems of methodology see Holmes and Robinson (1963), Bereday (1964), Holmes (1965), King (1968), Noah and Eckstein (1969).

Certainly, judging by the number of university chairs in comparative education, this is one sector of the field which is poorly represented in Britain. The number of scholars whose appointments enable them to engage in this kind of work on a full-time basis probably does not exceed a score (Scotland has only one!), and except in one or two centres of higher learning it tends to be regarded as peripheral. No doubt this explains why H. J. Butcher's *Educational Research in Britain* (1968 and 1970: cited under Educational Psychology, p. 94) contains no mention of comparative education. True, the annual conferences of the British section of the Comparative Education Society usually muster well over a hundred participants, but a review of the research literature indicates that only a handful of them are in a position to make serious, regular contributions. Comparative education, it has to be recognized, is *not* the field for aspiring young academics who want to get on in the world! As a consequence, for the most part, it continues to be taught in colleges and university departments of education in a hand-to-mouth, jejune fashion. The situation, moreover, is not improved by the lack of an adequate textbook.

How far all this is due to insular-mindedness and how far to sheer lack of opportunity is an interesting question. If it cannot be attributed to any lack of interest on the part of students neither can it be due to any lack of relevance of comparative education as an ingredient in the training of teachers. Insular-mindedness must be partly responsible: how else to account for the fact that as late as November 1970 there was nothing in the British literature on post-war developments in West Germany, and until 1965 virtually nothing at all on current reforms in France – a country which might just as well have located itself in Central Asia so far as most educationists on this side of the Channel were concerned? British policy-making, complacent in calling itself pragmatic, often gives the impression of being strangely immune to foreign influences, or at any rate indifferent to them. It sees no reason to change its direction when presented with evidence which shows, for instance, that the narrow specialization which persists in the sixth form of grammar schools is a peculiarly English phenomenon. It prides itself in being unique, even if being unique means being out of step with the rest of the world.

Elsewhere, comparative studies have commanded the attention of governments – and substantial research grants – for the sake of throwing light on the elusive problems of the connection between the educational services and economic growth. International bodies like UNESCO and OECD, to mention only two, have at their disposal immense resources and the expertise of large staffs of highly trained personnel, yet it appears that the periodical reports issued by such bodies count for little in the deliberations of the authorities in the United Kingdom. To take only one illustration: Frank Bowles's UNESCO study *Access to Higher Education* (1963) quotes figures showing that whereas forty-eight member states had some kind of tripartite or two-track system of secondary schools and only seven had adopted the comprehensive principle in 1950, by 1959 the former had dropped to twenty-seven and the latter had risen to thirty-seven. It is unnecessary to remark that this unmistakable international trend, and the whole mass of evidence from other sources pointing in the same direction, did not prevent a Conservative government from trying to put the clock back immediately after the General Election of June 1970. Apart from the Robbins investigation (*Higher Education*, 1963: cited under Sociology of Education, p. 136), it is not unfair to say that most of the official reports on British education have a way of going about their business and making their recommendations without ever bothering to look outside these islands.

If it is true that comparative education begins at home, we might do worse than take note of what distinguished visitors to this country have to say about our peculiar system of education. D. J. Koerner's *Reform in Education* (1968) may not be the kind of book which is normally classified under the heading of comparative education: for all that, it is a candid, unflattering appraisal of current practices and trends which deserves to be taken seriously by English readers. Coming as it does from an American, however, the chances are that the advice will fall on deaf ears. As talk of going into Europe increases, and when or if the time approaches when talk translates itself into action, some modification of this introverted frame of mind may be anticipated: as it is, the verdict must be that the British climate of opinion is not one in which comparative education can be expected to flourish.

Against this, lack of opportunity is undoubtedly a serious handicap. Foreign travel now goes further and faster than ever before, but relatively few educationists in this country can bargain for extended periods of residence and study abroad. It is no accident, therefore, that ethnographic, cross-cultural studies like those typified by L. Warren's *Education in Rebhausen* (1967) and J. Singleton's *Nichū: A Japanese School* (1967) do not figure at all in the British literature. It is not simply that Communist China is to all intents and purposes out of bounds or that Latin America is too far away: much more problematical is the difficulty of arranging regular feedback of information and personnel from countries much nearer home. If anything, facilities for students wishing to engage in research abroad are more generous than they are for members of the academic staff responsible for teaching them: the trouble is that the facilities are not used in the best possible way (as part of their first degree work, in modern languages for example, thousands of British undergraduates are required to spend up to one whole year abroad, yet although the majority of them eventually proceed to take a course of teacher training, how often do they use their opportunities to begin investigations which might be the basis for a thesis at the M.Ed. stage?). Exchange schemes and the eastbound transatlantic traffic in books ensure that there is no lack of information about developments in the U.S.A. The *World Year Book of Education*, indeed, represents an annual triumph of Anglo-American collaboration in the international field of comparative education. Some European countries, notably Sweden, provide their own information services for the English-speaking world. Others do not, with the result that it is left to a minority of a minority of British educationists, i.e. those who have the time, the interest, the training and the financial backing, to undertake any worthwhile investigations.

Increasingly, however, comparative education makes demands which are beyond the reach of even the ablest and most privileged individual, so that nothing less than large-scale team research will suffice. In this respect, the U.S.A. has enormous advantages not only in financial resources but also in being able to draw on large numbers of scholars with the necessary linguistic and anthropological qualifications. Part of the trouble with the British concept of comparative education is that it is limited to descriptions of national systems which belong in one way or other to the Western tradition – usually those of the U.S.A., the U.S.S.R., France, Germany and the Scandinavian countries – leaving the more exotic ones beyond its reckoning and its ken.

There remains, of course, that growing sector variously referred to as the 'backward', 'developing' or 'emerging' nations. For some unexplained reason these do not 'count' as comparative education in academic circles. Strictly speaking, no doubt, they call for separate treatment. Here, thanks to Britain's erstwhile colonial connections, but mainly because of the urgent requirements of nation-building in these newly independent states, the record of progress is rather more favourable. Britain's contribution, it should be pointed out, is not to be gauged solely in terms of material aid (which to date has amounted to rather less than one per cent of the gross national product annually), but rather in terms of the guidance afforded by some of her most experienced educationists and administrators. New nations cannot afford to wait until academics develop comparative education as a prescriptive and predictive science; and it cannot go unremarked that most of the respected British names in the 'Third World' – Sir Eric Ashby, Adam Curle, E. B. Castle, etc. – are not the same ones that are prominent in the literature of comparative education.

What is happening, clearly, is that comparative education is ceasing to be a spectatorial, academic study and is flexing its muscles as it prepares to enter the sphere of practical planning. In Dr King's view (*Comparative Studies and Educational Decision*, 1968), 'The affinity which comparative education has with *applied* science in the social field (economics or forensic medicine for example) lies in the application of that knowledge or skill to readjustments of a useful kind. First, it can show how education in its widest sense is or can be distributed between schools, industries, and other socio-political organizations – a dynamic study in times of such rapid change. Secondly, it can show how greater overall satisfaction or efficiency in some detail can be achieved. Such satisfactoriness can be helped by proposing hypotheses, or by demonstrating feasibility or priority.

'Yet comparative appraisal of this kind is far more likely to be effective by relating itself to a practical series of articulated decisions in the public field of education. Such decisions might be about the structure of schools and their "flow" into later opportunity; they might concern curriculum and orientation, or deal with enrolment and retention and life-linkage of some kind. They might, on the other hand, deal with productivity and effectiveness in certain contingencies, or with the pull-and-thrust of learning, teaching and training. Our questions might attempt to analyse training and retraining (both personal and professional) along a developmental scale. And so on. Thus comparative study – contextually undertaken and with direct practical relevance to decision – can help to provide that vital framework of decision: a public and publicized and institutionally linked *strategy of choice*.'

This sounds fine but scarcely squares with King's admission that all we have at present is an 'ill assorted scatter of specialists'. At the risk of labouring the point, comparative education is not far enough advanced on the developmental scale to justify any high-flown claims for its efficacy and reliability as a guide to policy-making. In all probability it has more to learn from the economists, the cultural anthropologists, the technological forecasters and the curriculum developers than they have from it. And if this sounds harsh to the point of being unkind, let it be said at once that education systems which pride themselves on being 'advanced' stand to gain as much in the way of understanding how to improve their provision as do those characterized as 'under-developed'.

Since their inception, UNESCO and its offspring, the International Institute for Educational Planning, have been advising countries throughout the world on ways and means of establishing systems of education in accordance with their needs and resources. Among the lessons learned from this hard-won experience two are of outstanding importance. First, it is now recognized that education systems pass through natural stages akin to those in the developmental psychology of the growing child: they do not spring fully fledged from the head of Jove nor can they be engineered all-of-a-piece like a new petrochemical plant. According to Walt Rostow, there are five steps leading to economic self-sufficiency, none of which can be skipped. According to C. E. Beeby (*The Quality of Education in Developing Countries*, 1966), who bases his conclusions on Rostow's economic theory, there are four stages in the maturation of an education system depending upon the level of professional competence of teachers. In the first stage teachers are partly educated but entirely untrained; in the second they are partly trained and partly educated; in the third they are well educated but still only partly trained; in the fourth – still not reached anywhere in the world – they are well educated and fully trained.

Even more important is the recognition that a country's educational 'needs' cannot be considered apart from its culture, its religion, its politics, its history and its traditions. Educational planning is not simply a matter of enlisting a team of experts from one country for the sake of promoting greater industrial productivity in another, though more often than not this is what the authorities in the host country look for from foreign aid programmes. 'Educational planning is not a magic formula that will come up with ready-made solutions', says Dr Diez-Hochleitner (in the *World Year Book of Education*, 1965).

'It is an instrument to channel all knowledge about education and related disciplines into the preparation and implementation of long-term and short-term development plans.' In so far as it calls for a team of all the talents, therefore, the task confronting the would-be planner is essentially the same whether he is working in the field of comparative education, in curriculum study (see pp. 60–71) in educational administration and management (see pp. 144–62) or educational technology (see pp. 190–206).

Bibliography

Fortunately, there is no lack of information services here:

1 BRISTOW, T. and HOLMES, B. *Comparative Education through the Literature.* L, Butterworth, 1968. pp. 181. A well annotated guide. Intended for librarians and lecturers, it is classified under (*a*) General textbooks, (*b*) Background books (including novels – an all-too-rare link with *real* literature!), (*c*) National area studies, (*d*) Cross-cultural and case studies, (*e*) Library tools and research.

2 HOLMES, B. and ROBINSON, S. B. *Relevant Data in Comparative Education.* Hamburg, UNESCO Institute for Education, 1963. pp. 143. Not so up-to-date, but in some respects more wide ranging than 1 above.

3 *Annual Educational Bibliography.* Geneva, International Bureau of Education, annually. Classified and annotated; see under the opening section, 'Generalities' and 'Systems of education'.

4 *Studies in Comparative Education.* Washington, D.C., U.S. Department of Health, Education & Welfare, annually.

5 *Education within the Commonwealth.* National Book League, 1965 (revised annually). Exhaustive annotated reading list.

6 *Education in the Commonwealth.* L, Commonwealth Institute, 1968. pp. 23. For advanced studies.

7 COUCH, M. (ed.) *Education in Africa: A Select Bibliography.* Education Libraries Bulletin, U of L Institute of Education, 1962, 1965. pp. 121.

8 INTERNATIONAL INSTITUTE FOR EDUCATIONAL PLANNING. *Educational Planning: A Bibliography.* Paris, UNESCO, 1964. pp. 137.

The list that follows is more supplementary and suggestive than exhaustive. It includes a number of works published since the Bristow-Holmes compilation, which remains the standard work of reference for British readers. The classification adopted is as follows:

1 Source books
2 Textbooks and general studies
3 National area studies
   3.1 Europe
      3.1.1 U.S.S.R.
      3.1.2 France
      3.1.3 West Germany
      3.1.4 Scandinavia
      3.1.5 Other European countries
   3.2 America
      3.2.1 U.S.A.
      3.2.2 Canada
      3.2.3 Central and South America
   3.3 Asia
      3.3.1 Middle East
      3.3.2 China
      3.3.3 Japan
      3.3.4 India
      3.3.5 Pakistan
   3.4 Africa
   3.5 Australasia
      3.5.1 Australia
      3.5.2 New Zealand
4 Educational development and educational planning

1 Source Books

COUNCIL FOR CULTURAL COOPERATION. *Education in Europe. School Systems: A Guide.* Strasbourg, Council of Europe, 1965. pp. 356.

LAUWERYS, J. A. and SCANLON, D. G. (eds.) *World Year Book of Education.* L, Evans, annually. Authoritative articles by leading experts from countries all over the world, centring each year upon a theme of common concern, e.g. Examinations, The Education Explosion, Education in Cities, etc. Indispensable.

POIGNANT, R. *Education and Development in Western Europe, the United States and the U.S.S.R.* NY, Teachers College P, 1969. pp. 329. Material slightly dated, heavy going but a useful comprehensive survey.

UNESCO. *World Survey of Education.* L, Evans.

1 *Handbook of Educational Organizations and Statistics,* 1955. pp. 943.

2 *Primary Education,* 1958. pp. 1387.

3 *Secondary Education,* 1961. pp. 1482.

4 *Higher Education,* 1966. pp. 1433.

Digests of the basic facts about education systems from Albania to Zanzibar.

—— *International Guide to Educational Documentation 1955-1960.* Paris, UNESCO, 1963. pp. 700.

Note: More fully documented source material is to be found in the UNESCO series *Educational Studies and Documents* (1953–), and in UNESCO's *Educational Abstracts* (quarterly).

2 Textbooks and General Studies

BEREDAY, G. Z. F. *Comparative Method in Education.* NY, Holt, Rinehart & Winston, 1964. pp. 318. The best available textbook for graduate students; outlines various approaches and illustrates them with chapters on indoctrination in Poland, scientific potential in the U.S.S.R. and U.S.A., teacher performance in England, France and Germany, control of curricula in Denmark, U.S.A., U.S.S.R. and India.

—— (ed.) *Essays on World Education.* L, OUP, 1969. pp. 374. The crisis of supply and demand; discusses (*a*) the theoretical assumptions in comparative education, (*b*) the place of the social sciences in comparative education, and (*c*) a taxonomy for comparative education.

CRAMER, J. F. and BROWN, G. S. *Contemporary Education.* 2nd ed. NY, Harcourt, Brace & World, 1965. pp. 598. Outlines basic factors influencing national systems, analyses administration, control and finance; describes schools in action in U.S.A., England, France, Australia, Canada, U.S.S.R. and West Germany; includes area studies of Japan, India and Communist China. Recommended.

HANS, N. *Comparative Education.* L, Routledge, 1949, 3rd ed. 1967. pp. 360. Widely used in its day; now seriously outdated.

HOLMES, B. *Problems in Education.* L, Routledge, 1965. pp. 322.

KING, E. J. *Other Schools and Ours.* L, Methuen, 1958. pp. 268. Readable accounts of past and present developments in Denmark, U.S.A., U.S.S.R., India, etc.; suitable introduction for non-graduates.

—— *World Perspectives in Education.* L, Methuen, 1962. pp. 380. Lengthy and rather wordy discussion of some major problems confronting different national systems.

—— *Comparative Studies and Educational Decision.* L, Methuen, 1968. pp. 192. Envisages the emergence of comparative education as a predictive science.

—— *Education and Development in Western Europe.* Reading, Mass., Addison-Wesley, 1969. pp. 448.

KOERNER, J. D. *Reform in Education: England and the United States.* L, Weidenfeld & Nicolson, 1968. pp. 332.

MALLINSON, V. *An Introduction to the Study of Comparative Education.* L, Heinemann, 1960. pp. 268. Good in parts; outdated.

MOEHLMAN, A. H. *Comparative Educational Systems.* NY, Center for Applied Research in Education, 1963. pp. 114. Outlines a theory of cultural morphology (national style) and illustrates it with reference to European, Asian, African and American culture areas.

NOAH, H. J. and ECKSTEIN, M. A. *Toward a Science of Comparative Education.* NY, Macmillan, 1969. pp. 222. Mainly methodological.

PETERSON, A. D. C. *A Hundred Years of Education.* 2nd ed. L, Duckworth, 1960. pp. 274. Not listed in other bibliographies, but not to be overlooked; an excellent historical review of European problems and developments.

THUT, I. N. and ADAMS, D. *Educational Patterns in Contemporary Societies.* NY, McGraw-Hill, 1964. pp. 494.

ULICH, R. R. *The Education of Nations.* C, Mass., Harvard UP, 1961. pp. 325. A cosmic view.

VAIZEY, J. *Education in the Modern World.* L, Weidenfeld & Nicolson, 1967. pp. 256. Factual *aperçus*; compresses a wealth of useful information into a small space.

3 National Area Studies

3.1 EUROPE

Note: Detailed, up-to-date accounts of systems of education in European and other countries are presented in the Pergamon Press series *Society, Schools and Progress.*

3.1.1 *U.S.S.R.*

BEREDAY, G. Z. F. and PENNAR, J. *The Politics of Soviet Education.* L, Stevens/Atlantic Books, 1960. pp. 217.

BEREDAY, G. Z. F., BRICKMAN, W. W. and READ, G. H. (eds.) *The Changing Soviet School.* NY, Riverside P; L, Constable, 1960. pp. 514. Based on a field study by members of the U.S. Comparative Education Society. Part 1 outlines the historical, social and ideological background; Part 2 describes the organization of the system.

CHAPMAN, J. V. (ed.) *Education in the Soviet Union.* L, College of Preceptors, 1962. pp. 111.

COUNTS, G. S. and LODGE, N. P. *The Challenge of Soviet Education.* NY, McGraw-Hill, 1957. pp. 330.

DE WITT, N. *Education and Professional Employment in the U.S.S.R.* Washington, D.C., National Science Foundation, 1961. pp. 856. Monumental study, clearly expounded, magnificently documented.

GRANT, D. (ed.) *The Humanities in Soviet Higher Education.* U of Toronto P, 1960. pp. 96.

GRANT, N. *Soviet Education.* Harmondsworth, Penguin Books, 1964. pp. 190. Much the best bird's eye view by a British observer; strongly recommended.

INTERNATIONAL INSTITUTE FOR EDUCATIONAL PLANNING. *Educational Planning in the U.S.S.R.* Paris, UNESCO, 1968. pp. 28.

LEVIN, D. *Soviet Education Today.* L, MacGibbon & Kee, 1963. pp. 304. 'Inside story', highly personal, by authoress who taught in Moscow pre-1939.

MAKARENKO, A. S. *Problems of Soviet School Education.* Moscow, Central Books, 1965. pp. 154. Four lectures by the renowned Russian educator on methods of child-rearing, discipline, curriculum, work-based courses, the place of the individual in the collective, etc.

NOAH, H. J. (ed. and tr.) *The Economics of Education in the U.S.S.R.* NY, Praeger, 1969. pp. 227.

REDL, H. B. (ed.) *Soviet Educators on Soviet Education.* NY, Collier-Macmillan, 1965. pp. 256. Includes articles by Makarenko and Krupskaya.

ROSEN, S. M. *Significant Aspects of Soviet Education.* Washington, D.C., U.S. Dept of Health, Education & Welfare, Bulletin 15, 1965. pp. 22. Examines the effects of Khruschev's 'Life and Work' reforms.

SHORE, M. J. *Soviet Education: Its Psychology and Philosophy.* NY, Philosophical Library, 1947. pp. 346.

3.1.2 *France*

Note: For advanced study there is an exhaustive bibliography, *Education in France,* compiled by the Institutes of Education Librarians and published by the University of Southampton Institute of Education (1964; pp. 59). This gives details of research theses, articles and other documents relating to French education available in British universities.

CAPELLE, J. *Tomorrow's Education: The French Experience.* O, Pergamon P, 1967. pp. 236. Masterly review of on-going reforms by a front-runner, former Recteur of Nancy, who does not disguise his crusading zeal.

CLARK, J. M. *Teachers and Politics in France.* NY, Syracuse UP, 1967. pp. 197. Doctoral study of French teachers' professional association (*Fédération de l'Éducation Nationale*) as a pressure group.

FRASER, W. R. *Education and Society in Modern France.* L, Routledge, 1963. pp. 151. Confused political in-fighting in the pre-Gaullist era; only helpful if the reader is *au fait* with French life and affairs.

HALLS, W. D. *Society, Schools and Progress in France.* O, Pergamon P, 1965. pp. 216. The best introduction to recent and current transformations.

MALE, G. A. *Education in France.* Washington, D.C., U.S. Dept of Health, Education & Welfare, Office of Education, 1963. pp. 205.

WYLIE, L. *Village in the Vaucluse.* C, Mass., Harvard UP, 1957. pp. 345. Ethnographic study of a rural community and its school in the Midi.

3.1.3 *West Germany*

HALLS, W. D. *Society, Schools and Progress in Germany.* O, Pergamon P, 1965. pp. 216. On a par with this author's study of France (see section 3.1.2 above).

HUEBENER, T. *The Schools of West Germany: A Study of German Elementary and Secondary Schools.* NYUP, 1962. pp. 181. Describes main types of school, curricula, methods and current reorganization.

HYLLA, E. J. and KEGEL, F. O. *Education in Germany.* Frankfurt am Main, Hochschule für Internationale Pedagogische Forschung, 1958. pp. 79.

SAMUEL, R. and THOMAS, R. H. *Education and Society in Modern Germany.* L, Routledge, 1949. pp. 191. Covers period from early nineteenth century to end of Nazi regime; brief, slanted chapter on post-war reconstruction.

WARREN, R. L. *Education in Rebhausen.* NY, Holt, Rinehart & Winston, 1967. pp. 114. Cross-cultural case study of a rural school in southwest Germany.

3.1.4 *Scandinavia*

DAHLLOF, S. Z. and OBERG, H. *Secondary Education in Sweden.* Stockholm, National Board of Education, 1965. pp. 104.

DIXON, C. W. *Society, Schools and Progress in Scandinavia.* O, Pergamon P, 1965. pp. 212.

HJELMTVEIT, N. *Education in Norway.* Oslo, Royal Norwegian Government Information Office, 1946. pp. 42. By a former Minister of Church and Education.

HOVE, O. *An Outline of Norwegian Education.* Oslo, Royal Norwegian Ministry of Foreign Affairs, 1955. pp. 79.

HUSÉN, T. and BOALT, G. *Educational Research and Educational Change: The Case of Sweden.* NY, Wiley, 1968. pp. 233. The most authoritative, detailed account of the reforms effected by research and development policies in a national system, which has earned the reputation as a pace-maker in educational innovation.

HUUS, H. *The Education of Children and Youth in Norway.* U of Pittsburgh P, 1960. pp. 247.

MARKLUND, S. and SODERBERG, P. *The Swedish Comprehensive School.* L, Longmans, 1968. pp. 128.

NELLEMAN, A. *Schools and Education in Denmark.* Danish Information Handbooks. Det Dansk Selskab, 1964. pp. 154.

ORGANIZATION FOR ECONOMIC COOPERATION AND DEVELOPMENT. *Reviews of National Policies for Education: Sweden.* Paris, OECD, 1969. pp. 62.

ORRING, J. *School in Sweden.* Stockholm, National Board of Education, 1969. pp. 162.

THOMSEN, O. B. *Some Aspects of Education in Denmark.* U of Toronto P, 1967. pp. 105.

3.1.5 *Other European Countries*

Note: In addition to the Pergamon Press *Society, Schools and Progress* series, case studies of Greece, Spain, Turkey and Yugoslavia are to be found in the OECD reports dealing with *The Mediterranean Regional Project: An Experiment in Planning by Six Countries.*

GRANT, N. *Society, Schools and Progress in Eastern Europe.* O, Pergamon P, 1969. pp. 390. Includes up-to-date accounts of Czechoslovakia, Hungary, Poland, Rumania and Bulgaria.

MALLINSON, V. *Power and Politics in Belgian Education 1815 to 1961.* L, Heinemann Educ., 1963. pp. 256. Mainly historical analysis of the explosive forces – religious, cultural and political – in the cockpit of Europe.

RICHMOND, W. K. *Educational Planning: Old and New Perspectives.* L, Michael Joseph, 1966. pp. 257. Compares post-war developments in Hungary and Czechoslovakia with those in England.

Education in Czechoslovakia. Prague, Státní Pedagické Nakladatelsví, 1958.

3.2 AMERICA

3.2.1 *U.S.A.*

BEREDAY, G. Z. F. and VOLPICELLI, L. (eds.) *Public Education in America: A New Interpretation of Purpose and Practice.* NY, Harper & Row, 1958. pp. 212. Many-sided re-evaluations by leading American educationists; reflects post-Sputnik anxieties.

DE YOUNG, C. A. and WYNN, D. R. *American Education.* 5th ed. NY, McGraw-Hill, 1964. pp. 538. Standard work for students and teachers.

GOOD, H. G. *A History of American Education.* 2nd ed. NY, Macmillan, 1962. pp. 610. 1607 to 1955.

GORER, G. *The American People.* NY, Norton, 1948. pp. 246. Offers some interesting insights into American culture and national character. (Arguable that Sinclair Lewis, Hemingway and Norman Mailer, etc., offer truer ones!)

HARTFORD, E. F. *Education in these United States.* NY, Macmillan, 1964. pp. 576.

KANDEL, I. L. *American Education in the Twentieth Century.* C, Mass., Harvard UP, 1957. pp. 247. Authoritative if dated.

KEPPEL, F. *The Necessary Revolution in American Education.* NY, Harper & Row, 1966. pp. 201. Notable review of recent changes in policy, curriculum projects, etc., by a former U.S. Commissioner for Education. Strongly recommended.

KING, E. J. *Society, Schools and Progress in the U.S.A.* O, Pergamon P, 1965. pp. 260. The best introduction by a British writer.

REINHARDT, E. *American Education: An Introduction.* Rev. ed. NY, Harper & Row, 1960. pp. 458. Textbook for teachers in training.

RICHMOND, W. K. *Education in the U.S.A.* L, Redman, 1956. pp. 227. Readable, largely obsolete.

THOMAS, R. *The Search for a Common Learning: General Education 1800–1960.* NY, McGraw-Hill, 1962. pp. 324. Major historical study of the permanent tension between Jeffersonian and Jacksonian in American democracy; 'quality' versus 'equality'.

WOODRING, P. *A Fourth of a Nation.* NY, McGraw-Hill, 1957. pp. 255. Well written, often witty plea for a more critical theory and practice; marks the end of the slap-happy Life Adjustment era in American education.

3.2.2 *Canada*

DOMINION BUREAU OF STATISTICS. *The Organization and Administration of Public Schools in Canada.* 3rd ed. Ottawa, Queen's Printer, 1966. pp. 206.

—— *A Bibliographical Guide to Canadian Education.* Ottawa, Queen's Printer, 1964. pp. 55. Indispensable.

KATZ, J. (ed.) *Canadian Education Today: A Symposium.* Scarborough Ontario, McGraw-Hill, 1956. pp. 243.

—— *Society, Schools and Progress in Canada.* O, Pergamon P, 1969. pp. 168. The best introduction for British students.

PHILLIPS, C. E. *The Development of Education in Canada.* Scarborough, Ontario, Gage, 1957. pp. 626. Mainly historical.

3.2.3 *Central and South America*

BENJAMIN, H. R. W. *Higher Education in the American Republics.* NY, McGraw-Hill, 1965. pp. 224.

GALE, L. *Education and Development in Latin America.* L, Routledge, 1969. pp. 192. A reliable, all-purpose introduction.

HAUCH, C. C. *The Current Situation in Latin American Education.* Washington, D.C., U.S. Dept of Health, Education & Welfare, Office of Education Bulletin No. 21, 1963. pp. 30.

HAVIGHURST, R. J. and MOREIRA, J. R. *Society and Education in Brazil.* U of Pittsburgh P, 1965. pp. 263. Standard work.

LYONS, R. F. (ed.) *Problems and Strategies of Educational Planning: Lessons from Latin America.* Paris, UNESCO, International Institute for Educational Planning, 1965. pp. 117.

MYERS, C. N. *Education and National Development in Mexico.* Princeton UP, 1963. pp. 147. Standard work.

ORGANIZATION FOR ECONOMIC COOPERATION AND DEVELOP-
MENT. *Education, Human Resources and Development in Argentina.*
Paris, OECD, 1967. pp. 465.

3.3 ASIA

ADAMS, D. *Education and Modernization in Asia.* Reading, Mass.,
Addison-Wesley, 1970. pp. 207. National case studies: Japan, India,
China.

3.3.1 *Middle East*

ARASTEH, R. *Education and Social Awakening in Iran.* Leyden, Brill,
1962. pp. 144.

AVIDOR, M. *Education in Israel.* Jerusalem, Zionist Organization, 1957.
pp. 179.

BENTWICH, J. *Education in Israel.* L, Routledge, 1965. pp. 200.

BOKTOR, A. *The Development and Expansion of Education in the United
Arab Republic.* American U in Cairo P, 1963. pp. 182.

KAZAMIAS, A. M. *Education and the Quest for Modernity in Turkey.* L,
Allen & Unwin, 1966. pp. 304. Historical introduction followed by
account of the transformation from traditional Islamic to secular-
political culture.

KLEINBERGER, A. F. *Society, Schools and Progress in Israel.* O, Pergamon P, 1969. pp. 354. To be read in conjunction with BENTWICH
(above).

LERNER, D. *et al.* (eds.) *The Passing of Traditional Society: Modernizing
the Middle East.* NY, Free P, 1958. pp. 466.

3.3.2 *China*

FRASER, S. (ed.) *Chinese Communist Education: Records of the First
Decade.* Nashville, Vanderbilt UP, 1965. pp. 542. Speeches, articles
and official documents.

HU CH'ANG-TU. *Chinese Education under Communism.* NY, Columbia
U, Teachers College Bureau of Publications, 1962. pp. 157.

ORLEANS, L. A. *Professional Manpower and Education in Communist
China.* Washington, D.C., U.S. Government Printing Office, 1961.
pp. 260.

PRICE, R. F. *Education in Communist China.* L, Routledge, 1970. pp.
308. The most comprehensive, up-to-date survey for British readers.

TSANG CHIU-SAM. *Society, Schools and Progress in China.* O, Pergamon
P, 1968. pp. 353.

3.3.3 *Japan*

HALL, R. K. *Education for a New Japan.* New Haven, Conn., Yale UP, 1949. pp. 503. Post-war Americanization; dated.

KAIGO, T. *Japanese Education: Its Past and Present.* Tokyo, Society for International Cultural Relations, 1965.

PASSIN, H. *Society and Education in Japan.* NY, Columbia U, Teachers College Bureau of Publications, 1965. pp. 347.

SINGLETON, J. *Nichū: A Japanese School.* NY, Holt, Rinehart & Winston, 1967. pp. 125. Cross-cultural study; a good introduction for readers who are wholly unfamiliar with the Japanese way of life.

3.3.4 *India*

AIRAN, J. W. *et al.* (eds.) *Climbing a Wall of Glass: Aspects of Educational Reform in India.* Bombay, Manaktalas, 1965. pp. 176.

RAMANATHAN, G. *Educational Planning and National Integration.* India and L, Asia Publishing House, 1965. pp. 252.

SANTHANAM, K. I. *Transition in India and other Essays.* India and L, Asia Publishing House, 1964. pp. 292.

SARGENT, SIR J. *Society, Schools and Progress in India.* O, Pergamon P, 1968. pp. 264.

SHRIMALI, K. *Education in Changing India.* India and L, Asia Publishing House, 1965. pp. 258. In-and-out-of-office speeches by former Minister of Education.

3.3.5 *Pakistan*

CURLE, A. *Planning for Education in Pakistan.* L, Tavistock, 1966. pp. 222.

PAKISTAN PLANNING COMMISSION. *Second Five Year Plan: 1960–65.* Karachi, Government Printer, 1960. pp. 414. See Chapter 14, 'Education and Training'.

RAHMAN, F. *New Education in the Making of Pakistan.* L, Cassell, 1953. pp. 165. Lectures and addresses by the then Minister of Education.

3.4 AFRICA

CASTLE, E. B. *Growing up in East Africa.* L, OUP, 1966. pp. 284.

CHESSWAS, J. D. *Educational Planning and Development in Uganda.* Paris, UNESCO, International Institute for Educational Planning, 1966. pp. 97.

COUCH, M. (ed.) *Education in Africa: A Select Bibliography.* U of L Institute of Education, Education Libraries Bulletin. Part 1, 1962, pp. 121; Part 2, 1965, pp. 116.

FOSTER, P. J. *Education and Social Change in Ghana.* L, Routledge, 1965. pp. 322.

HUNTER, G. *Education for a Developing Region.* L, Allen & Unwin, 1963. pp. 119.

LEWIS, L. J. *Society, Schools and Progress in Nigeria.* O, Pergamon P, 1965. pp. 176.

MOUMOUNI, A. *Education in Africa.* Tr. P. N. OTT. L, André Deutsch, 1968. pp. 320. Major work by an African educationist; offers a critical commentary on developments south of the Sahara 1816–1960 and outlines a programme for the future fitted to African needs and aspirations.

NDUKA, O. *Western Education and the Nigerian Cultural Background.* Ibadan, OUP, 1964. pp. 168. Considers the effects of Westernization, the implications of the Ashby Commission Report and the long term prospects.

SCANLON, D. G. (ed.) *Traditions of African Education.* NY, Columbia U, Teachers College P, 1964. pp. 184.

WILLIAMS, P. *Aid In Uganda – Education.* L, Overseas Development Institute, 1966. pp. 152.

WILSON, J. *Education and Changing West African Culture.* NY, Teachers College P, 1963. pp. 125.

3.5 AUSTRALASIA

Note: For a fuller bibliography, see *Education within the Commonwealth* (National Book League, London, 1965). The numerous publications of the Australian Council for Educational Research and the New Zealand Council for Educational Research should also be consulted.

3.5.1 *Australia*

AUSTIN, A. G. *Australian Education 1788–1900.* Carlton, Victoria, Pitman, 1961. pp. 282. Traces the evolution of the public system from the colonial period.

BARCAN, A. *A Short History of Education in New South Wales.* Sydney, Martindale P, 1965. pp. 338.

COWAN, R. W. T. (ed.) *Education for Australians.* Melbourne, Cheshire, 1964. pp. 298. A symposium.

FOGARTY, R. *Catholic Education in Australia 1806–1950.* Carlton, Victoria, Melbourne UP, 1959. 2 vols. pp. 255 and 257.

MCLEAN, D. (ed.) *It's People that Matter: Education for Social Change.* Sydney, Angus & Robertson, 1970. pp. 384. Virile cross-section of academic opinion.

PARTRIDGE, P. H. *Society, Schools and Progress in Australia.* O Pergamon P, 1968. pp. 264. A good introduction.

3.5.2 *New Zealand*

CURRIE, SIR G. (Chairman) *Report of the Commission on Education in New Zealand.* Wellington, Government Printer, 1962. pp. 885.

ROTH, H. *A Bibliography of New Zealand Education.* Wellington, New Zealand Council for Educational Research, 1964. pp. 234.

UNESCO. Studies on Compulsory Education. *Compulsory Education in New Zealand.* Paris, UNESCO, 1952. pp. 130.

4 Educational Development and Educational Planning

Since adaptation to rapidly changing circumstances is necessarily a feature of *any* education system in the modern world, it is not surprising that development plans are the order of the day. Inevitably, then, this section is something of a mixed bag. Some titles refer to programmes in the developing countries, others to planning strategies in advanced industrial societies. At this point problems in comparative education merge with those in educational administration (management and organization), curriculum study and curriculum development, economics of education and educational technology, to which cross-reference should be made.

ANDERSON, C. A. and BOWMAN, M. J. (eds.) *Education and Economic Development.* L, Cass, 1966. pp. 436. Proceedings of a conference on the role of education in the early stages of building a national system.

ARMITAGE, P., SMITH, C. and ALPER, P. *Decision Models for Educational Planning.* L, Allen Lane, 1969. pp. 124. First steps towards a computable model of the education system as a whole.

ASHBY, SIR E. *Universities: British, Indian, African.* L, Weidenfeld & Nicolson, 1966. pp. 576. A study in the ecology of higher education.

BEEBY, C. E. *The Quality of Education in Developing Countries.* C, Mass., Harvard UP, 1966. pp. 139. New Zealander's perceptive essay; sees development as dependent upon a four-stage evolution in the professional competence of teachers. Strongly recommended.

BOWLES, F. *Access to Higher Education: The International Study of University Admissions.* Paris, UNESCO. 2 vols. vol. 1, 1963, pp. 212; vol. 2, 1965, National studies. pp. 648.

BUCKLEY, W. *Modern Systems Research for the Behavioral Scientists.* Chicago, Aldine, 1968. pp. 525. A source book; for advanced students.

COOMBS, P. H. *The World Educational Crisis: A Systems Analysis.* NY, OUP, 1968. pp. 252. How to feed minds and mouths in the population explosion. A global study, not to be ignored.

CURLE, A. *Educational Strategy for Developing Countries: A Study of Educational and Social Factors in Relation to Economic Growth.* L, Tavistock, 1963. pp. 192.

—— *Educational Problems in Developing Societies.* NY, Praeger, 1969. pp. 170

HANDY, H. W. and HUSSAIN, K. M. *Network Analysis for Educational Management.* Englewood Cliffs, Prentice-Hall, 1969. pp. 186. See under Educational Administration, section 3 (p. 160).

LEWIS, L. J., and LOVERIDGE, A. J. *The Management of Education.* L, Pall Mall P, 1965. pp. 124. For teachers and administrators in developing countries.

LOWE, J., GRANT, N. and WILLIAMS, T. D. (eds.) *Education and Nation Building in the Third World.* Edinburgh, Scottish Academic P, 1970. pp. 258.

LYONS, R. F. (ed.) *Problems and Strategies of Educational Planning.* Paris, UNESCO, 1965. pp. 117. Lessons from Latin America.

ORGANIZATION FOR ECONOMIC COOPERATION AND DEVELOPMENT. *Education and Economic Development.* Paris, OECD, 1966. pp. 296.

—— *Organizational Problems in Planning Educational Development.* Paris, OECD, 1966. pp. 109.

PLATT, W. J. *Research for Educational Planning.* Paris, UNESCO, International Institute for Educational Planning, 1970. pp. 67. Notes on emergent needs.

RICHMOND, W. K. *Educational Planning: Old and New Perspectives.* L, Michael Joseph, 1966. pp. 257.

SPOLTON, L. *The Upper Secondary School.* O, Pergamon P, 1967. pp. 298.

TINBERGEN, J. and BOS, H. C. *et al. Econometric Models of Education: Some Applications.* Paris, OECD, 1965. pp. 99.

WOODHALL, M. *Cost-Benefit Analysis in Educational Planning.* Fundamentals of Educational Planning 13. Paris, UNESCO, International Institute for Educational Planning, 1970. pp. 49.

9 *The Economics of Education*

Another late arrival – it seems only yesterday that writers like John
Vaizey were voices in the wilderness – economics is rapidly emerging
as a major contender in the field of educational studies. It may not be
everyone's cup of tea exactly but there is a real sense in which it can
be said to be everybody's business. In these commentaries the point has
been made more than once that the production of books about education
is susceptible to the same laws of supply and demand as operate in other
spheres. The same is true of the educational services themselves. The
nexus between governmental grants and regulations serves as a reminder
that planning authorities have always had some notion, however dim and
easygoing, of the importance of cost-effectiveness, and the nineteenth-
century system of 'Payment by Results' may be seen as an early and
crude attempt to ensure that the public received value for money in the
running of its elementary schools. Significantly, the need for similar
safeguards was never felt in the independent schools for whose clientele
there was a visible return from the outlay in fees in the shape of improved
life chances and lucrative life earnings: as Dean Gaisford shrewdly
observed, the point of studying Classics was that it led to positions of
considerable emolument. Although it has been left to economists to
make explicit the implications of the concept of human capital it is as
well to recognize that the concept has long been implicit in upper and
middle class ways of thinking.

Being less amenable to 'deferred gratification', working class culture
has on the whole been disinclined to share this belief that education is
ipso facto a Good Thing which invariably pays handsome dividends in
the long run. Education, nevertheless, feeds on itself. Built into its
very nature in modern industrial societies is an Oliver Twist effect
which guarantees a steady rise in levels of aspiration and expectation,
and hence a growing demand for more and better services. The history
of popular education in Britain may be seen as largely a record of missed
opportunities and little-and-too-late policies, yet it was only a matter of
time before meritocratic motives became well nigh universal.

As the scale of operations has increased, the problems of allocating
and deploying resources, which, if not necessarily as scarce as is often

supposed, are always limited, have become more complex – and the case for treating them like any other nationalized industry or commercial enterprise has become more difficult to resist. For developing countries, needless to say, the economic aspects take precedence over all others. Governments, like individuals, profess to want education for a variety of reasons. Obviously, however, the ideal of education as a 'human right' carries a good deal less force than the idea of education as means of advancing national and personal development. Whether or not, as the saying goes, we are all Marxists nowadays, there is no denying that economic considerations loom large in our daily lives. Today, the acumen of the businessman is needed even in academic circles, once the haven for world-forsaking dons and absent-minded professors. Fund raising for research projects is now as much of an art as playing the stock market, and no less chancy for those who do not know the ropes.

British educational thought has been tardy in reacting to this go-getting mood. From the *Crowther Report* on (1959: cited under Educational Theory, p. 50), a series of official reports has adduced evidence which indicates that Britain's relatively poor showing in the world economic growth league must in some way be connected with the education system's failure to meet the nation's manpower needs. 'In some way connected' – but how? Certainly not by direct cause and effect. Tempting as it is to ascribe the failure to an elitist preference for 'liberal' studies and a dogged refusal to recognize what amounts to a wholesale wastage of talent, the evidence remains inconclusive. Even so, the suspicion has grown that the inputs in the educational services are not being matched by comparable outputs. Various methods of measuring educational outputs have been devised, all of them highly ingenious, but to date none of them has proved totally convincing.

With costs escalating, nevertheless, the authorities have been forced to call upon the advice of economists. It was perhaps symptomatic of their unreadiness that the Robbins Committee felt obliged to invite an American expert to write the relevant chapter in their report on *Higher Education* (Bowen, 1963), and that they preferred to make the pressure of demand for university places the main criterion for their recommendations rather than rely on dubious estimates of future manpower needs and cost-benefit anaysis. Symptomatic, too, that only five years later the Committee of Vice-Chancellors agreed to call a conference on university productivity!

Since 1963 British research into the economics of education has made its own mark, although it is still confined to one or two centres and has yet to make much of an impact on, or find its proper niche in, college and university department of education courses. Generally speaking, the latter do not have lecturers who are competent to interpret it. Moreover, the difficulties arising from this gap between advanced research and teaching are compounded in the literature, which makes few concessions to the average reader. Many a student is deterred when, on the very first page, he comes across such expressions as 'aggregate production functions' and 'international factor endowments', which leave him darkling. An elementary introduction to the subject is sorely needed. J. Vaizey's *The Economics of Education* (1962) is as good as any, but somewhat outdated. W. K. Richmond's *The Education Industry* (1969: cited under Educational Technology, p. 204) is a layman's attempt to expound some of the basic issues, concepts and techniques. J. A. Lauwerys (ed.), *Education and Economy* (1969), reproduces papers from the 1954, 1956, 1967 and 1968 issues of the *World Year Book of Education*, which are at once authoritative and readable. M. Woodhall in *Educational Research in Britain 2*, edited by H. J. Butcher and H. B. Pont (1970: cited under Educational Psychology, p. 94), gives a synoptic view of recent and current explorations of the field.

In the first instance, economists are concerned with what, on the face of them, are simple matters of accountancy – how the educational services are financed and how the money is spent. In the event, these turn out to be exceedingly complicated. At a rather more problematical level, again, economists interest themselves in such questions as: How can the contribution of education to economic growth be evaluated? How do the two interact? How can techniques like cost-benefit analysis and manpower forecasting help to improve standards of efficiency in the use of resources in the education system? What guidance can they afford the planners? How to disentangle the pay-off from policies of 'investment' from the pay-off in terms of 'consumption'? Assuming that 'whatever is exists in some amount' (incidentally, an assumption that provides the starting point for the psychometrist and other social scientists), what can be done to measure educational outputs and productivity? At a still higher level, attempts to answer these questions have led to research into the possibilities of devising computable models of the education system as a whole. Once these are perfected – it must be emphasized that the models are still at a rudimentary stage of development – the planners will have at their disposal the kind of mathematical ready reckoner which will enable them to predict the outcomes of this or that policy with a fair degree of accuracy. That at least is the dream. But unless the gap between advanced research and teaching is closed, and the indications are that it is widening all the time, the outcome could easily become an Orwellian nightmare. Why? Simply because decision-making, given the necessary know-how, might cease to be shared. To repeat, the economics of education is everybody's business.

M. Blaug's *Economics of Education: A Selected Annotated Bibliography* (2nd ed. 1970) is the indispensable work of reference. Additional references are to found in Section B3 of *Educational Planning: A Bibliography*, compiled by the International Institute for Educational Planning (UNESCO, 1964: cited under Comparative Education, p. 169). No attempt has been made to duplicate these: the following list is restricted to some of the more recent, noteworthy contributions to the literature.

Bibliography

ABT, C. *Design for an Education System Cost-Effectiveness Model*. Paris, OECD, 1967.

ANDERSON, C. *The Social Context of Educational Planning*. Paris, UNESCO, 1967. pp. 35.

ARMITAGE, P., SMITH, C. and ALPER, P. *Decision Models for Educational Planning*. L, Allen Lane, 1969. pp. 124. Preliminary analysis of stocks, flows and bottlenecks in the English education system; envisages a computable model which will assist planners to quantify variables which have hitherto been at the mercy of guesswork.

BEEBY, C. E. (ed.) *Planning and the Educational Administrator*. Paris, UNESCO, 1967. pp. 36. One of a series of short monographs on *The Fundamentals of Educational Planning* (see also ANDERSON, HALLAK, POIGNANT, and VAIZEY and CHESSWAS).

—— *Qualitative Aspects of Educational Planning*. Paris, UNESCO, 1969. pp. 302. Symposium with economists, sociologists and educationists discussing the other side of the cost-benefit equation.

BLAUG, M. (ed.) *Economics of Education: A Selected Annotated Bibliography*. 2nd ed. O, Pergamon P, 1970. Also Harmondsworth, Penguin Books, 1968-9. 2 vols. pp. 448 and 398. Papers by leading authorities on such topics as the concept of human capital, cost-benefit analysis, manpower forecasting and educational planning.

—— *An Introduction to the Economics of Education*. L, Allen Lane, 1970. pp. 363. Comprehensive; for advanced students.

BLAUG, M., LAYARD, R. and WOODHALL, M. *The Causes of Graduate Unemployment in India*. L, Allen Lane, 1969. pp. 312.

BLAUG, M., PESTON, M. and ZIDERMAN, A. *The Utilization of Educated Manpower in Industry*. Edinburgh, Oliver & Boyd, 1967. pp. 106.

BOWEN, W. G. *Economic Aspects of Education*. Princeton UP, 1964. pp. 122.

—— 'Assessing the economic contribution of education: an appraisal of alternative approaches'. Appendix 4 *in* COMMITTEE ON HIGHER EDUCATION, *Higher Education (The Robbins Report)*. Cmnd. 2145-IV. L, HMSO, 1963. pp. 335.

BOWMAN, M. J., DEBEAUVAIS, M., KOMAROV, V. and VAIZEY, J. (eds.) *Readings in the Economics of Education*. Paris, UNESCO, 1968. pp. 943. The best buy for advanced students. Wide selection of articles by an international team of all the talents, including Strumilin's 1929 essay on 'The cheapest and most effective way of creating a productive labour force'.

COMMITTEE ON THE MORE EFFECTIVE USE OF TECHNICAL COLLEGE RESOURCES. *On the Use of Costing and Other Financial Techniques in Technical Colleges (The Capps Report)*. L, HMSO, 1969. pp. 178. Cold, hard look at the factors that determine expenditure; almost certainly foreshadows a new style of governmental surveillance of the educational services.

COOMBS, P. *et al.* (eds.) *New Educational Media in Action*. UNESCO, International Institute for Educational Planning, 1967. pp. 175. Case studies for planners.

DIRECTORATE FOR SCIENTIFIC AFFAIRS. *Educational Policy and Planning: Austria*. Paris, OECD, 1967. pp. 437.

—— *Educational Policy and Planning: Sweden*. Paris, OECD, 1968. pp. 448. Records of economic growth and educational development in two very different countries.

—— *Methods and Statistical Needs for Educational Planning*. Paris, OECD, 1967. pp. 363. A handbook for planners. Urges the need for uniformity in methods of compiling educational/economic statistics in order to facilitate accurate intercountry comparisons.

—— *Budgeting, Programme Analysis and Cost-Effectiveness in Educational Planning*. Paris, OECD, 1968. pp. 304. Definitive accounts of new approaches and new techniques, stressing the importance of long-range goals.

—— *Study on Teachers*. Paris, OECD, 1969. 7 vols. Investigations into the worldwide phenomenon of teacher shortage.

—— *Economic and Social Aspects of Educational Planning*. Paris, OECD, 1969.

EDDING, F. *Methods of Analysing Educational Outlay*. Paris, UNESCO, 1966. pp. 70. Masterly.

HALLAK, J. *The Analysis of Educational Costs and Expenditure*. Paris, UNESCO, 1969. pp. 69. Short monograph in the *Fundamentals of Educational Planning* series.

HARTLEY, H. J. *Educational Planning – Programming – Budgeting: A Systems Approach*. Englewood Cliffs, Prentice-Hall, 1968. pp. 290.

HOLLISTER, R. *A Technical Evaluation of the First Stage of the Mediterranean Regional Project*. Paris, OECD, 1967. pp. 188. Interim assessment of the vast manpower-planning exercise carried out in Italy, Greece, Spain, Portugal, Yugoslavia and Turkey; of interest to the comparative educationist as well as the economist.

LAUWERYS, J. A. (ed.) *Education and the Economy*. L, Evans, 1969. pp. 140.

LEITE, M. J., LYNCH, P., SHEEHAN, J. and VAIZEY, J. *The Economics of Educational Costs*. Lisbon, Centro de Economica e Financas. Vol. 1 *Cost and Comparisons: A Theoretical Approach*, 1968, pp. 137; Vol. 3a *Capital and Reforms in Education*, 1969, pp. 161. Highly technical reviews of problems of large-scale educational finance.

MACLURE, J. S. *Learning Beyond Our Means?* L, Councils & Education P, 1968. pp. 39. Readable estimate of the effects of governmental cut-back of spending on education.

NOSHKO, K., MONOSZON, E., ZHAMIN, V. and SERVERTSEV, V. *Educational Planning in the U.S.S.R.* Paris, UNESCO, 1968. pp. 295. Explains how the Soviet education system is geared to industrial manpower requirements.

PEACOCK, A., GLENNERSTER, H. and LAVERS, R. *Educational Finance: Its Sources and Uses in the United Kingdom*. Edinburgh, Oliver & Boyd, 1968. pp. 90. Probably the most thorough investigation into the costs of education in this country so far; more significant for its methodology than for its actual findings, being based on 1962–3 data.

POIGNANT, R. *The Relation of Educational Plans to Economic and Social Planning*. Paris, UNESCO, 1967. pp. 51.

ROBINSON, E. A. G. and VAIZEY, J. (eds.) *The Economics of Education*. NY, Macmillan, 1966. pp. 781. Useful papers by Edding, Dennison, Vaizey, etc.

SCHRAMM, W., COOMBS, P. H., KAHNERT, F. and LYLE, J. (eds.) *The New Media: Memo to Educational Planners.* Paris, UNESCO, International Institute for Educational Planning, 1967. pp. 175.

—— *New Educational Media in Action: Case Studies for Planners.* Paris, UNESCO, International Institute for Educational Planning, 1967. 3 vols. pp. 203, 226, 198.
Appraisals of the cost-effectiveness of some major projects in ETV, etc.

SMITH, C. S. *The Costs of Further Education: A British Analysis.* O, Pergamon P, 1970. pp. 202. Finds the existing system of finance inefficient and favours an alternative based on vouchers.

THONSTAD, T. *Education and Manpower: Theoretical Models and Empirical Applications.* Edinburgh, Oliver & Boyd, 1969. pp. 176.

VAIZEY, J. and CHESSWAS, J. D. *The Costing of Educational Plans.* Paris, UNESCO, 1967. pp. 63. Another monograph in *The Fundamentals of Educational Planning* series. The series as a whole is an invaluable source of information and ideas.

VAIZEY, J. and SHEEHAN, J. *Resources for Education.* L, Allen & Unwin, 1968. pp. 176. Economic analysis of education in the U.K. 1920–65; vigorous rewrite of Vaizey's earlier work *The Costs of Education.*

WEST, E. G. *Education and the State.* Institute of Economic Affairs, 1965. pp. 242. Stimulating, provocative and not very convincing argument in favour of state finance as distinct from state *provision* of education; advocates free enterprise with vouchers to allow parents freedom of choice.

10 *Educational Technology*

What *is* educational technology? Latest fad or epoch-making advance? Back in the 1950s it went by a less pretentious name, audiovisual aids – and to the rank and file of teachers this is still what it denotes. Its conflation dates from the early 1960s when programmed learning and teaching machines made headlines news, since when it has assumed ever more portentous proportions.

The reasons for this heady progress are not far to seek. As the number of bits and pieces of equipment available for teachers has increased – first, film projectors, radio sets and gramophones, then cassette-loaded and overhead projectors, language laboratories, portable tape recorders, calculating machines and closed circuit television, later still desk-top computers, electronic video recordings, feedback classrooms, etc., etc. – so has the need to lump them together under some kind of conceptual framework, however rough and ready. As a consequence, the small talk now current in academic circles is interspersed with all manner of esoteric catch-phrases – 'systems approaches', 'multi-media usage', 'communication channels' and the like. From being a side-show, educational technology looks like becoming the big tent. Blown up with hot air, say the critics.

Promise or threat? It could be either; and the chances are that it will be neither. What cannot be doubted is that the philosophical disputes which have arisen in educational theory and practice in the past will be revived with greater urgency as the impact of technology becomes more apparent. On the one hand, there are those who maintain that technology is the most dynamic force in the modern world and who welcome it as the springboard for a new humanism; on the other, those who regard it with abhorrence as a depersonalizing influence. The two camps are nicely described by Austwick ('Towards a Technology of Instruction' in G. Baron and W. Taylor (eds.) *Educational Administration and the Social Sciences*, 1969): 'Self-styled liberals or progressives clutch their children about them ready to defend to the death the personal element of education – the direct human contact between teacher and taught, the so-called meeting of minds; whilst taxonomists, systems analysts, the white-coated faceless ones, reduce education to a collection of measurables – a predictable, controllable, automated process in which the child passes through a clinically controlled environment to emerge at the end duly charged and docketed.' In one sense, these opposing attitudes reflect the difference between tough-minded and tender-minded appraisals – between men who are haunted by the prospects opened up by social engineering and fearful of the advent of 1984. Albeit in different ways, Sir Eric Ashby (1958), B. F. Skinner (1968) and Sir Leon Bagrit (1965) typify the former position; Jacques Ellul (1965) and J. W. Krutch (1956) the latter.

Being so rough and ready, the concept of educational technology requires closer scrutiny than it has received so far by some of its leading proponents. In fact, most of those engaged in this field are too absorbed in their work to reflect deeply, if at all, about its implications. As a result, what they have to say on the subject often sounds impressive only because it is couched in an elaborate jargon which serves as a smoke screen for an abysmally low level of discourse. To conclude that the enormous research literature which has grown up around programmed learning alone is mostly moonshine would be unfair, but it can hardly be denied that it contains more chaff than wheat. The cause of educational technology is ill served by treating it as a bandwagon for second-raters, merchant adventurers, poseurs and the jet set. Its pros and cons need to be weighed with the utmost care, always bearing in mind that technology itself is essentially neutral and amoral; bearing in mind also that the choice before us is not a straightforward one between the machinations of mad scientists and the last ditch stance of latter-day Luddites.

There are at least three areas in which technological developments are bound to influence education willynilly: (1) in methods of teaching and curriculum design, (2) in patterns of organization within educational institutions, (3) in administration, in particular as regards the utilization of manpower and material resources. Whether we like it or not, the relationship between man and machines is now so intimate as to amount to a symbiosis. The teacher who refuses to have any truck with mechanical devices – hardware in the jargon of the trade – has as little survival value as a soldier who fights his battles with bow and arrows. Instrumentation alters styles of presentation; instrumentation alters the learning situation: above all, instrumentation alters the options open to teachers and pupils by extending the range of possible experience. It is easy to see, therefore, why the concept of educational technology is so appealing to intellectual empire builders. To their way of thinking, it is all-embracing.

Educational technology has three main objectives: (1) to rationalize the use of resources available for education by making it a less labour-intensive activity, (2) to individualize the learning process, and (3) to extend and enrich the range of learning experiences.

On the first score, the efforts made so far must be accounted a failure. Worthy as it is, the aim of increasing educational outputs through substituting machinery for manpower has proved to be considerably more difficult than was at first supposed. To some extent, this can be attributed to the inherent conservatism of the teaching profession, but this is far too facile an explanation. The fact of the matter is that the cost of expensive mechanical devices like teaching machines, language laboratories and closed circuit television networks has not, on the whole, been justified in terms of their long-term effectiveness. None of them has helped significantly to alleviate the shortage of teachers – or to ease the work load of existing staff. Like new toys, overhead projectors have been welcomed with open arms by many teachers, only to be consigned to the store cupboard later on in favour of the old-fashioned blackboard. Teaching machines have been tried out and abandoned, either because they did not fit in with normal classroom procedures or because they were found to be little better than page-turners anyway. Language laboratories, even when properly serviced, are apt to stand idle for days at a time unless they are managed by skilled operators. The situation, indeed, is rather like that which would exist in a motorway culture in which there were no automobiles, only carburettors, brake systems, headlamps and the rest all waiting to be assembled in order to become a going concern. Today, the teacher has bits and pieces of equipment lying around all over the place; and if, at times, he complains that they do not add up and cause him more trouble than they are worth, who shall blame him?

Understandably, then, educational technologists are having to turn their attention to the cost-effectiveness aspects. At the same time, improvements in instrumentation are likely to take place more rapidly than improvements in the training of teachers. Inability to exploit the advantages offered by mechanical devices may well prove to be a barrier to progress.

Programmed learning

As regards the problem of catering for individual differences, the programmers can rightly claim to have gone part of the way towards breaking the lockstep of conventional classroom teaching. In so far as they have striven to perfect systematic techniques of instruction they are more entitled than most to call themselves educational technologists. Against this, some of their earlier claims (e.g. that self-instructional devices could do the job without assistance or supervision from teachers, that self-pacing produced the essential features of individual tutoring, that success for all was virtually guaranteed, etc.) have been shown to be exaggerated. Though they have been effective enough in industrial training , i.e. in situations where competent instructors are not available or in short supply, teaching machines of the kind marketed so far have been too crude to have more than a limited usefulness in schools. For most purposes, programmed texts have been found capable of achieving their objectives without going to the trouble of installing them in a cheat-proof metal box. On the hardware side, programmers are now more inclined to pin their faith on computer assisted instruction. For the majority, however, it is a case of back to the drawing board, to what is loosely referred to as a systems approach to problems of learning and instruction.

Is programmed learning the caterpillar from which the perfect imago of educational technology will eventually take flight ? During its short life it has undergone some remarkable changes. Although fixed-sequence, linear programmes of the Skinner type are by far the most numerous – most of them dealing with mathematical, scientific and technical subjects, incidentally – programming techniques have become more fluid in recent years. Several of the 'principles' alleged to be basic in the early 1960s, e.g. the insistence on small steps, immediate reinforcement, low error rates, overt responses, etc., have been drastically modified, if not altogether discredited. It is instructive, for instance, to note the change of viewpoint between Leith (*A Handbook of Programmed Learning*, 1964) and the same writer's second thoughts (*Second Thoughts on Programmed Learning*, 1969). Nevertheless, it would be wrong to jump to the conclusion that nothing of any consequence can be salvaged from the wreckage of a decade and more of hard slogging on the part of the programmers. The advances made in the specification of learning objectives and in testing-as-you-go assessment procedures represent solid gains. In fairness, too, it has to be said that most programmes do the job for which they are intended.

The fact remains that they have made relatively little headway in the schools. So far as publishers are concerned they are a drug on the market. Apart from one or two outstanding exceptions, e.g. R. F. Mager (1962,

1968), most of them are inordinately dull. In the first flush of enthusiasm which greeted the onset of programmed learning Holland and Skinner's *The Analysis of Behaviour* (1961) was well received by all and sundry: today, by contrast, it seems stale, flat and unprofitable. All of which goes to prove the point made by Sidney Pressey long before 1945: that it is not enough that a learning device passes all its tests in the laboratory – it must be seen to pass them in the average classroom with average pupils and with average teachers.

Not that the slowness in moving on from the bench test stage to general usage is confined to programmed learning by any means: the same difficulty has been encountered in curriculum projects (cf. Curriculum Study), as well as in the audiovisual field. Oettinger's *Run, Computer, Run* (1969) is a timely and amusing reminder that similar snags are certain to be encountered in getting computer-assisted instruction off the ground.

Systems Theory and Its Applications

If educational technology has not ushered in the age of automation overnight and if the quest for tailor-made learning for individual pupils has proved to be singularly elusive, its advocates are sustained by the unshakeable conviction that the third objective – to extend and enrich the range of learning experiences – is already well within their reach. No one doubts for a moment that schools broadcasting and television have played an immensely important part in the education of millions of children. The same is true of educational film. The fact that the cognitive gains as measured by examination 'results' may seem rather tenuous does not mean that the contribution of the mass media has been negligible. Hitherto the trouble with most of the investigations into the effects of television and radio, e.g. Himmelweit *et al.* (*Television and the Child*, 1958) and Trenaman (*Communication and Comprehension*, 1967), has been that they have been so literate-minded as to miss the point, so that it is scarcely surprising that they reported no significant differences. Since its inception, the Schools Broadcasting Council has never tired of stressing that its aim is to provide not so much an information service as a fund of vivid, imaginative, emotional experience which teachers otherwise cannot hope to supply.

Which media can most appropriately be used to achieve given learning objectives? What are the peculiar properties of motion film with or without a sound track, of black and white *vis-à-vis* colour film, of film strip, of slide-tape, of wall charts ? How does film differ from television ? When is recorded sound more powerful than a visual image ? These and a host of related questions concerning the 'grammar' of the various media are now increasingly exercising the minds of educational technologists. How to bring all the *disjecta membra* together under the roof of an overarching theory which will be at once descriptive, explanatory and predictive ? That is the question.

Whether it expresses itself in the form of programmed learning, of management studies and organization theory (*v.* educational administration) or so-called curriculum development (*v.* curriculum study), faith in techniques of regulation and control is a characteristic of life in advanced industrial societies. Systems theory, in fact, has a number of origins: in mathematics, in biology, in industrial psychology and sociology (network analysis, operational research, queueing theory, games theory, *et al.*), but most spectacularly, perhaps, in communication engineering. Because of this diverse genealogy, 'general systems theory' as expounded by writers such as Talcott Parsons may appear to have little in common with that of cyberneticists like Norbert Wiener (*Cybernetics*, 1948; *The Human Use of Human Beings*, 1951) and Ross Ashby (*An Introduction to Cybernetics*, 1968). In the sense that 'systems are isomorphic', however, they are all symptomatic of a converging trend in the contemporary movement of ideas. For 'planning' from now on read 'systems thinking'!

In a sense, systems theory represents the apotheosis of a process which has been going on ever since the methods of the social sciences first began to invade the educational field. G. H. Bantock in *Education and Values* (1965: cited under Educational Theory, p. 49) describes how completely taken aback he was when a distinguished academic proffered the opinion that 'education', as studied in the universities, had become largely a technical subject: 'Then, of course, I came to realize that, to a large extent, he was right – "education" had become increasingly a matter of research into child development and learning theory, into implication for social structure and the effects of social environment into method and teaching aids, into backwardness and special school problems, into organization and administration. It had, in fact, developed into a technology into a set of theoretical structures designed to facilitate the achievement of defined ends; its aim was efficiency.'

But if educational technology is all-embracing it is as well to recognize that this is because technology itself is all-embracing. Systems thinking, in other words, is machine-minded. Jacques Ellul (1965) puts his finger on the cause: 'Technique integrates the machine into society. It constructs the kind of world the machine needs and introduces order where the incoherent banging of machinery heaped up ruins. It clarifies, arranges, and rationalizes; it does in the domain of the abstract what the machine did in the domain of labour. It is efficient and brings efficiency to everything. Technique integrates everything. It avoids shock and sensational events. Man is not adapted to a world of steel; technique adapts him to it. It changes the arrangements of this blind world so that man can be part of it without colliding with its rough edges, without the anguish of being delivered up to the inhuman. Technique thus provides a model; it specifies attitudes that are valid once and for all. The anxiety aroused in man by the turbulence of the machine is soothed by the consoling hum of a unified society.

'As long as technique was represented exclusively by the machine, it was possible to speak of "man and the machine". The machine was an external object, and man (though significantly influenced by it in his professional, private and psychic life) remained none the less independent. He was in a position to assert himself apart from the machine; he was able to adopt a position with respect to it.

'But when technique enters into every area of life, including the human, it ceases to be external to man and becomes his very substance. It is no longer face to face with man but is integrated with him, and it progressively absorbs him. In this respect, technique is radically different from the machine. This transformation, so obvious in modern society, is the result of the fact that technique has become autonomous.'

Simply because it is internalized, however, machine-mindedness is *not* obvious to those who, not content with the applications of technology *in* education, want to speed the passage towards a fully developed technology *of* education. Maybe, after all, they are the faceless ones and plain folk who cannot make head or tail of what they are up to are right to fear them. Maybe those teachers whom Dr Briault (*Learning and Teaching Tomorrow,* 1969) complains of as being bemused with 'me and my children' attitudes are instinctively applying a touch of the brakes that is needed, not simply dragging their heels. The situation in which we find ourselves is one in which those in front cry 'Forward!' and those behind cry 'Back!' If we are to preserve an open mind, therefore, ambivalence may be a necessary virtue, even if to preserve an open mind means thinking with the blood. In an open system, when all is said and done, there can be no accepting the axiom that education is ultimately reducible to a set of variables or a computable model.

Confined to the domain of the abstract, education soon wilts and dies.

Bibliography

There is no lack of information services in this burgeoning field.

1 The National Council for Educational Technology has commissioned its own *An Annotated Select Bibliography of Educational Technology*. Prepared by M. ERAUT and G. SQUIRES, this was published by Councils and Education Press in 1971. pp. 90.

2 *Survey of British Research into Audio-Visual Aids*, published by and available from the Educational Foundation for Visual Aids, 33 Queen Anne Street, London W1.

3 A bibliography on educational broadcasting is obtainable from the Information Officer, Schools Broadcasting Council, BBC, London W1.

4 BOARD, B. *The Effect of Technological Progress on Education: A Classified Bibliography from British Sources 1945–57*. Institute of Production Engineers, 1959. pp. 141.

5 DODD, W. E. and ENGLAND, A. *Programmed Instruction and Teaching Machines: An Annotated Bibliography*. Stoke-on-Trent Libraries, 1965. pp. 168. Dated, but the best of its kind in Britain.

6 GEE, R. D. *Teaching Machines and Programmed Learning: A Guide to the Literature*. 2nd ed. HERTIS (Herts County Council Technical Library Information Service), 1965. pp. 128.

7 HEPWORTH, J. B. *The Language Laboratory*. Manchester Libraries Committee, 1966. pp. 29. Contains 224 entries.

8 SCHRAMM, W. *Research on Programmed Instruction: An Annotated Bibliography*. Washington, D.C., U.S. Dept of Health, Education & Welfare, 1964. pp. 114.

9 CAVANAGH, P. and JONES, C. *Yearbook of Educational and Instructional Technology*. L, Cornmarket P, 1969–70. pp. 459. Indispensable work of reference; lists available programmes in print. details of hardware – teaching machines, projectors, tape recorders, language laboratories, etc.

10 MCALEESE, W. R. and UNWIN, D. *Microteaching: A Bibliography*, Coleraine, New U of Ulster, Education Centre, 1970. pp. 32. Contains 236 entries, not annotated.

The present bibliography is arranged under the headings of:
1 The concept of educational technology

2 The use of teaching aids
3 Programmed learning and teaching machines
4 Computer assisted instruction
5 Systems theory and its applications
6 Media and communication

1 The Concept of Educational Technology

ASHBY, SIR E. *Technology and the Academics*. L, Macmillan, 1958. pp. 118. 'Apprehending a technology in its completeness . . . is the essence of technological humanism.'

BAGRIT, SIR L. *The Age of Automation*. L, Weidenfeld & Nicolson, 1965. pp. 88. Reith lectures on the theme of a brave new world that is just around the corner (if we hurry).

BRIAULT, E. W. *Learning and Teaching Tomorrow*. NCET Occasional Paper 2. L, Councils & Education P, 1969. pp. 16. Assesses present and future trends.

ELLUL, J. *The Technological Society*. L, Cape, 1965. pp. 496. Sees the laws of technological advance as immutable, beyond human control, and takes a dim view of the destiny of the man-machine.

HUTCHINS, R. M. *The Learning Society*. L, Pall Mall P, 1968; Harmondsworth, Penguin Books, 1970. pp. 142. Sees the education system as a technology, doubts whether it can be controlled.

KRUTCH, J. W. *The Measure of Man*. L, Redman, 1956. pp. 261. Bitter attack on social engineering.

MCLUHAN, M. *Understanding Media*. L, Routledge, 1964, and various eds. pp. 359. Essential reading despite its obscurantism and eccentricities of style.

RICHMOND, W. K. (ed.) *The Concept of Educational Technology: A Dialogue for Yourself*. L, Weidenfeld & Nicolson, 1970. pp. 254. An open-ended programmed reader.

SKINNER, B. F. *The Technology of Teaching*. NY, Appleton-Century-Crofts, 1968. pp. 271. Behaviourist view on the shaping of behaviour.

2 The Use of Teaching Aids

Inability to exploit the advantages of mechanical devices may well prove to be the Achilles heel of educational technology. Learning to operate them, like learning to drive a car, is not an accomplishment that comes from reading manuals of instruction, though in the absence of adequate pre-service and in-service training for teachers, such manuals have their uses.

ADAM, J. B. and SHAWCROSS, A. S. *The Language Laboratory.* L, Pitman, 1963. pp. 72.

ATKINSON, N. J. *Modern Teaching Aids.* L, Maclaren & Sons, 1966. pp. 224. A practical guide to audiovisual techniques in education.

BUNG, K. (ed.) *Programmed Learning and the Language Laboratory: Collected Papers.* Research Publications Services. 2 vols. 1967, pp. 279; 1968, pp. 243.

COPPEN, H. *Aids to Teaching and Learning.* O, Pergamon P, 1968. pp. 240. Comprehensive, down to earth; good bibliography.

DIEUZEIDE, H. *Teaching Through Television.* Paris, OECD, 1969. pp. 71.

GIBSON, T. *The Use of ETV.* L, Hutchinson Educ., 1970. pp. 127.
—— *The Practice of ETV.* L, Hutchinson Educ., 1970. pp. 189. Illustrated handbook for students and teachers; recommended.

GOLDSMITH, M. (ed.) *Mechanisation in the Classroom.* L, Souvenir P, 1963. pp. 236. Interesting symposium, somewhat dated.

KINROSS, F. *Television and the Teacher.* L, Hamish Hamilton, 1968. pp. 138.

MAY, M. A. and LUMSDAINE, A. A. *Learning from Films.* New Haven, Conn., Yale UP, 1959. pp. 357.

MOIR, G. (ed.) *Teaching and Television: ETV Explained.* O, Pergamon P, 1967. pp. 170.

POWELL, L. S. *A Guide to the Overhead Projector.* L, British Association for Commercial and Industrial Education, 1964. pp. 52.
—— *A Guide to the Use of Visual Aids.* L, BACIE, 1968. pp. 54.
—— *Communication and Learning.* L, Pitman, 1969. pp. 218. Illustrated guide to the theory and practice of audiovisual techniques.

RICHMOND, W. K. *Teachers and Machines.* L, Collins, 1965. pp. 272. Relates programming techniques to a background of educational theory.

ROMISZOWSKI, A. J. *The Selection and Use of Teaching Aids.* L, Kogan Page, 1968. pp. 168.

SIMPSON, M. *Film Projecting without Tears or Technicalities.* L, National Committee for Audio-Visual Aids in Education, 1966. pp. 51. Just the thing for those with five thumbs on both hands.

STACK, E. M. *The Language Laboratory and Modern Language Teaching.* 2nd ed. L, OUP, 1970. pp. 248.

TAYLOR, G. (ed.) *The Teacher as Manager.* L, Councils & Education

P/NCET, 1970. pp. 166. Essential background information for decision-making and the effective deployment of resources for learning in schools; strongly recommended.

TROW, W. C. *Teacher and Technology: New Designs for Learning.* NY, Appleton-Century-Crofts, 1963. pp. 198. An approach to teaching as a man-machine system.

TUCKER, N. *Understanding the Mass Media.* CUP, 1966. pp. 198. Packed with suggestions for everyday classroom practice; highly recommended.

TURNER, J. D. *Introduction to the Language Laboratory.* U of LP, 1965. pp. 110.

—— *Programming for the Language Laboratory.* U of LP, 1968. pp. 263.

—— (ed) *Using the Language Laboratory.* U of LP, 1969. pp. 156.

VERNON, P. J. (ed.) *The Audio-Visual Approach to Modern Language Teaching.* L, National Committee for Audio-Visual Aids in Education, 1965. pp. 80.

VINCENT, A. *The Overhead Projector.* L, National Committee for Audio-Visual Aids in Education, 1964, 1970. pp. 68.

WEISGERBER, R. A. *Instructional Process and Media Innovation.* Chicago, Rand McNally, 1968. pp. 569.

WESTON, J. *The Tape Recorder in the Classroom.* 3rd ed. L, National Committee for Audio-Visual Aids in Education, 1968. pp. 132.

3 Programmed Learning and Teaching Machines

Is programmed learning the caterpillar from which the perfect imago of educational technology will eventually take flight, we asked? Judging by its own prolific literature, it is certainly undergoing a process of rapid change, if not a metamorphosis. With the situation as fluid as it is, anything published on the subject before 1965 may be reckoned more or less obsolete.

AUSTWICK, K. *Teaching Machines and Programmed Learning.* O, Pergamon P, 1963. pp. 188.

—— *Register of Programmed Instruction in the Field of Education and Training in Commerce and Industry.* L, BACIE. Vol. 1, 1966, pp. 40; vol. 2, 1968, pp. 190.

BAJPAI, A. C. and LEEDHAM, J. F. *Aspects of Educational Technology IV.* L, Pitman, 1970. pp. 522.

BARRY, W. S. *Programmed Instruction in BEA.* O, Pergamon P, 1967. pp. 47.

BRETHOWER, D. M. *et al. Programmed Learning: A Practicum.* Ann Arbor, U of Michigan P, 1964. pp. 237. In the form of a self-instructional programme.

CALLENDER, P. *Programmed Learning: Its Development and Structure.* L, Longmans, 1969. pp. 120. Concise summary.

DE CECCO, J. P. (ed.) *Educational Technology: Readings in Programmed Instruction.* NY, Holt, Rinehart & Winston, 1964. pp. 479. American symposium.

DETERLINE, W. A. *An Introduction to Programmed Instruction.* Englewood Cliffs, Prentice-Hall, 1963. pp. 131. An oldy, but still a goody.

DUNN, W. R. and HOLROYD, C. (eds.) *Aspects of Educational Technology II.* L, Methuen, 1969. pp. 688. Proceedings of 1968 Glasgow APL conference; notable paper by Landa.

GLASER, R. (ed.) *Teaching Machines and Programmed Learning II.* Washington D.C., DAVI, 1965. pp. 831. Source book follow-up on LUMSDAINE and GLASER (below).

HOLLAND, J. G. and SKINNER, B. F. *The Analysis of Behavior.* NY, McGraw-Hill, 1961. pp. 337. Square One for beginners; serves a dual purpose: (*a*) as an introduction to operant conditioning, (*b*) as an introduction to linear programming. Now mainly of historic interest.

KAY, H. (ed.) *Teaching Machines and Their Use in Industry.* L, Dept of Scientific & Industrial Research/HMSO, 1963. pp. 32.

KAY, H., DODD, B. and SIME, M. *Teaching Machines and Programmed Instruction.* Harmondsworth, Penguin Books, 1968. pp. 173. Probably the best all-round account for British students.

LEEDHAM, J. and UNWIN, D. *Programmed Learning in the Schools.* L. Longmans, 1965. pp. 162.

—— (eds.) *Aspects of Educational Technology I.* L, Methuen, 1967, pp. 544. Proceedings of 1966 APL Loughborough conference; papers by F. H. George and L. Stolurow on computer-assisted instruction.

LEITH, G. O. M. *et al. A Handbook of Programmed Learning.* 2nd ed. U of Birmingham Institute of Education, 1966. pp. 152.

—— *Second Thoughts on Programmed Learning.* Occasional Paper No. 1. L, Councils & Education P, 1969. pp. 16. 'And oh, the difference to me!'

LUMSDAINE, A. A. and GLASER, R. (eds.) *Teaching Machines and Programmed Learning.* Washington, D.C., DAVI, 1960, 1968. pp. 724. Standard source book.

MAGER, R. F. *Preparing Objectives for Programmed Instruction.* Palo Alto, Calif., Fearon, 1961. pp. 62. An absolute must; exemplary specimen of a branching programme, which makes its points most effectively.

—— *Developing Attitude Toward Learning.* Palo Alto, Calif., Fearon, 1968. pp. 104. Rather less effective, but makes refreshing reading.

MAGER, R. F. and BEACH, K. M. *Developing Vocational Instruction.* Palo Alto, Calif., Fearon, 1969. pp. 83. Tips for industrial training.

MANN, A. P. and BRUNSTROM, C. K. (eds.) *Aspects of Educational Technology III.* L, Pitman, 1970. pp. 404. Proceedings of London APL conference; curate's egg collection of papers.

MARKLE, S. M. *Good Frames and Bad.* NY, Wiley, 1964. pp. 278. A grammar for programme writers.

MONTAGNON, P. and BENNETT, R. (eds.) *What is Programmed Learning?* L, BBC, 1965. pp. 104. Answers most of the questions.

OFIESH, G. D. and MEIERHENRY, W. C. (eds.) *Trends in Programmed Instruction.* Washington, D.C., DAVI, 1964. pp. 289. A reader.

POPHAM, W. J. and BAKER, E. L. *Systematic Instruction.* Englewood Cliffs, Prentice-Hall, 1970. pp. 166.

—— *Planning an Instructional Sequence.* Englewood Cliffs, Prentice-Hall, 1970. pp. 138.

—— *Establishing Instructional Goals.* Englewood Cliffs, Prentice-Hall, 1970. pp. 130.

Three volumes typifying the *nouvelle vague* in which programmed learning and curriculum development tend to coalesce.

ROWNTREE, D. *Basically Branching.* L, Macdonald, 1966. pp. 224.

SMITH, W. I. and MOORE, J. W. (eds.) *Programmed Learning: Theory and Research.* L, Van Nostrand, 1962. pp. 240.

TABER, J. I., GLASER, R. and SCHAEFFER, H. H. *Learning and Programmed Instruction.* Reading, Mass., Addison-Wesley, 1965. pp. 182. A good, readable exposition of applied learning theory.

4 Computer Assisted Instruction

The use of computers in education has been discussed off and on ever since the beginnings of programmed learning, but apart from one or two experimental projects relatively little progress can be recorded in Britain so far. The promises held out for the design of a genuinely adaptive teaching machine, i.e. one that monitors the learner's performance and responds to his individual needs, have yet to be fulfilled.

Research papers on CAI and other computer-based techniques are to be found in the *Aspects of Educational Technology* series, as well as in the source books and symposia listed above.

BRODERICK, W. R. *The Computer in School*. L, Bodley Head, 1968. pp. 144.

COULSON, J. E. (ed.) *Programmed Learning and Computer-based Instruction*. NY, Wiley, 1962. pp. 291.

GOODLAD, J. I., O'TOOLE, J. F. and TYLER, L. F. *Computers and Information Systems in Education*. NY, Harcourt, Brace & World, 1966. pp. 152. Readable review of the state of the art, future developments, etc.

NATIONAL COUNCIL FOR EDUCATIONAL TECHNOLOGY. *Computers for Education*. Working Paper 1. L, NCET, 1969. pp. 44. Report of a feasibility study of the potential applications.

—— *Computer Based Learning*. L, NCET, 1969. pp. 138. Programme for research and development.

OETTINGER, A. G. *Run, Computer, Run*. C, Mass., Harvard UP, 1969. pp. 303. Recognizes the practical snags.

SASS, M. A. and WILKINSON, W. D. *Symposium on Computer Augmentation of Human Reasoning*. NY, Spartan Books, 1965. pp. 235.

SCOTTISH EDUCATION DEPARTMENT. *Computers and the Schools*. Edinburgh, HMSO, 1969. pp. 20.

STOLUROW, L. M. *Teaching by Machine*. Washington, D.C., U.S. Dept of Health, Education & Welfare, 1961. pp. 173

—— 'A computer-assisted instructional system in theory and research', *in* LEEDHAM, J. and UNWIN, D. (eds.) *Aspects of Educational Technology I* (see above, section 3).

—— 'CAI: problems and perspectives', *in* DUNN, W. R. and HOLROYD, C. (eds.) *Aspects of Educational Technology II* (see above, section 3).

5 Systems Theory and Its Applications

Tyros are apt to be left floundering here. Without a thorough grasp of the basic concepts in communication theory and cybernetic principles, most students will be well advised to tread warily in a literature which is decidedly uneven in quality. Being highly technical, the best (Wiener, Ashby, Pierce) is difficult; the worst is gibberish.

RECALL (*Review of Educational Cybernetics and Applied Linguistics*), published three times a year by Research Publication Services, is a useful source for those interested in a 'multi-media approach'.

ARMITAGE, P., SMITH, C. and ALPER, P. *Decision Models for Educational Planning*. L, Allen Lane, 1969. pp. 124. First steps towards a computable model of the education system as a whole.

ASHBY, W. R. *An Introduction to Cybernetics*. L, Methuen, 1956. pp. 396. Paperback ed. 1964, pp. 308. Abstruse but rewarding.

BARON, G. and TAYLOR, W. (eds.) *Educational Administration and the Social Sciences*. L, Athlone P, 1969. pp. 192. As good an introduction as any for beginners.

EMERY, F. E. (ed.) *Systems Thinking*. Harmondsworth, Penguin Books, 1969. pp. 400.

GEORGE, F. H. *The Brain as Computer*. O, Pergamon P, 1961. pp. 413.

GUILBAUD, G. T. *What is Cybernetics?* L, Heinemann, 1959. pp. 126. Gives a readable answer.

PIERCE, J. R. *Symbols, Signals and Noise*. L, Hutchinson, 1962. pp. 307. Sound exposition of the essentials of information and communication theory.

RICHMOND, W. K. *The Education Industry*. L, Methuen, 1969. pp. 237. Chapters 10–12 deal with systems theory, systems engineering, etc.

ROMISZOWSKI, A. J. (ed.) *The Systems Approach to Education and Training*. L, Kogan Page, 1970. pp. 95. Good in parts.

SMITH, K. U. and SMITH, M. F. *Cybernetic Principles of Learning and Educational Design*. NY, Holt, Rinehart & Winston, 1966. pp. 529. Standard U.S. textbook on programmed-learning-plus.

WIENER, N. *Cybernetics*. NY, Wiley, 1961 (first pub. 1948). pp. 212.
—— *The Human Use of Human Beings*. L, Eyre & Spottiswoode, 1951. New ed. Sphere, 1969. pp. 192.
Last on the list and by far the best of the bunch; either of these classic texts is indispensable.

6 Media and Communication

Whether or not the medium is the message, research into the educational effectiveness of the various media, into the properties of each of them, and into the effects of media exposure is now receiving a good deal of attention.

Belatedly, it may be thought. Here again, students should be warned that any findings to date will need to be revised as research probes become more refined than they are at present.

ARANGUREN, J. L. *Human Communication*. L, Weidenfeld & Nicolson, 1967. pp. 253. Survey of modern theories for the general reader.

BAILLEY, K. V. *The Listening Schools*. L, BBC, 1957. pp. 184. Survey-review of schools broadcasting.

BRIGGS, L. J., CAMPEAU, P. L., GAGNÉ, R. M. and MAY, M. A. *Instructional Media: A Procedure for the Design of Multi-Media Instruction: A Critical Review of Research and Suggestions for Future Research*. Pittsburgh, American Institutes for Research, 1967. pp. 176.

HALLORAN, J. D. *The Effects of Mass Communication*. Leicester UP, 1965. pp. 84. With special reference to television.

—— *Attitude Formation and Change*. Leicester UP, 1967. pp. 168.

—— (ed.) *The Effects of Television*. L, Panther, 1970. pp. 224.

HIMMELWEIT, H. T. et al. (eds.) *Television and the Child*. L, OUP, 1958. pp. 522. Exhaustive, inconclusive investigation; findings no longer to be trusted.

MACLEAN, R. *Television in Education*. L, Methuen, 1968. pp. 176. Level-headed account mercifully free from mystique; recommended.

MCQUAIL, D. *Research and School Broadcasting*. L, BBC, 1965. pp. 27.

MEE, ELLEN, C. *Audio-Visual Media and the Disadvantaged Child*. Working Paper No. 3. L, NCET, 1970. pp. 97.

MIALARET, G. *The Psychology of Audio-Visual Aids in Primary Education*. L, Harrap/UNESCO, 1966. pp. 228. One of the few authentic research reports available; strongly recommended.

NATIONAL COMMITTEE FOR AUDIO-VISUAL AIDS IN EDUCATION. *Visual Aid Year Book*. L, NCAVA, annually. A useful source.

PARRY, J. *The Psychology of Human Communication*. U of LP, 1967. pp. 224. Good introduction to information theory.

ROBINSON, J. and BARNES, N. (eds.) *New Media and Methods in Industrial Training*. L, BBC, 1968. pp. 224.

SCHOOLS BROADCASTING COUNCIL FOR THE UNITED KINGDOM. *School Broadcasting and Primary Education: A Background Note on BBC School Broadcasting*. L, BBC, 1964. pp. 27. Policy statement.

SHRAMM, W. (ed.) *The Process and Effects of Mass Communication*. Urbana, U of Illinois P, 1954. pp. 586

—— (ed.) *The Science of Human Communication*. NY, Basic Books, 1963. pp. 158.

SCHRAMM, W., COOMBS, P. H., KAHNERT, F. and LYLE, J. (eds.) *The New Media: Memo to Educational Planners*. Paris, UNESCO, International Institute for Educational Planning, 1967. pp. 175.

—— *New Educational Media in Action: Case Studies for Planners*. Paris,

UNESCO, International Institute for Educational Planning, 1967. 3 vols. pp. 203, 226, 198. Evaluations of some major projects in educational technology.

SCUPHAM, J. *Broadcasting and the Community*. L, Watts, 1967. pp. 264.

—— *ETV East and West. Japan and Britain: A Survey*. L, British Film Institute, 1967. pp. 17.

—— *The Revolution in Communications*. NY, Holt, Rinehart & Winston, 1970. pp. 206. Stimulating, informed discussion covering the whole gamut from radio to satellites; strongly recommended.

TANSLEY, P. J. and UNWIN, D. *Simulation and Gaming in Education*. L, Methuen Educ., 1969. pp. 112.

TRENAMAN, J. M. *Communication and Comprehension*. L, Longmans, 1967. pp. 232. Reports one of the few rigorously controlled experimental investigations into the relative effectiveness of radio, television and print. Note, however, that 'comprehension' excludes any subliminal or affective aspects of learning

UNWIN, D. (ed.) *Media and Methods*. Maidenhead, McGraw-Hill, 1969. pp. 219. Instructional technology in higher education.

WILLIAMS, R. *Communications*. Harmondsworth, Penguin Books, 1970. pp. 192.